READ ALL ABOUT IT

Mastering Reading Comprehension and Critical Thinking Skills

Ethel Tiersky

Esther Dickstein

National Textbook Company
a division of *NTC Publishing Group* • Lincolnwood, Illinois USA

Articles from *USA TODAY* are republished by
permission of Gannett New Media Services, a division
of Gannett Satellite Information Network, Inc.,
1000 Wilson Boulevard, Arlington, Virginia 22229.

Acknowledgments: Susan Bokern, Michelle Mattox, Silvia Molina, Tom Turco.

Published by National Textbook Company, a division of NTC Publishing Group,
4255 West Touhy Avenue, Lincolnwood (Chicago), Illinois 60646-1975 U.S.A.
© 1995 NTC Publishing Group and Gannett New Media Services.
Manufactured in the United States of America.
Library of Congress Catalog Number: 94-68736.

5 6 7 8 9 0 VL 9 8 7 6 5 4 3 2 1

CONTENTS

INTRODUCTION

Read All About It: Mastering Reading Comprehension and Critical Thinking Skills is a compilation of forty-five articles from *USA TODAY,* a respected, prominent, and accessible newspaper.

We have selected a wide range of interesting articles in the areas of news, editorials and opinions, money, sports, education, lifestyles, and science. You'll read about the fiftieth anniversary of D-Day, the end of apartheid in South Africa, and weddings at the Mall of America.

As you explore issues in the news, you will strengthen your reading and critical thinking skills. The exercises that accompany the articles are designed to help you better understand the articles' main points and language.

In addition, special "Focus on the Newspaper" discussions at the end of each section help you understand the kinds of information you can expect to find in the newspaper and provide hands-on practice in analyzing various types of articles.

The exercises that accompany the articles follow a definite pattern to help you get the most out of *Read All About It.* Here is an outline of their contents:

Previewing the Article

- Stimulates interest in and understanding of the topic or subject.

Before You Read

- Provides discussion questions that encourage you to get the most out of your reading time.

As You Read

- Prompts you to look for important dates and information as you read each article.

Getting the Message

- Allows you to confirm your comprehension of the article with fill-in-the-blank and true-false questions.

Playing with Words

- Asks you to define words or phrases found in the article by using context clues.

Digging beneath the Surface

- Encourages you to respond to and talk about the article.

Going beyond the Text

- Provides collaborative opportunities for you to gain access to the thinking processes of others and to build knowledge related to the article.

Making Connections

- Provokes you to explore the interrelatedness of articles that deal with similar issues or topics.

We hope you enjoy reading the material in this book and that it leads you to a greater appreciation for the importance of reading in general and the reading of the daily newspaper in particular.

Ethel Tiersky
Esther Dickstein

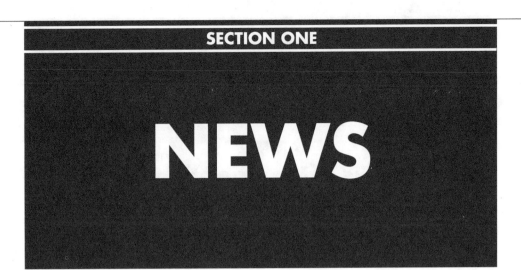

NEWS

USA SNAPSHOTS®

A look at statistics that shape your finances

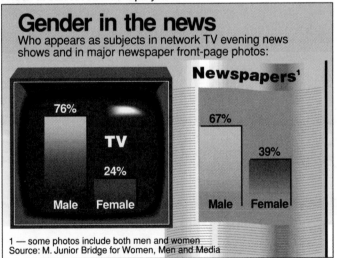

Gender in the news

Who appears as subjects in network TV evening news shows and in major newspaper front-page photos:

TV

76% Male
24% Female

Newspapers[1]

67% Male
39% Female

1 — some photos include both men and women
Source: M. Junior Bridge for Women, Men and Media

By Deirdre Schwiesow and Elys A. McLean, USA TODAY

ARTICLE 1A
A woman's love vs. a tribe's cultural quest

ARTICLE 1B
Race is often adoption issue

PREVIEWING THE ARTICLES

In recent years, the news media have focused public attention upon several poignant stories regarding the adoption of children. Disputes between biological parents and adoptive parents have created real-life drama and raised complex legal questions. Whose rights and needs should be given greatest priority—those of the adopted child, the biological parents, or the adoptive family? Article 1A describes a case with an additional wrinkle. In this case, it is not a biological parent who wants to regain custody of the adopted child; rather it is the child's tribe that is laying claim to her. Kayla American Horse's tribe is trying to exert its legal right to decide upon custody of its children. Article 1A presents the two sides of a story that, thus far, has no ending.

Article 1B deals with the larger legal and social questions raised by Kayla's case. Should people who want to adopt children be allowed to raise children of another race? Are transracial adoptions harmful to children? Will minority groups be significantly diminished by this practice? Or could transracial adoptions lead to greater understanding and appreciation of one race for another?

BEFORE YOU READ

1. Do you think a child should be removed from a family that he or she has been living happily with for several years? Do you think the rights of biological parents or an ethnic group are more important than those of the adopted child? Discuss these questions as a class.

2. Discuss the advantages and disadvantages of transracial adoptions. What does society gain by allowing such adoptions? What problems can they create?

AS YOU READ

Imagine that you are one of the lawyers hired by Kayla's tribe to argue for her return to the Standing Rock Sioux reservation. As you read this article, look for good arguments that you could use to build a strong case. Jot them down.

A woman's love vs. a tribe's cultural quest

By Patricia Edmonds
USA TODAY

1 ASHLAND, Ky.—When Loni Rye first saw 8-month-old Kayla American Horse, the almond-eyed baby wore a shirt that read, "Somebody in South Dakota Loves Me."

2 Now, somebody in South Dakota wants Kayla back.

3 More than a decade after the Standing Rock Sioux tribe gave "temporary custody" of Kayla to Rye and her husband, tribal leaders want the girl—now 11—to leave her Kentucky home and return to their South Dakota reservation.

4 The case pits the intensely personal against the cultural and political: a woman's love for the child she raised vs. a tribe's quest to keep its children in their own culture.

5 A Kentucky circuit judge has ruled it's in Kayla's best interest to stay with Rye. But the Standing Rock tribal court seeks to overturn that ruling, on the grounds that a 1978 federal law gives tribes ultimate jurisdiction over the custody of Indian children.

6 Rye's mother, Marcella, whom Kayla calls grandmother, says the tribe "just wants to prove a legal point—even if it would absolutely tear the child to pieces."

7 But Steve Moore of the Native American Rights Fund says cases like Kayla's are pursued because "Indian children are the lifeblood of Indian tribes." With hundreds of custody fights every year, Moore says, "the very vitality of tribes is threatened."

8 Now that school is out for Kayla, the bubbly 5th-grade graduate should be capering into summer, giggling over her school yearbook and practicing her cheerleading routines.

9 Instead, she says, she feels sad to see "my mom and my grandmother crying." And she plots where she would hide if anyone came to take her from the people she calls her family.

10 In late 1983, a Sioux woman named Effie American Horse was struggling with alcoholism and couldn't care for her infant daughter Kayla. Paternity never was officially established, but Kayla's father is believed to be Kim Weasel's brother.

11 Kim and his wife, Loni, had two toddlers of their own when they saw baby Kayla during a visit to the Standing Rock reservation. "I thought she was the cutest thing I'd ever seen," Loni recalls, "and my sister-in-law said Effie was looking for someone to raise her."

12 In January 1984, the tribal court declared Kayla its ward, and Kim and Loni Rye Weasel her custodians "until further notice." The couple, living off the reservation, raised Kayla with their own children for nearly a decade.

13 During those years, court records say, the tribe showed no interest in Kayla. When the Weasels asked for financial help three years ago to have a hole in Kayla's heart repaired, the tribe refused.

14 When the pair separated last year, Kim returned to the Standing Rock reservation. Loni—whose own heritage is one-fourth Cherokee and Choctaw—took back the name Rye and moved to Kentucky.

15 In January, sheriffs served Rye with a tribal court order, rescinding custody and saying the tribe would send an agent to take Kayla to the reservation for new custody proceedings.

By Elaine Alexander

TOGETHER FOR NOW: Loni Rye with Kayla American Horse, the 11-year-old she has raised for more than a decade.

16 "I always had the fear they could come and get her," Rye says. "But I thought if I had her 10 years, surely they wouldn't ask for her back."

17 Rye got a Boyd County Circuit Court order staying Kayla's removal. Since then, tribal and state courts have jousted over jurisdiction.

18 The tribe cites the federal Indian Child Welfare Act of 1978, passed to help stem the tide of adoptions off reservations. Unlike other cross-cultural adoption and custody cases where laws may be vague, this act is clear: "Where an Indian child is a ward of a tribal court, the Indian tribe retains exclusive jurisdiction" over the child's placement, it says.

19 The act gives tribal courts the right to decide custody disputes—unless a state court shows "good cause" for taking jurisdiction.

20 In April, Boyd County Circuit Judge C. David Hagerman ruled he had good cause to keep the case, because Kayla "has had no contact" with her tribe since her infancy; is "happy and well-adjusted" in her Kentucky home; and "would suffer considerable trauma from being removed from the only family she knows."

21 Standing Rock attorneys appealed Hagerman's decision and have asked the Kentucky Supreme Court to decide the case. That request is pending.

22 Rye's lawyer, James Moore, says the high court should refuse the case, lest the custody of an 11-year-old turn into a "turf" war on tribal rights.

23 It's not clear how many custody cases end with Indian children going back to the reservation, says Toby Grossman of the American Indian Law Center in Albuquerque. But when most tribes number in the low thousands, she says, even one case "is terribly significant."

24 Lawyer Richard Guarnieri says his client, the Standing Rock tribe, is only asserting its jurisdictional rights under the Indian Child Welfare Act. If Rye, Weasel or others want custody, he says, they can seek it in tribal court.

25 It is unclear whether Kim Weasel is seeking Kayla's return, or custody; he could not be located for comment. Standing Rock court officials referred calls to their lawyers.

26 Rye's family has set up a defense fund for Kayla's legal bills and collected 1,000 signatures on petitions circulated in Ashland, pleading that Kayla be allowed to stay.

27 For all this effort, Rye concedes, "I'm afraid the tribe will win." But she sees Kayla's face cloud up as she says it, so she moves to reassure.

28 "We're a family," Rye declares. "And we're going to get to stay that way."

Race is often adoption issue

By Desda Moss
USA TODAY

1 After two decades of highly charged debate, policies affecting adoptions across racial and cultural lines are, once again, in flux:

2 The Senate passed a bill in March that bars agencies that receive federal funds from delaying the placement of a child because of race, color or national origin. The bill, introduced by Sen. Howard Metzenbaum, D-Ohio, and Sen. Carol Moseley-Braun, D-Ill., was a response to the rising number of minority children in foster care and long delays in finding permanent homes.

3 A similar bill has been introduced in the House.

4 In Florida, starting in January, the law requires that race be given no greater weight than other factors in determining adoption placement. Texas adopted a similar law last fall.

5 In the 1960s, transracial adoptions were on the rise.

6 But after 1972, when the National Association of Social Workers called the practice tantamount to "cultural genocide," agencies sharply curtailed such placements.

7 Same-race preference is the policy in 45 states, and the law in three: Minnesota, California and Arkansas.

A. After reading Article 1A, mark the following statements true or false.

_____ 1. According to paragraphs 7 and 18, non-Indian couples rarely want to adopt Native American babies.

_____ 2. Paragraph 23 suggests that Native American cultures place great emphasis upon the needs of the community.

_____ 3. Kayla wants to live with her biological mother.

_____ 4. The tribal court never gave Loni Rye permanent custody of Kayla.

_____ 5. The tribal court's effort to regain Kayla began after Loni Rye moved the family to Kentucky.

_____ 6. According to paragraph 20, Kayla had been visiting her tribe regularly until the move to Kentucky.

_____ 7. Paragraph 25 implies that Kim Weasel may have encouraged his tribe to demand Kayla's return.

B. According to Article 1B, which of the individuals and groups listed below favor or have no objection to transracial adoption and which oppose it? Put a check (✓) in the appropriate column.

	Pro	Con
1. The Florida legislature	_____	_____
2. The Minnesota legislature	_____	_____
3. The Texas legislature	_____	_____
4. The National Association of Social Workers	_____	_____
5. Senator Howard Metzenbaum	_____	_____
6. Senator Carol Moseley-Braun	_____	_____

PLAYING WITH WORDS

A. Complete the following sentences with the legal vocabulary listed below. All of these words appeared in Article 1A.

appealed	jurisdiction	proceedings	staying
circuit	overturn	quest	vitality
custody	pending	rescinded	ward

1. Loni Rye won a victory in Kentucky's _____ court.

2. The tribal attorneys have _____ the case to Kentucky's Supreme Court.

3. The Supreme Court has not yet decided whether or not to hear this case. The case is

_____ .

4. Loni Rye wants to retain _____ of Kayla American Horse.

5. In 1984, Kayla was declared a _____ of the tribal court, and that court gave the Weasels temporary custody.

6. In January 1994, the tribal court _____ the Weasels' custody and sent an agent to Kentucky to take Kayla back to the South Dakota reservation.

7. In response, Loni Rye got a court order in Kentucky _____ the tribal order.

8. Loni Rye could ask the Standing Rock tribal court for custody of Kayla in legal _____ on the reservation.

B. With a partner, decide upon a good definition for each phrase listed below. The phrases are all from Article 1B. Use a dictionary and context clues to help you. The paragraph where each phrase is used is indicated in parentheses.

1. *two decades* (1) _____

2. *highly charged* (1) _____

3. *in flux* (1) _____

4. *minority children* (2) _____

5. *foster care* (2) _____

6. *transracial adoptions* (5) _____

7. *cultural genocide* (6) _____

8. *sharply curtailed* (6) _____

9. *same-race preference* (7) _____

C. Find the meanings of each word part listed below.

1. *trans-* _____

2. *geno-* _____

3. *-cide* _____

DIGGING BENEATH THE SURFACE

If you were the circuit court judge hearing Kayla's case, which of the following factors would you consider when making your decision? Discuss the factors in small groups. Then mark each statement "R" for relevant or "I" for irrelevant. Compare your answers with other groups' in the class.

_____ 1. Loni Rye is part Indian.

_____ 2. Loni Rye and Kim Weasel no longer live together.

_____ 3. Kayla wants to continue to live with Loni Rye.

_____ 4. Loni Rye has other children, her own biological offspring.

_____ 5. The Standing Rock Sioux tribe refused to pay for Kayla's heart surgery.

_____ 6. An Indian tribe has the right to decide the custody of an Indian child.

_____ 7. A state court can take jurisdiction from a tribal court if it can show good reason for doing so.

_____ 8. Kayla is a happy, friendly child with many interests.

_____ 9. If non-Indian families adopt Indian children in great numbers, some American Indian cultures may disappear.

_____ 10. Loni Rye took Kayla to another state, far from the reservation on which she was born.

_____ 11. Kayla had no contact with her tribe while she was living in South Dakota.

_____ 12. Kayla will hide if anyone tries to take her from Loni Rye.

GOING BEYOND THE TEXT

A. *Learning Together*

1. Working in small groups, develop a compromise plan that could settle Kayla's case. Write it up as if you were a judge deciding this case in a circuit court.

2. With a partner, discuss Loni Rye's situation and how she could have avoided it. What mistakes do you think she made? What steps could she have taken to protect Kayla from this situation? What do you think Loni Rye should do next?

3. Visit a local courtroom with a few of your classmates. Afterwards, discuss what you learned about how the law operates. Discuss the courtroom proceedings that confused you. List the various people you saw in the courtroom, and discuss what their jobs were.

B. *Responding in Writing.* Choose one of the following writing projects.

1. Scan the articles on Native Americans in two general encyclopedias. (The heading may be "Indians, American.") Look for information about the influences of American Indian cultures on mainstream American life today. Consider foods, clothing, transportation, medications, language, ideas, arts and crafts, and so on. Write a summary of the influences you found. Indicate which two encyclopedias you read.

2. Imagine that you are Kayla. Write an open letter to the circuit court judge and the tribal court expressing your viewpoint.

3. Read Barbara Kingsolver's novel *Pigs in Heaven,* which deals with a situation similar to Kayla's. Then write an essay comparing the book to the situation described in this article.

MAKING CONNECTIONS

Kayla's situation has certainly brought a lot of stress into her life. In the "Science, Health, and Behavior" section of this book, you will find an article containing advice on how to handle stress. Read "Learn to lighten up and live longer." Then decide how you would advise Kayla to deal with the stress in her life.

ARTICLE 2A
Cities deciding that it's time for teen curfews

ARTICLE 2B
Girl Scout bounces banking industry

ARTICLE 2C
"Great terrain robbery": Up to $10 billion in gold

ARTICLE 2D
Brazil hits brakes on phones

PREVIEWING THE ARTICLES

Americans have come to expect their government to provide many things for them. Foremost among these is protection—from crime, dangerous products, unfair business practices, and so on. The trouble is that protection often brings with it a limitation on someone's freedom.

Legislating protection is a complicated issue. For example, many people object to laws that require them to wear safety belts when riding in a car or helmets when riding on a motorcycle or bicycle. These people say that they have the right to risk injury or death if they choose to. But, their opponents point out, if they don't wear the safety belt or the helmet and an accident leaves them paralyzed, who pays their medical bills?

The following four articles deal with the role of government in protecting the interests of citizens. Articles 2A, 2B, and 2C deal with situations in the United States—teen curfews, unfair banking practices, and the sale of American land to foreign companies. Article 2D describes a Brazilian law that forbids cellular phone usage while driving a car. Would Americans feel safer on the roads if this country had such a law? Which do we value most—safety or freedom?

BEFORE YOU READ

1. Discuss rules and laws in your school or community. In your opinion, do some of them limit individual freedom with little or no benefit to the community?

2. Discuss the purpose of curfews. When are local or national governments likely to institute one? Could an American city legally institute a curfew for adults?

AS YOU READ

As you read these articles, try to think of ways in which governments (local and national) protect you and limit your freedom.

Cities deciding that it's time for teen curfews

By Mark Potok
USA TODAY

1 DALLAS—Melissa Vela, 16, says she should be allowed to walk the streets of her neighborhood, even late at night. But her mother disagrees, Melissa says.

2 "My mom tries to argue about it, but I just go to my room," says the Dallas teen, strolling through a shopping mall.

3 Now, the city of Dallas is taking her mother's side.

4 Since the U.S. Supreme Court last week let stand a controversial city curfew on teen-agers, Dallas—along with hundreds of other cities nationwide—has been doing its best to keep kids under 17 inside late at night.

5 Under the law, children are barred from public places after 11 on week-nights and midnight on weekends. The curfew lasts until 6 a.m. Since the curfews began May 1, more than 100 youths have been ticketed; fines run to $500. Others have been warned.

6 Curfews have been used since at least early this century, but Dallas' court victory may have opened the floodgates.

7 "We expect this Supreme Court decision will encourage many communities to look at curfews," says Doug Peterson at the National League of Cities. "It is one more tool in their toolbox."

8 With violent crime among teens up 57% in the past decade, city after city has imposed curfews, but some have been struck down as overly broad. Dallas' law was upheld, in part, because of the many exceptions it provides—for children running errands for parents, going to jobs and taking part in school- or church-sponsored activities.

9 "More cities are going to go this route because they're desperate," says Assistant City Attorney Don Postell, who helped draft Dallas' law. "We're losing kids at astronomical levels."

10 In many cities, the American Civil Liberties Union has argued that curfews curtail teens' freedom of assembly and speech and, in effect, criminalize a class of people. The ACLU argues curfews can be enforced primarily against inner-city youth, mainly minorities.

11 "Now police can just go up to anyone they don't like the looks of without a reason," says Yale student Sabrina Qutb, 19, who helped challenge Dallas' law in court.

12 "We believe children ought to be in at some reasonable hour," says Joe Cook, regional ACLU director in Dallas. "But that decision belongs to the parents, not police officers and politicians."

13 Still, curfews are booming:

▶ In Denver, enforcement of a new curfew for youths under 18 begins tonight. Violators face fines up to $50.

▶ Orlando, Fla., officials plan to enforce a new curfew, applying only to the downtown bar district, late this week.

▶ In Cedar Hill, a Dallas suburb of about 24,000 people, an ordinance that closely parallels Dallas' law was passed in late May. Enforcement of the law, including tickets of up to $500, begins at month's end.

▶ Dickinson, N.D., is expected to approve today a curfew banning teens from the streets between 11 p.m. and 5 a.m. on school nights, and from 1 to 5 a.m. on weekends.

▶ Fort Worth officials expect to adopt a law patterned on Dallas' statute.

14 Many adults are delighted.

15 "It's the devil's workshop if you're outside after 9," says Rosie Prettyman, 69, of Dallas. "The government has to step in. If they're smart enough to put a man on the moon, they're smart enough to make some kind of control system for these kids."

16 But experts such as Yale sociologist Albert Reiss say it's not clear if curfews prevent crime. "We've been trying in this country for at least 80 years to decide if curfews are effective. Nobody's ever been able to show they are, and there are a lot of reasons to conclude that they are not."

17 Brandy Montgomery, 15, is livid.

18 "I hate it," she says, adding that most of her friends regularly break the Dallas curfew. "I understand how bad crime is, but this is a free country. If we want to risk our lives staying out late, we should be able to do that."

By Susan Weers

FACING DALLAS CURFEW: Melissa Vela, with boyfriend Billy Duron

---

Girl Scout bounces banking industry

By Janet L. Fix
USA TODAY

1 Ten-year-old Ryan Cobb took on the banking industry and won Wednesday.

2 The Girl Scout from Arlington, Va., went to Capitol Hill because her credit union charged her $39 after a $15 check written by a cookie customer bounced. "It was somebody else's mistake," she told a House subcommittee.

3 Committee members lashed out at banks, claiming the industry is gouging consumers with excessive charges, especially those on people who receive a bad check.

4 "Ryan's story illustrates the devastation that bank fees have on the most vulnerable consumers," said Rep. Joe Kennedy, D-Mass., who invited Ryan to testify.

5 Bankers contend the fees are fair.

6 Ryan's bank battle began when her father helped her open a checking account at State Department Credit Union. When a check for boxes of cookies bounced twice, Ryan was charged $24. And that made her $7 school lunch check bounce. The cost: $15.

7 Her high-profile testimony struck a chord. Noticing Ryan's photo with a story about the issue in Wednesday's *Washington Post,* the credit union refunded her $39 with an apology and a $100 check to the Girl Scouts.

"Great terrain robbery": Up to $10 billion in gold

By Linda Kanamine
USA TODAY

1 WASHINGTON—"The biggest gold heist since the days of Butch Cassidy"—a bargain sale of 1,793 acres of gold-rich federal land was reluctantly approved Monday by Interior Secretary Bruce Babbitt.

2 Canada-based Barrick Goldstrike Mines Inc. now owns the sagebrush-covered hills in Carlin, Nev., and an estimated $10 billion in gold below. Cost: $5 an acre or $8,965.

3 "These are public assets basically being given away," Babbitt says. "It's a ripoff."

4 It's also the law.

5 The 1872 Mining Act, passed to encourage Western settlers, gives those who stake a valid claim on public land cheap access to minerals, without having to pay royalties.

6 Even today, mining companies can file patents to buy that land for $2.50 to $5 an acre.

7 "That barren rock in a desolate desert didn't have any value until Barrick came along, started exploring, took the risk and invested $1 billion" to mine there, says Barrick vice president Vince Borg.

8 But Babbitt—standing by a giant blue bank check made out to Barrick for $10 billion and signed "The American People"—used the day to push for mining law reform.

9 Senate and House conferees will have to work out big differences in their bills.

10 Babbitt says he wants royalties, greater environmental protection and an end to the federal land giveaways.

11 More than 500 other patent applications are pending with the Bureau of Land Management and Forest Service.

12 Says Sierra Club's Kathryn Hohmann: "This is the great terrain robbery."

Brazil hits brakes on phones

By James R. Healey
USA TODAY

1 Hang up and drive.

2 If you don't, Brazil will bust you. It's now a crime in that country to use a cellular phone while driving, even when stopped at a stop light.

3 Exception: Voice-activated phones that let drivers keep hands on the wheel.

4 Violators can be fined up to $25.20. Repeaters can lose their drivers' licenses.

5 A U.S. study says only lighting a cigarette is more distracting. Experts say that distraction causes wrecks.

6 A 1990 phone study, by the American Automobile Association Foundation, says drivers age 26 to 50 take an average 0.9 of a second longer to react in an emergency while making a phone call.

7 At 30 mph, their cars travel 37 feet during that delay. Drivers over 50 average 1.4 seconds, or nearly 62 feet.

8 A complex conversation, such as a business deal, slows reaction time about 0.8 of a second for most drivers.

9 But experts say no data directly link phones to crashes, making it difficult to justify a ban in the USA.

10 But the real reason anti-phone laws aren't likely, says Jim Baxter, head of the National Motorists Association: "A lot of elected officials like to use cellular phones."

A. After reading Article 2A, select the best completion for each statement.

1. According to Article 2A, _____ .

    a. curfews are effective in curtailing crime

    b. the number of American cities with curfews has been increasing

    c. teenagers like curfews

    d. the ACLU agrees with the U.S. Supreme Court on the curfew issue

2. Teenagers don't like curfews because _____ .

    a. they don't understand the dangers of being out late

    b. they want to decide for themselves whether to risk the danger of late hours

    c. they have no respect for the law

    d. their parents approve of them

3. When people under age eighteen violate a curfew, the punishment is usually _____ .

    a. a short jail sentence

    b. a fine

    c. a caning

    d. being grounded for a month

4. Curfews have been used in various places in this country _____ .

    a. only recently

    b. for at least 80 years

    c. only in Texas

    d. since May 1994

B. After reading Articles 2B and 2C, discuss the answers to these questions with a partner.

1. In Article 2B, who was Ryan Cobb complaining about? What was the House subcommittee complaining about?

2. In Article 2C, who was criticizing the land purchase? Why?

PLAYING WITH WORDS

A. Use context clues to determine the meaning of each italicized expression from Article 2A. The paragraph in which each expression is used is indicated in parentheses. Match each word or phrase in the first column with its literal meaning in the second column by writing the correct letter on each blank line.

_____ 1. *let stand* (4)

_____ 2. *opened the floodgates* (6)

_____ 3. *one more tool in their toolbox* (7)

_____ 4. *overly broad* (8)

_____ 5. *at astronomical levels* (9)

_____ 6. *inner-city* (10)

_____ 7. *booming* (13)

a. very high amounts

b. a time and place to learn evil ways

c. an area in or near the center of a city

d. very similar to; following the same pattern

e. increasing; growing in popularity

f. allow to remain in effect

g. another way of working on a problem

_____ 8. *closely parallels* (13) h. caused a great increase in something by making that action possible

_____ 9. *the devil's workshop* (15) i. applying to too many people or situations

B. Use context clues to determine the meaning of each italicized word or phrase as it is used in Article 2B. Circle the best definition. The paragraph in which each word or phrase is used is indicated in parentheses.

1. *credit union* (2)
   a. an organized group of workers in the credit industry
   b. an association for pooling the savings of members

2. *bounced* (2)
   a. went down and up again
   b. was not cashable due to insufficient funds in the account

3. *gouging* (3)
   a. physically injuring
   b. overcharging a lot

4. *vulnerable* (4)
   a. rich
   b. weak in some way; not able to put up a good defense

5. *high-profile* (7)
   a. noticeable
   b. a long nose and large forehead

6. *testimony* (7)
   a. the presentation of facts and answers to questions
   b. an emotional appeal for help

7. *struck a chord* (7)
   a. played musical notes together
   b. caused a response

8. *refunded* (7)
   a. established a second fund
   b. returned money

DIGGING BENEATH THE SURFACE

A. In Article 2A, the reporter presents the viewpoints of several different groups (teenagers, parents, and so on). In the chart below, list five of these groups. How does each group feel about curfews for teenagers? Check (✓) pro or con.

Group	Pro	Con
1. _____	_____	_____
2. _____	_____	_____
3. _____	_____	_____
4. _____	_____	_____
5. _____	_____	_____

B. In groups of two or three students, answer these questions about Article 2C.

1. This article uses an analogy (extended comparison) to make its point. What two "robberies" are compared? Were both robberies real?

2. Is the giant blue bank check a real check? What does it symbolize?

3. What are royalties? Why would they help to solve the problem?

A. *Learning Together*

1. In 1993, the state of Illinois passed a law requiring motorists to turn on their headlights when using their windshield wipers. Discuss this law in small groups, and decide if you think it is a good law or not. Why or why not? Compare your group's decision with the other groups'.

2. With a partner, discuss the headlines of all four articles. Note the uses of puns.

B. *Responding in Writing.* Choose one of the following writing projects.

1. Write a curfew law for your community. Indicate the ages and the hours it would apply to. Include any exceptions you think would be necessary to keep the law from being too broad.

2. Should behavior while driving a car be more restricted than it is in your community? Should drivers be forbidden to smoke, eat, or drink while behind the wheel? Should they be required to keep both hands on the wheel at all times? Write a short composition expressing your opinion.

3. Write a letter to the Secretary of State's office in your state. Ask for information about restrictions or legal obligations in some area of interest to you (safety belt laws or teen work restrictions, for example). Ask what members of the affected group are required to do or are restricted from doing. Mail your letter. When you get a response, read or post it in class.

4. Do a telephone survey. Find out what kinds of limitations the shopping malls in your community place upon customers. For example, can they shop without shoes? Can they bring their dogs in the mall? Can they bring their babies in strollers? Are there any special regulations for those under age eighteen? Report your findings to the class.

MAKING CONNECTIONS

Compare and contrast the general impression of American youngsters in Article 2A with the impression created by Article 3 ("Children committed to cleanup") in the "Science, Health, and Behavior" section. Which article better describes the youngsters you know? Do you think American children and teenagers know how to spend their time in constructive ways?

ARTICLE 3A
Minority boom in Texas, Calif.

ARTICLE 3B
Immigrants' status: Many factors in the mix

PREVIEWING THE ARTICLES

The population of the United States has always been a great ethnic mix. In the past, the United States was commonly referred to as a *melting pot.* Today, many people call it a *salad bowl.* The new metaphor (unlike the old one) suggests that various ethnic groups share a common national culture but also keep their individual cultural identities.

So, if this nation has always had cultural diversity, what is changing? American immigrants used to be predominantly white and European. Now, the country's population is on its way to becoming a majority of minorities. A recent Census Bureau report predicts that, by about the year 2050, the nation's various ethnic minorities added together will total more than the number of white, non-Hispanics. Two factors are causing this change—increasing Asian and Hispanic immigration and high birth rates among minority groups.

Article 3A tells which states are experiencing this change soonest and when it will become a national phenomenon. How will the nation be altered by this more pronounced multiculturalism? That is left for the reader to ponder.

Article 3B focuses on recent immigrants. In the 1980s, there were nine million new immigrants—the largest number ever to come in one decade. What factors determine which ethnic groups prosper and which groups struggle in their new country? This article provides some interesting answers.

BEFORE YOU READ

1. Define and discuss the word *stereotype.* Are stereotypes usually correct? Are they always wrong? What are some stereotypes that Europeans believe about Americans? What ethnic stereotypes have you heard? When you became acquainted with people of that ethnic group, did the stereotype fit the individual?

2. In recent years, schools, communities, advertisers, and the news and entertainment media have all tried to respond to the new multiculturalism in the United States. Have you noticed any changes? Discuss your observations with classmates.

AS YOU READ

1. Article 3A talks about states becoming divided by having very different populations. As you read, look for the two main types of populations that states will have.

2. In Article 3B, look for the various factors that affect the family income of immigrants.

Minority boom in Texas, Calif.

By Margaret L. Usdansky
USA TODAY

1 Minorities will be a majority of Californians by the year 2000, while Texas will turn "majority minority" before 2015, new population figures released by the Census Bureau today show.

2 That puts both states decades ahead of the nation. Blacks, Hispanics, Asians and Native Americans aren't expected to make up more than half of the USA's population until after 2050, although minorities already account for more than half the populations of Hawaii and New Mexico.

3 Much of the population growth of minorities is due to immigration, says University of Michigan demographer William Frey: "The national trend is one of increasing separation between those states which are getting most of the immigrants and those states that are not."

4 Frey says the trend is likely to create "sharp divides . . . between parts of the country that are becoming older and whiter and parts that are becoming younger and more ethnically diverse."

5 The new Census Bureau report—a catalog of state and national population growth through 2020—also shows:

▶ The nation's population will reach 325.9 million in 2020, up 25% from 260.7 million now.

▶ There will be 166 million women, making up 50.9%, and 159.9 million men.

▶ Whites still will make up the largest number of Americans, though they will not be as big a percentage as they are now. The white population, though numbering 254.8 million, will shrink from today's 83.3% to 78.2% in 2020.

▶ Rapid immigration from Latin American and high birth rates mean Hispanics will overtake blacks, becoming the nation's largest minority group by the year 2010. By 2020, there are expected to be 51.2 million Hispanics, or 15.7% of the population, up from 9.7% now.

▶ Blacks will be the second largest minority at 45.4 million, or 13.9%, up from 12.5%.

▶ Asians and Pacific Islanders will have the fastest growth of any group, rising to 22.6 million, or 6.9%, from 3.4%.

▶ Native Americans will increase their share of the population, from .8% to .9%, or 3.1 million people.

6 The report also found that New York, already falling to third place this year as Texas becomes the second-largest state, will take another hit in 2018, when Florida bumps up to No. 3, pushing the Empire State into fourth place.

7 California will remain the largest state, with 14.7% of the population in 2020, compared with 12.2% today.

8 More than half of California's growth will come from immigration, the rest from an excess of births over deaths.

9 "California is the major magnet for immigration from overseas," attracting almost 40% of immigrants, says Carl Haub of the Washington, D.C. Population Reference Bureau.

10 But the Golden State isn't nearly as popular with people already in the USA. The Census Bureau expects California to have a net loss of more than 4 million residents between 1993 and 2020, more than any other state except New York.

Immigrants' status: Many factors in the mix

By Margaret L. Usdansky
USA TODAY

¹ Some of the immigrants who came to America in the 1980s were met not with open arms, but with resentment and misunderstanding as debate raged over the impact of 9.5 million new residents in a decade—a record.

² But a new Census Bureau report sheds some light where there has been a lot of heat. The report, the largest review of immigrants ever undertaken, ultimately both challenges and confirms some stereotypes about the nearly 20 million people in the USA who were foreign born.

³ Interpreting the numbers can be tricky: The status of immigrant groups has a lot to do with when they arrived here and what skills and education they brought with them.

⁴ For example, the study says European immigrants are less likely to have a college education than immigrants from Asia, South America or Africa.

⁵ But it also finds that Europeans have higher household incomes than the other groups.

⁶ Those numbers seem contradictory. The explanation lies in when most members of the groups arrived.

⁷ The typical European immigrant arrived before 1950 and is older than the average immigrant from Asia, South America or Africa, many of whom came in the 1980s.

⁸ And, since college attendance has grown in recent decades—in the USA and abroad—young immigrants are far more likely to have a degree than older adults.

⁹ But despite fewer degrees, the European immigrants are better off economically because they've been here longer and have become established.

¹⁰ Among the factors to consider when comparing groups:

▶ Household and family income: Highly educated immigrant groups and those commonly in managerial and professional jobs have high incomes. But the number of people in a household has a big effect, too.

Filipino immigrants, for example, have the second-highest median household income—$45,419—of the groups surveyed. But they also have many households with at least five members. And 30.9% of all Filipino families have at least three workers in them—higher than any other group.

▶ Poverty: Poverty is closely tied to how long immigrants have been here, with groups here longest far better off.

Immigrant groups with the highest poverty rates tend to be mainly recent arrivals, and many—including Laotians and Cambodians, the groups with the highest poverty rates—are also refugees who fled with little wealth.

▶ Education: Education reflects the quality and length of schooling in countries immigrants come from. But it also says something about who is able to immigrate from a particular place.

For instance, immigrating from far-off places—such as India or Africa—requires an expensive airline ticket and can usually only be afforded by members of the well-educated middle- and upper-classes. Cost is not such a barrier for immigrants coming from closer places, making it easier for less educated people from places such as Mexico and Central America to come to the USA.

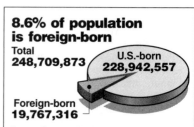

8.6% of population is foreign-born

Total 248,709,873

U.S.-born 228,942,557

Foreign-born 19,767,316

Immigrant groups larger than 100,000

Rank	Place of birth	Total
1	Mexico	4,298,014
2	Philippines	912,674
3	Canada	744,830
4	Cuba	736,971
5	Germany	711,929
6	United Kingdom	640,145
7	Italy	580,592
8	Korea	568,397
9	Vietnam	543,262
10	China	529,837
11	El Salvador	465,433
12	India	450,406
13	Poland	388,328
14	Dominican Republic	347,858
15	Jamaica	334,858
16	Former Soviet Union	333,725
17	Japan	290,128
18	Colombia	286,124
19	Taiwan	244,102
20	Guatemala	225,739
21	Haiti	225,393
22	Iran	210,941
23	Portugal	210,122
24	Greece	177,398
25	Laos	171,577
26	Ireland	169,827
27	Nicaragua	168,659
28	Hong Kong	147,131
29	Peru	144,199
30	Ecuador	143,314
31	Yugoslavia	141,516
32	Guyana	120,698
33	France	119,233
34	Cambodia	118,833
35	Trinidad and Tobago	115,710
36	Hungary	110,337
37	Honduras	108,923
38	Thailand	106,919

Source: Census Bureau
By Stephen Conley, USA TODAY

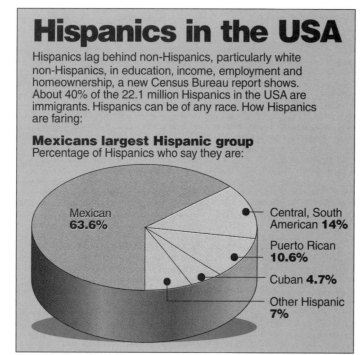

Hispanics in the USA

Hispanics lag behind non-Hispanics, particularly white non-Hispanics, in education, income, employment and homeownership, a new Census Bureau report shows. About 40% of the 22.1 million Hispanics in the USA are immigrants. Hispanics can be of any race. How Hispanics are faring:

Mexicans largest Hispanic group
Percentage of Hispanics who say they are:

Mexican **63.6%**

Central, South American **14%**

Puerto Rican **10.6%**

Cuban **4.7%**

Other Hispanic **7%**

Source: U.S. Census Bureau

By J. L. Albert, USA TODAY

GETTING THE MESSAGE

A. Scan Article 3A for the information needed to complete the following sentences.

1. The United States will become a "minority majority" nation after the year
   _____ .

2. In 1994, the population of the United States was _____ .

3. In the year 2020, the population of the United States will be _____ .

4. In 1994, the largest ethnic minority in the United States was _____ .

5. In 2020, the largest ethnic minority in the country will be _____ .

6. From 1995 to 2020, the ethnic group that will increase by the greatest percentage is
   _____ .

7. In 2018, the four states with the largest populations will be:

   #1 _____   #2 _____

   #3 _____   #4 _____

8. California is sometimes called the _____ state, and New York is
   sometimes called the _____ state.

9. The population of California is now _____ . In 2020, it will be
   _____ . (To compute this, use the U.S. population figures in
   paragraph 5 and the California percentages in paragraph 7.)

B. After reading Article 3B, indicate if each of these statements is true or false.

   _____ 1. In the 1980s, more immigrants came to the United States than ever before in
   the nation's history.

   _____ 2. Younger, newer, better educated immigrants usually earn more than older,
   less educated immigrants who have been in the country longer.

   _____ 3. A key factor affecting an immigrant's earnings is how long he or she has been
   living in the United States.

   _____ 4. People who come from far-away countries tend to be wealthier and more
   educated than those who come from nearby countries.

   _____ 5. The U.S. population today includes about twenty million foreign-born.

C. According to Article 3B, many factors affect the financial position of an immigrant family.
   List four of these factors.

   1. _____

   2. _____

   3. _____

   4. _____

PLAYING WITH WORDS

A. In Article 3A, scan each paragraph indicated for a word that means the opposite of the word listed. (The paragraph numbers are in parentheses.) Use a dictionary for help, if necessary.

1. *majority* (1): _____

2. *withheld* (1): _____

3. *similar* (4): _____

4. *expand* (5): _____

5. *slow* (5): _____

6. *decrease* (5): _____

7. *shortage* (8): _____

8. *gain* (10): _____

B. Work with a partner to circle the correct definitions for these groups of words from Article 3B. The paragraph in which each phrase is used is indicated in parentheses.

1. *with open arms* (1)
    a. warmly, eagerly
    b. suspiciously

2. *debate raged* (1)
    a. they fought physically
    b. they argued emotionally

3. *sheds some light* (2)
    a. explains
    b. hides

4. *challenges and confirms* (2)
    a. proves all of it
    b. suggests that part may be wrong and part correct

5. *interpreting the numbers* (3)
    a. deciding what they mean
    b. adding them up

DIGGING BENEATH THE SURFACE

A. Article 3B discusses the status of various immigrant groups by dividing them into two large categories. What are these two groups?

B. In Article 3B, reread paragraphs 3–8. What two facts seem to be contradictory? What further information explains this seeming contradiction?

C. According to Article 3B, the Census Bureau report confirms some stereotypes that people have about immigrants, but it challenges others. Working in small groups, make a list of some common stereotypes about new immigrants. Then decide if the report supports or disproves each idea. Appoint one member of your group as the reporter to tell your conclusions to the class.

A. *Learning Together*

1. Article 3A talks about the U.S. population in 2020 as if these statistics are facts. But they are only projections, predictions about the future. Many things could happen in the United States or in the world that would cause the population to grow less rapidly or even decline. Work with a partner to play the following game against other pairs of students: You have ten minutes to write down as many circumstances as you can think of that would keep the population of the United states from growing 25 percent in the next fifty-five years. Use your imagination. List anything possible, even if it is not likely. The team with the longest list wins.

2. New immigrants are sometimes resented, according to the first paragraph of Article 3B. Jot down some reasons why. Share your ideas with a partner and then with another pair of students. Then see if the four of you can think of any way to decrease this resentment. Appoint one student as the recorder (to take notes on your discussion) and another as the reporter (to summarize your discussion for the entire group).

3. With a partner, choose one of the countries listed in the chart of countries that have sent more than 100,000 immigrants to the United States. Read about your country in encyclopedias and geography books. Find five interesting facts about it, and write each fact on a 3" × 5" notecard. Write the name of the country on the other side of the card. In class, point out your country on a map of the world, and read your cards to the class. After all the cards have been read, combine them, shuffle the deck, and use them to play a trivia game called "What Country Is It?" The student who answers the most cards correctly gets to keep the game.

B. *Responding in Writing.* Choose one of the following writing projects.

1. Interview someone who has come to the United States within the past five years. Ask why the person came, what difficulties he or she faced, and what aspects of American life were new and surprising. Write up your interview as a newspaper article. Select the most interesting interviews to publish in a classroom newsletter.

2. Read about the history of census-taking in an encyclopedia, and write a summary of what you learned.

3. In the library, look at a famous reference book entitled *The Statistical Abstract of the United States.* This book has been revised annually since 1878. Look through a recent copy and find some interesting statistics on an immigration-related topic to write about.

Article 3B notes that poverty is a serious problem for recently arrived immigrants. Read Article 1A in the "Education" section ("Poverty impairs children's IQs") to see how poverty affects schoolchildren.

ARTICLE 4A
Key task: Funding equality

ARTICLE 4B
Kindness of whites is recalled

PREVIEWING THE ARTICLES

The lines snaked back and forth. Some were a mile long. People stood in darkness, hot sunlight, and driving rain. What were they seeking? A ticket to a World Series game or a rock concert? No, this was South Africa, where millions of blacks were voting for the first time in their lives—"a blessed day," said one shantytown resident. Voting began on April 27, 1994, and continued for several days. It took a few more days to tabulate the results. When the votes were counted, Nelson Mandela, leader of the African National Congress (ANC), became South Africa's first black president. His party had won 63 percent of the votes cast. After 342 years of white domination and 44 years of apartheid, South Africa entered a new era.

South Africa has a new leader, a new flag, a new constitution, and a new season of hope. What next? What must the new government accomplish? Its major goals are to achieve unity, improve living conditions, increase employment opportunities, and end violence. Mandela took over a country in which the 75 percent black population has an average annual income of $3,240 and in which the black unemployment rate is 33 percent.

Article 4A deals with the challenges that face Mandela and the ethnic rainbow of citizens now governing some 41 million South Africans. Article 4B is a profile of Nelson Mandela, a man whose courage, determination, and ability to forgive have amazed the world.

BEFORE YOU READ

1. Find the continent of Africa and the country of South Africa on a world map. What do you think the climate is like in South Africa? How many countries are in Africa? Take a guess. Then check your answer in a recently published reference book.

2. Look up South Africa in an encyclopedia and read about apartheid. Discuss some of the restrictions it placed upon black South Africans.

AS YOU READ

While reading Article 4A, jot down a list of needs that must be addressed to improve the lives of black South Africans.

Key task: Funding equality

By Jessica Lee
USA TODAY

1 KWANDEBELE, South Africa—Artist Francina Ndimande sits on a reed mat in her spacious studio, surrounded by hollowed-out ostrich eggs she's preparing to paint.

2 Her lavish geometric-design paintings and beadwork are sold in galleries in Johannesburg and Paris.

3 Her art has taken her from a home with no electricity or plumbing to a substantial income and the kind of life few blacks here even know about.

4 Did she vote? Ndimande chuckles: "Yes. And, probably now, I might go ahead and build my gallery"—and fulfill her dream of setting up a business outside of her home.

5 To Nelson Mandela, on the verge of being elected South Africa's first black president, her dream matches his hopes for black entrepreneurs: economic equality.

6 "They say there will never be a market-driven economy," Mandela said in an interview Sunday, "until the position of blacks is raised to the same level as that of whites."

7 But for Mandela to achieve that vision, and for Ndimande to open her business, much must be done and billions must be expended.

8 "Decent roads, telephones, clean water, electricity, education, adequate housing, and the single most important thing, jobs. And they will require state spending," says political analyst and author Allister Sparks. "But it must be done without damaging the growth of the economy."

9 That is the reality as Mandela attempts to turn his political rhetoric into national policy. He can't be too lavish or move too fast in rewarding supporters, despite the economic gulf between the races.

10 A major hurdle for planners is determining what is needed in Mandela's constituency. The government has only a very loose idea of how many blacks are in the country.

11 Population estimates in black areas were made by flying over and counting houses, then guessing at the number of occupants. That method put the black population at 31 million in a country of 41.6 million.

12 But as the election revealed, the count was vastly short.

13 Without an accurate count, planners are guessing.

14 Still, Mandela is pushing forward. He has revealed an ambitious public works plan for South Africa that would:
▶ Create jobs and training for 2.5 million over 10 years.
▶ Build 1 million homes in five years.
▶ Connect electricity to 2.5 million homes in five years.
▶ Provide free education.

15 The price tag is hotly debated. The African National Congress estimates an outlay of $3.3 billion. Rivals, especially in President F.W. de Klerk's National Party, put the cost at 15 times that.

16 Mandela sees available money from reordering de Klerk's priorities. "The last government spent 10 billion rand ($3 billion) on guns and ammunition and only 2 billion ($600 million) on housing. We are going to reverse that."

17 Citing the conclusion of the 1993 report by the World Bank, Mandela says: "In South Africa at the present moment, there is no market system in the proper sense of the word. On the Johannesburg Stock Exchange, more than 80% of the shares that are quoted are owned by five conglomerates."

18 "We want the South Africans to invest in their own country instead of exporting and investing abroad. . . . It is going to be necessary for us to rely on local investments."

19 To attract investors, he says, "we have to be very careful" with appointments to the central bank and finance ministry. He won't discuss names.

20 Mandela also envisions a greater economic participation in the crowded and crime-plagued black townships.

21 In Katlehong and Soweto, sprawling townships surrounding Johannesburg, trailers and buses serving as dry cleaners, carry-outs, and even hotels sit along the streets or in fields.

22 Their black owners were not permitted to own property. But nothing could stop their drive to become entrepreneurs.

23 Managerial skills have been hard to come by, because apprenticeship programs were closed to blacks. Blacks finish high school in their 20s, cabbie Alfred Mamabolo says. "They have to work, then go (to school), work, then go back."

24 Few scholarships are available even to those with excellent grades, similar to the situation for U.S. blacks prior to passage of civil rights laws.

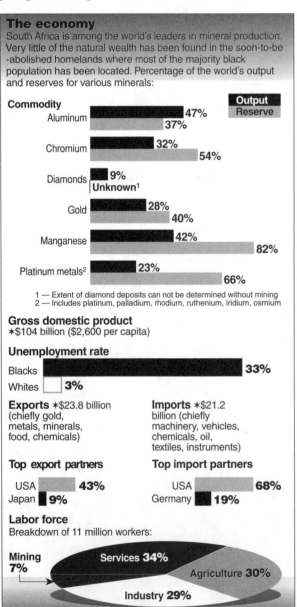

The economy
South Africa is among the world's leaders in mineral production. Very little of the natural wealth has been found in the soon-to-be-abolished homelands where most of the majority black population has been located. Percentage of the world's output and reserves for various minerals:

Commodity — Output / Reserve

Commodity	Output	Reserve
Aluminum	47%	37%
Chromium	32%	54%
Diamonds	9%	Unknown[1]
Gold	28%	40%
Manganese	42%	82%
Platinum metals[2]	23%	66%

1 — Extent of diamond deposits can not be determined without mining
2 — Includes platinum, palladium, rhodium, ruthenium, iridium, osmium

Gross domestic product
✱$104 billion ($2,600 per capita)

Unemployment rate

Blacks	33%
Whites	3%

Exports ✱$23.8 billion (chiefly gold, metals, minerals, food, chemicals)

Imports ✱$21.2 billion (chiefly machinery, vehicles, chemicals, oil, textiles, instruments)

Top export partners

USA	43%
Japan	9%

Top import partners

USA	68%
Germany	19%

Labor force
Breakdown of 11 million workers:

Mining 7%
Services 34%
Agriculture 30%
Industry 29%

By Julie Stacey, USA TODAY

By Denis Farrell, AP

WORTH THE EIGHT-HOUR WAIT: Voters in the black township of Soweto, in the southwest suburbs of Johannesburg, loop their way toward the ballot box. At some polling places, waiting time stretched to eight hours and more.

25 Says Alexandra resident Mary Setshedi, 23, who wants to be an accountant: "They did accept me at the University of Cape Town, but there was no financial assistance."

26 Mandela also must deal with a 500,000-strong bureaucracy, almost all white.

27 "The ANC will want to bring many of their senior people into the top jobs," says de Klerk spokesman Richard Carter.

Kindness of whites is recalled

By Jessica Lee
USA TODAY

1 JOHANNESBURG, South Africa— Nelson Mandela, at some point in his 75 years, has played roles in South Africa similar to those of Thurgood Marshall, Malcolm X and the Rev. Martin Luther King Jr.

2 Mandela, on his way to becoming South Africa's first black president, sidetracks during an hour-long interview Sunday to trace memories of his life as a civil rights lawyer, and revolutionary.

3 He speaks with no bitterness or anger of the wrongs he suffered under South Africa's apartheid policy, which tried to make blacks into social, economic and political inferiors.

4 Racism left Marshall crusty and resentful at the end of his life. It propelled Malcolm X to preach eye-for-an-eye vengeance for most of his. It kept King on his knees in prayer.

5 But Mandela never mentions apartheid's racist core, which turned him from a lawyer to a convict serving 27 years for fighting apartheid. Instead, he speaks of the generosity, friendship and respect that whites extended to him.

6 He tells of a time 30 years ago when apartheid laws prevented him from suing to protect a black man uprooted from his Johannesburg home on the whim of a clerk.

7 Mandela says he was able to persuade white authorities to remedy the tragedy.

8 "Invariably, these leading officials . . . attached normal human considerations and they reversed the decision of the clerk," he says. "I found cooperation throughout."

9 White men came to his aid repeatedly during his four-year trial for treason, even enabling him to continue practicing law. "It was my livelihood," he says.

10 Mandela says his treason trial "was heard from 9 o'clock (a.m.) to 1 o'clock (p.m.). The afternoon would be free. I was able to arrange that all the (client) cases in which I was involved should be heard in the afternoon. They met me in that regard, prosecutors, policemen, magistrates."

11 But it was while serving life in prison,

By Dixie D. Vereen, USA TODAY

SPEAKING OF RESPECT: White friendships have helped Nelson Mandela endure, and overcome, apartheid's racist core.

breaking rocks on Robben Island off Cape Town, that Mandela formed friendships with white men so deep he continues to nurture them.

12 Guards ignored prison rules to bring him blankets, newspapers and other kindnesses.

13 To show his thanks, Mandela has invited two jailers to attend his inauguration May 10.

14 Mandela also shows no bitterness toward governments, such as Japan's, that violated worldwide economic sanctions imposed against South Africa.

15 "We could not normalize relations with the National Party (apartheid's creator) and not with those who merely fitted into a situation and committed lesser crimes," he says.

16 Mandela smiles with pride while relating tales of his upbringing in the "absolutely democratic" tradition of his Xhosa clan in the Transkei region on the Indian Ocean.

17 The clan "resisted white penetration for 100 years using an ox shield and a spear against gunpowder."

18 As a youth, he says, "it was easy to

want to be part of that tradition. But, of course, I broke with that tradition when there was a forced marriage and I ran away from home" before marrying.

19 Mandela later married a colleague in the African National Congress. Winnie Mandela campaigned to focus the world's attention to her husband when he was jailed.

20 Shortly after his release, at a time when police had linked her to a township gang implicated in the fatal beating of a teen-age boy, they separated.

21 Now, he says, the marriage is irrevocably broken.

22 "I have got my own view of what a marriage should be. She probably has got her own view. It was regrettable that I had to take a decision to separate from her. Nothing has happened to induce me to revise my stand."

23 Her view is different. In a recent interview, she said the two are still in love.

24 Mandela is cool on that point. "I cannot stop her from having certain sentiments. . . . Nothing has changed."

A. After reading Article 4A, select the best completion for each statement.

1. Paragraphs 1–5 are about an artist. She is an example of _____ .

   a. the economic prosperity of South African blacks

   b. the hope that in the new South Africa blacks will be able to own businesses

   c. the importance of the visual arts in South Africa

   d. the fact that many blacks have artistic talent

2. According to paragraphs 10–12, _____ .

   a. the South African government knows exactly how many blacks live in South Africa

   b. there are 31 million blacks in South Africa

   c. there are probably a lot more than 31 million blacks in South Africa

   d. there may be fewer than 31 million blacks in South Africa

3. According to paragraph 15, Mandela's government will increase spending for _____ .

   a. bureaucracy

   b. military equipment

   c. housing

   d. rands

4. According to paragraphs 22–24, South African blacks have had trouble learning how to run businesses because _____ .

   a. they have no interest in business

   b. there are no businesses in the black communities

   c. all South African businesses are operated by the government

   d. apprenticeship programs in management were closed to blacks

B. Article 4A discusses many changes that are needed to improve economic conditions for South African blacks. Name four of them.

1. _____

2. _____

3. _____

4. _____

A. Circle the correct meaning of each of these phrases from Article 4A. The paragraph in which each phrase is used is indicated in parentheses. In addition to context clues, use a dictionary for help, if necessary.

1. *spacious studio* (1)
   a. large studio
   b. small studio

2. *lavish geometric-design paintings* (2)
   a. simple paintings
   b. fancy paintings

3. *a substantial income* (3)
   a. a very good income
   b. a low income

4. *his hopes for black entrepreneurs* (5)
   a. he wants more blacks to become artists
   b. he wants more blacks to own their own businesses

5. *a market-driven economy* (6)
   a. prices are determined by competition and supply and demand
   b. people drive cars to the markets

6. *billions must be expended* (7)
   a. billions must be spent
   b. billions must be taken in by the government through increased taxes

7. *political rhetoric* (9)
   a. persuasive speech and writing designed to win votes
   b. political ambitions

8. *economic gulf between the races* (9)
   a. the races live far apart
   b. there is a big difference between the average incomes of blacks and whites

9. *The price tag is hotly debated* (15)
   a. people disagree about how much will have to be spent
   b. no one wants to determine the price

10. *reordering the priorities* (16)
    a. ordering priorities for the second time
    b. changing ideas about what is considered most important

B. Reread Article 4B, scanning the paragraphs indicated below. Look for a word that means the opposite or almost the opposite of each word or phrase listed. The paragraph in which each word or phrase is used is indicated in parentheses.

1. *stays on a direct path* (2) _____

2. *integration* (3) _____

3. *forgiveness* (4) _____

4. *occasionally* (8) _____

5. *loyalty to one's country* (9) _____

6. *defense attorneys* (10) _____

7. *can be altered* (21) _____

DIGGING BENEATH THE SURFACE

A. Writers sometimes imply (suggest) ideas instead of stating them directly. The skillful reader gets these indirect messages by making inferences (conclusions based upon the information given). This is sometimes called "reading between the lines." Apply this skill to Article 4B. Decide which of the following statements are appropriate inferences. Then put a check in the "Yes" or "No" box. After each statement, write the number of the paragraph that helped you decide.

Inferences	**Yes**	**No**
1. Mandela is skillful at resolving conflicts peacefully.	_____	_____
2. Mandela often uses threats and confrontation to achieve his goals.	_____	_____
3. Mandela believes that a group member should obey the group's rules even when he or she considers them morally wrong.	_____	_____
4. Mandela does not approve of his wife's past behavior.	_____	_____
5. Mandela is a practical man.	_____	_____

B. Use the graphs that accompany the articles to answer the following questions.

1. The bar graphs on mineral output contrast South Africa's percentage of world output and reserves for several important minerals. For what three minerals does South Africa have more than half of the world's reserves?

   1. _____

   2. _____

   3. _____

2. According to the bar graph on unemployment, the unemployment rate of blacks in South Africa is ____ times that of whites.

3. Using the pie graph on sectors of the economy, find out how many actual workers in South Africa are employed in each of the following:

   1. service occupations _____

   2. mining _____

   3. industry _____

GOING BEYOND THE TEXT

A. *Learning Together*

1. With a partner, choose one African country to research. (Each pair should choose a different country.) One of you can look for basic information, such as the country's size, location, major products, and population. (In addition to encyclopedias, world almanacs, the *Reader's Guide to Periodical Literature,* and a periodical CD-ROM database will help you to find information.) The other partner can look for recent news stories about the country. (*Facts on File: A Weekly World News Digest* and the *New York Times Index* are excellent additional references to consult.) Then work together to prepare a short oral report (with visual aids) about your country.

2. Working in groups of four, select an African folktale to dramatize. Two excellent sources for stories are the following collections: *Bury My Bones but Keep My Words: African Tales for Retelling,* retold by Tony Fairman (Henry Holt and Co., 1991); and *When Lions Could Fly and Other Tales from Africa,* told by Nick Greaves (Barron's Educational Services, Inc., 1993). Each member of the group should be assigned a

specific task: for example, narrator, actor(s), director, or technical director (in charge of costumes, props, sound effects, and so on). Act out the story for the class. Then ask your classmates to write a statement about what they consider the theme and message of the tale.

B. *Responding in Writing.* Choose one of the following writing projects.

1. Article 4A points out that many blacks in South Africa live without electricity in their homes. Imagine that you had no electricity in your home. How would that affect your life? What would you miss most? How would you manage to get along? Write a brief composition on this topic.

2. To millions of South Africans and Americans, Nelson Mandela is a hero. Who is your hero? Write a composition about him or her. Note that Article 4B describes Mandela by using anecdotes, paraphrasing (the writer's restatement of someone else's words), and direct quotation (repeating the subject's exact words). Try to use at least two of these techniques in your composition.

MAKING CONNECTIONS

Article 1 in the "Sports" section ("Aaron paid a price for beating Ruth") describes Hank Aaron's experiences with racism in America. Compare his experiences with those of black South Africans under apartheid.

ARTICLE 5A
Real people fought, won "mythic" battle

ARTICLE 5B
Paratroopers relive jumps that landed in history

PREVIEWING THE ARTICLES

"They gave us our world," President Bill Clinton said of the Allied forces who invaded Normandy on D-Day, June 6, 1944. To the thousands who died there and the 35,000 American, British, and Canadian veterans who returned to Normandy in 1994 to commemorate D-Day's fiftieth anniversary, Clinton said, "We are the children of your sacrifice."

The term *D-Day* (meaning the secret date of a planned military invasion) goes back at least to World War I. But it is now forever linked to June 6, 1944. On that date, 175,000 Allied troops crossed the English Channel by air and sea. Thousands died on beaches with code names such as Omaha and Utah. But at day's end, eighty square miles of Normandy were in Allied hands. The Allied forces had broken through Hitler's Atlantic "wall." The liberation of Europe had begun. Article 5A summarizes that historic "longest" day.

D-Day anniversaries have been celebrated before and will, no doubt, continue in future decades. But probably none will be more poignant than the fiftieth. Veterans of that horrible yet wonderful day were mostly in their seventies and eighties by 1994. Yet about 20,000 veterans went to Normandy with their families for the historic day, as did huge fleets of ships and planes. Events included everything from solemn speeches, military parades, and cemetery visits to festive reunion parties, fireworks, dances, and streeet fairs. For many spectators, however, as described in Article 5B, the crowning moments came when thirty-eight veterans, ranging in age from sixty-eight to eighty-three, parachuted onto the beaches of Normandy, as they had done so many years ago.

BEFORE YOU READ

1. On a large map of Europe, locate England, France, Normandy, and the English Channel.

2. In small groups, share information about World War II. Discuss the famous bombing that caused the United States to enter the war and the bombings that led Japan to surrender. Discuss which countries fought on the Allied side and which fought on the Axis side.

AS YOU READ

1. As you read Article 5A, look for the reasons why the D-Day invasion was unusual.

2. Article 5B tells about thirty-eight elderly men who risked injury and death to relive a terrifying wartime experience. Why did they do this?

Real people fought, won "mythic" battle

By Andrea Stone
USA TODAY

1   The Allies had only the ancient victories of Julius Caesar and William the Conqueror to guide them as they crossed the English Channel on June 6, 1944—D-Day.

2   History's greatest amphibious invasion had begun. Before its end, 9,500 troops would be dead or wounded.

3   "I haven't figured out how many days I've lived on this Earth. But June 6th was the most dramatic," says Bob Slaughter, 69, of Roanoke, Va. "I left my youth over there. I have to go back and sort it all out."

4   As the USA honors its war dead this Memorial Day, it also prepares to commemorate next week's 50th anniversary of D-Day. The memories and images of the Normandy invasion cling as tenaciously as weary infantrymen to bloody Omaha Beach. More than just the opening salvo of a crucial military campaign, D-Day began the USA's transformation into a global power.

5   There would be bigger battles and another year left to fight in Europe and the Pacific. But never again would one single day loom so large, risk so much, prove so critical.

6   D-Day will endure beyond the men who took part in it.

7   "There aren't many moments in American military history that have been more important or been invested with more mythic proportions," says James P. Jones, Florida State University historian. "It was the turning point of the war."

8   More, "D-Day was the pivot point of the 20th century," says Stephen Ambrose, author of *D-Day: The Climactic Battle of World War II.* "It ensured the future of democracy."

9   As an 18-year-old paratrooper, Eugene Cook of King of Prussia, Pa., had no doubt "we were on the right side. . . . We really gave one whole generation back their life."

10   On D-Day, Nazi Germany had occupied and oppressed most of Europe for four years. The Allies had nibbled the edges of Hitler's "Fortress Europe" with landings in North Africa, Sicily and mainland Italy, but the continent's heart still lay beyond their reach.

11   Only on the Eastern Front did a massive army oppose Hitler. Yet, the Soviet Union could not fight alone forever.

12   So the world anxiously awaited the inevitable.

13   "The first 24 hours of the invasion will be decisive," German Field Marshal Erwin Rommel told an aide. "For the

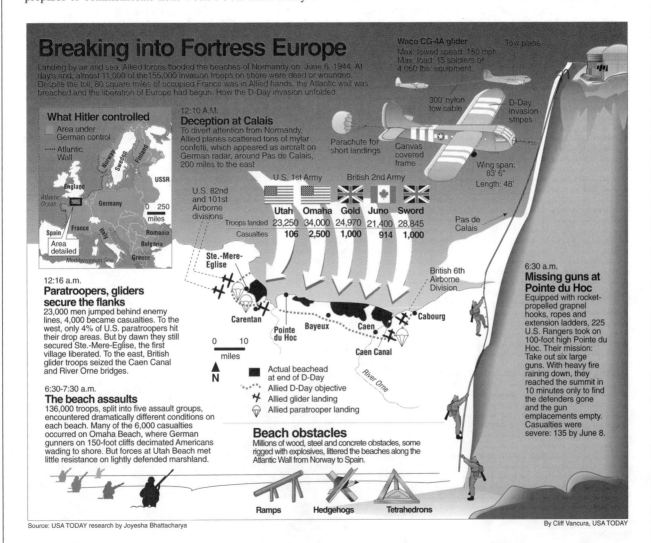

Breaking into Fortress Europe

Landing by air and sea, Allied forces flooded the beaches of Normandy on June 6, 1944. At day's end, almost 11,000 of the 155,000 invasion troops on shore were dead or wounded. Despite the toll, 80 square miles of occupied France was in Allied hands, the Atlantic wall was breached and the liberation of Europe had begun. How the D-Day invasion unfolded:

Waco CG-4A glider
Max. towed speed: 150 mph
Max. load: 15 soldiers or 4,060 lbs. equipment

Tow plane
300' nylon tow cable
D-Day invasion stripes
Parachute for short landings
Canvas covered frame
Wing span: 83' 6"
Length: 48'

What Hitler controlled
☐ Area under German control
····· Atlantic Wall

Norway, Sweden, Finland, England, Atlantic Ocean, Germany, USSR, Spain, France, Italy, Romania, Bulgaria, Greece, Mediterranean Sea
0   250 miles
Area detailed

12:10 A.M.
Deception at Calais
To divert attention from Normandy, Allied planes scattered tons of mylar confetti, which appeared as aircraft on German radar, around Pas de Calais, 200 miles to the east

U.S. 82nd and 101st Airborne divisions

Pas de Calais

	U.S. 1st Army		British 2nd Army		
	Utah	Omaha	Gold	Juno	Sword
Troops landed	23,250	34,000	24,970	21,400	28,845
Casualties	106	2,500	1,000	914	1,000

Ste.-Mere-Eglise

British 6th Airborne Division

12:16 a.m.
Paratroopers, gliders secure the flanks
23,000 men jumped behind enemy lines, 4,000 became casualties. To the west, only 4% of U.S. paratroopers hit their drop areas. But by dawn they still secured Ste.-Mere-Eglise, the first village liberated. To the east, British glider troops seized the Caen Canal and River Orne bridges.

Carentan, Pointe du Hoc, Bayeux, Caen, Cabourg, Caen Canal, River Orne

0   10 miles
N

6:30-7:30 a.m.
The beach assaults
136,000 troops, split into five assault groups, encountered dramatically different conditions on each beach. Many of the 6,000 casualties occurred on Omaha Beach, where German gunners on 150-foot cliffs decimated Americans wading to shore. But forces at Utah Beach met little resistance on lightly defended marshland.

■ Actual beachhead at end of D-Day
·⚔· Allied D-Day objective
✦ Allied glider landing
⊙ Allied paratrooper landing

6:30 a.m.
Missing guns at Pointe du Hoc
Equipped with rocket-propelled grapnel hooks, ropes and extension ladders, 225 U.S. Rangers took on 100-foot high Pointe du Hoc. Their mission: Take out six large guns. With heavy fire raining down, they reached the summit in 10 minutes only to find the defenders gone and the gun emplacements empty. Casualties were severe: 135 by June 8.

Beach obstacles
Millions of wood, steel and concrete obstacles, some rigged with explosives, littered the beaches along the Atlantic Wall from Norway to Spain.

Ramps   Hedgehogs   Tetrahedrons

Source: USA TODAY research by Joyesha Bhattacharya

By Cliff Vancura, USA TODAY

Allies, as well as Germany, it will be the longest day."

14 "Operation Overlord" took two years to plan and provision. When D-Day came, 175,000 men from the USA, Britain, Canada and six other nations would be ferried across 100 miles of water in 11,000 planes and 5,300 ships.

15 "It was as if the cities of Green Bay, Racine, and Kenosha, Wis., were picked up and moved—every man, woman and child, every automobile and truck—to the east side of Lake Michigan, in one night," Ambrose writes.

16 Still, the Allies initially landed just five divisions to the 60 German units in France.

17 And they were entrenched behind Hitler's "impregnable" Atlantic Wall, which stretched from the North Sea to Spain.

18 The 2,500-mile "wall" really consisted of millions of jagged steel landing craft obstacles, underwater and land mines, barbed wire fences, artillery batteries, concrete bunkers and pillboxes. It ate up nearly 20% of Germany's war effort.

19 "It was a construction feat unrivaled in human history, much bigger than the Great Wall of China," Ambrose says.

20 The wall was strongest near ports and the Pas de Calais, the channel's narrowest point and the closest to Germany's industrial Rhine-Ruhr area. Hitler expected the attack there.

21 Surprise was crucial. An elaborate allied deception campaign fed German confusion, indicating landing sites from Norway to the Balkans.

22 The real armies were set to land in Normandy June 5. But, though the fleet had already sailed, storms forced allied leader Gen. Dwight Eisenhower to postpone for 24 hours.

23 Without a break in the weather, D-Day would have to be put off two weeks until tides and moon were right again.

24 Allied meteorologists predicted that break, small though it was, for June 6. Eisenhower launched the invasion with a simple: "OK, we'll go."

25 Shortly after midnight, British glider infantry landed near Caen and seized bridges over the River Orne—blocking German reinforcements from the east. To the west, U.S. paratroopers scattered amid clouds and heavy fire. Though some drowned in flooded fields and others were shot hanging from trees, they diverted the Germans from the main invasion force that landed at dawn.

26 In what Gen. Omar Bradley called "the most dangerous mission of D-Day," U.S. Rangers scaled the heavily defended 100-foot cliffs at Pointe du Hoc to destroy six guns.

27 Of 225 Rangers, only 90 were left by June 8.

28 The worst fighting would come on Omaha Beach, which had just been secretly reinforced by crack German troops. Riddled with mines and obstacles beneath steep bluffs studded with machine-gun pillboxes, Omaha became a killing field for the 1st and 29th Infantry Divisions.

29 "I came pretty close to having my own stone marker," says Robert Miller, 69, of Pueblo, Colo., paralyzed there by a sniper's bullet.

30 Allied mistakes added to casualties. Many soldiers were dazed and seasick after hours in landing craft. Air support didn't bomb holes in the beaches, leaving infantry exposed.

31 The Germans also erred. Faulty weather forecasts convinced Rommel, the western commander, that it was safe to go home for his wife's birthday. Other senior officers were away at war games.

32 When the real war came, officials refused to wake Hitler. Normandy, they reasoned, was a feint. They ordered the bulk of German forces to stay near the Pas de Calais.

33 Ten hours would pass before Hitler sent two critical Panzer tank divisions to Normandy. By then, it was too late.

34 At day's end, the Allies had established a firm, if narrow, beachhead.

35 Vehicles and supplies were unloaded on the beach and from one of two artificial harbors, or "Mulberries," that had been towed from England.

36 Many who worked were black troops, then relegated to support units in the still-segregated armed forces.

37 Hard fighting through Normandy's hedgerows followed the landings. The battle would rage until Aug. 21, when the remnants of two German armies were trapped at Falaise. Three days later, the Allies entered Paris.

38 Allied forces would suffer greatly in the months ahead, especially in Operation Market Garden and the Battle of the Bulge. Later, they would stumble upon the horrors of Hitler's concentration camps.

39 "The war would get grimier after that," says Jones. "In many ways, D-Day was the last shining crusade. The last hurrah of heroism and bravery."

Paratroopers relive jumps that landed in history

By Andrea Stone
USA TODAY

1 AMFREVILLE, France—For 38 World War II veterans of the Return to Normandy Association, a commemorative parachute jump into a mud-choked marsh here Sunday provided a sense of closure.

2 "We left some of our youth here," said Thomas Rice, 73, of San Diego, his face blackened with burnt cork as it was when he landed before dawn on D-Day 50 years ago today. "We're coming back to get some of that youth. Now we're whole again."

3 Before the group could fulfill its dream of jumping into Normandy again, the veterans—age 67 to 83—had to overcome initial Pentagon objections and concerns about safety.

4 Yesterday's jump saw its share of bumps and bruises and one truly frightening moment.

5 Earl Draper, 70, of Inverness, Fla., the last veteran to jump before active duty paratroopers took to the skies, terrified onlookers when his sport parachute failed to open.

6 As hundreds gasped below, Draper tumbled in a spiral before cutting away his faulty streamer. A blue emergency chute opened just in time to deposit him behind the crowd.

7 Draper was helicoptered in stable condition to a French hospital to determine the extent of a back injury.

8 Elsworth Harger, 68, of Munising, Mich., suffered a bloody temple when his parachute risers whacked him in the head on the way down. But Harger, who wore a leather helmet with a Mohawk down the center, walked off the field on his own.

9 A veteran of more than 880 jumps, Harger said this one was "in memory of all the fallen comrades (and) to celebrate that we turned the world around."

10 Though they were followed by 500 members of the 82nd and 101st Airborne Divisions and 60 French paratroopers, the veterans in their tilted red berets and matching silk kerchiefs were the stars of the show.

By Eileen Blass, USA TODAY

IN MEMORY: Veteran paratrooper Gordon King, 70, of Merrill, Wis., carried photos of his two brothers-in-law and comrades killed in WWII.

11 Each veterans' landing brought cheers and applause. After the jump, former 82nd Airborne paratrooper Jack Dunn, 69, of Brookfield, Wis., played bagpipes as he led veterans to the reviewing area. Reporters and autograph seekers surrounded them.

12 "They are very courageous to jump at 70 years," said Jacques-Claude Leymond, a local resident.

13 Most of the men, many of whom parachute as a hobby, considered Sunday's jump a breeze compared with 50 years ago, when they were fired on in darkness by Germans.

14 But a small army of nurses, medics and doctors—including two heart specialists—positioned around the drop zone attested to concerns about the seniors' safety.

15 Their services weren't needed by most veterans. Some, however, did have bruised egos when, as 50 years earlier, they floated far afield from their designated drop zone.

16 "I didn't want to land with the cows so I steered to a nice dry field way out there. A couple of French gendarmes found me," said a smiling Howard Greenberg, 69, from Bay Village, Ohio.

17 Yet, Greenberg was serious about why he jumped: to honor two close friends killed in the war. "I carried their names in my pocket," he said. "In those days, we made a difference for freedom."

18 Gordon King, 70, of Merrill, Wis., also jumped to honor warriors of a half-century ago. In his pocket, he carried pictures of his wife's two brothers, one killed in North Africa, the other in Sicily; and a photo of "the man I jumped behind in Normandy," who later died in Holland.

19 "People shouldn't remember us," said King. Then, pointing to the old black and white photos he carried, he said, "That's what this whole thing is about."

GETTING THE MESSAGE

A. After reading Article 5A, select the best completion for each statement.

1. D-Day was the beginning of _____ .

   a. World War II

   b. the war on the Eastern front

   c. the Normandy invasion

   d. the defeat of the Allied forces

2. By the end of D-Day, the Allied forces had _____ .

   a. freed Normandy from Nazi control

   b. established a beachhead on Normandy

   c. suffered 15,000 casualties

   d. suffered severe losses in the Pacific

3. The German military forces were surprised by _____ .

   a. an Allied plan to invade France

   b. the location of the invasion

   c. code names used by Allied forces

   d. the nationalities of their attackers

4. The Allies might have been pushed off the Normandy beaches if _____ .

   a. they had lost fewer troops

   b. the Channel crossing had been smooth

   c. the Russian army had arrived in time

   d. German forces had arrived sooner

5. D-Day was an important Allied victory because _____ .

   a. it ended World War II

   b. good always triumphs over evil

   c. the Allies broke through Germany's Atlantic "wall"

   d. the Allies died bravely

B. After reading Article 5B, mark these answers true or false.

_____ 1. The Pentagon was eager to have these elderly paratroopers jump as part of the D-Day commemoration ceremonies.

_____ 2. Some of the jumpers missed the landing spot they were aiming for.

_____ 3. The 1944 and the 1994 jumps were made at the same time of day.

_____ 4. There was concern about the paratroopers' safety because most of them had not parachuted since 1944.

A. Use context clues to determine the meaning of each italicized word from Article 5A. Choose the best definition. The paragraph in which each word is used is indicated in parentheses.

1. *amphibious* (2)
   a. by air
   b. by land and water

2. *tenaciously* (4)
   a. easily
   b. with determination and firmness

3. *inevitable* (12)
   a. something that had to happen
   b. something uncertain

4. *crucial* (21)
   a. cruel but necessary
   b. extremely important

5. *meteorologists* (24)
   a. scientists who study meteors and the stars
   b. scientists who study weather and climate

6. *casualties* (30)
   a. soldiers who didn't fight hard
   b. people killed or injured

7. *erred* (31)
   a. made a mistake
   b. used good judgment

8. *feint* (32)
   a. false, counterfeit
   b. real, true

9. *critical* (33)
   a. essential, crucial
   b. insulting, finding fault with

10. *relegated* (36)
    a. given an inferior position
    b. given a higher position

B. After reading Article 5B, explain the meanings of the following phrases. Use a dictionary for help, if necessary. The paragraph in which each phrase is used is indicated in parentheses.

1. *initial Pentagon objections* (3) _____

2. *active duty paratroopers* (5) _____

3. *in stable condition* (7) _____

4. *bruised egos* (15) _____

5. *French gendarmes* (16) _____

DIGGING BENEATH THE SURFACE

A. Write the numbers of the paragraphs in Article 5A that do the following:

1. give a chronological account of D-Day _____

2. compare Allied and German forces _____

3. use figures of speech that compare the Allied forces and the continent of Europe to the human body _____

B. In Article 5A, the words *impregnable* (17) and *wall* (18) are in quotation marks. Why?

C. Article 5B suggest some reasons why thousands of veterans wanted to return to Normandy for the D-Day commemoration. List three of these reasons.

1. _____
2. _____
3. _____

GOING BEYOND THE TEXT

A. *Learning Together*

For this exercise, the class should split up into eight small groups. Each group will research the role that one of these men played during World War II: Franklin Roosevelt, Harry Truman, Winston Churchill, Charles de Gaulle, Joseph Stalin, Dwight Eisenhower, Benito Mussolini, and Adolf Hitler. After each group gives a short report to the class, match each man with the words he said. (There are two Churchill quotes.) Use a book of quotations, an American history book, or an encyclopedia for help, if necessary.

1. "The great masses of people . . . will more easily fall victims to a big lie than a small one." (1933) _____

2. "We have buried the putrid corpse of liberty." (1934) _____

3. "I cannot forecast to you the actions of Russia. It is a riddle wrapped in a mystery inside an enigma." (October 1939) _____

4. "France has lost the battle. But France has not lost the war." (June 1940)

   _____

5. "We will have no truce or parley with you [Hitler], or the grisly gang who work your wicked will. You do your worst and we will do our best." (July 1941)

   _____

6. "Yesterday, December 7, 1941—a date which will live in infamy—the United States was suddenly and deliberately attacked by naval and air forces of the Empire of Japan." _____

7. "You are about to embark upon the Great Crusade, toward which we have striven these many months. The eyes of the world are upon you. The hope and prayers of liberty-loving people everywhere march with you. . . ." (June 6, 1944)

   _____

8. "Sixteen hours ago an American airplane dropped one bomb on Hiroshima. . . . The force from which the sun draws its power has been loosed against those who brought war to the Far East." (August 6, 1945) _____

9. "A single death is a tragedy, a million deaths is a statistic." (quoted in *Inside Russia Today* by John Gunther, 1958) _____

B. *Responding in Writing.* Choose one of the following writing projects.

1. Interview someone who remembers the World War II years well. Plan your questions beforehand. Take notes or tape the interview. Then write an article about that person's experiences either on the battlefront or the homefront.

2. Write a biographical sketch of one of the World War II national or military leaders.

3. Research and write a summary of the various important roles of women in military and civilian life during World War II.

MAKING CONNECTIONS

The English Channel is now a less formidable barrier than it was when the Allied forces crossed it on D-Day. Today, a tunnel under the English Channel connects France and England. You can read about the Channel in the "Money" section of this book. In that article, you can also learn about other historic moments involving the Channel.

NEWS

The "Straight" News Story

The front page of the newspaper is where you will find the latest and most important news. The most significant story of the day becomes the lead article. The newspaper's biggest headline is over this story, and there is often a photograph with it. In many papers, the lead story is placed in the left-hand column, right below the first word of the banner headline. In other papers, the lead story is centered, sometimes under a picture.

"Straight" (or "hard") news stories are written in an objective style. Journalists include only the facts, never their own opinions, reactions, or judgments. Any comment upon what happened comes from experts, observers, or those directly involved in or affected by the event. If the article is about a controversial subject, people with opposing viewpoints are quoted and, ideally, given equal space in the article.

An objective news story does not reveal the author's viewpoint. However, a story can be "slanted" in one direction or another by the inclusion or exclusion of certain facts, by the amount of space given to various facts or quotations, and by the location of various pieces of information in the article. A fact mentioned briefly near the end of the article is less likely to be noticed than information presented earlier and in greater detail. In deciding what kind of slant to give a story, journalists consider the interests and educational level of their paper's typical reader.

Exercise 1: Comparing Two News Articles

Read the front pages of two different daily newspapers on the same day. Choose two articles about the same event (preferably the lead story). Compare them by answering the following questions.

1. Are both stories objective, presenting facts without comment upon them and giving equal space to both sides if the story is controversial?

2. Do the stories seem about the same, or do they emphasize different aspects of the news event?

3. Does one story take a more negative view of the information than the other does?

4. Which reporter made a greater effort to get as much information as possible?

5. Could you switch the stories (put each in the other paper), or is there something about the content, language level, slant, or style that would make each story seem out of place in the other paper?

6. In your opinion, which story is better? Why?

The Five Ws

Who, what, when, where, and *why*—these are the standard questions that every good news story must answer. (In some stories, *how* must be included, too.) Journalists try to get all or most of this information into the lead (the opening paragraph) because that's what readers expect. Many readers scan leads to get the gist of stories. Then they read further only those articles of interest to them.

Straight news stories never end with a "punch," as feature stories sometimes do. After the lead, the writers present the details in order of decreasing importance. The last paragraph or two usually provide nonessential background. Then, if the last inch or two of the story is cut for lack of space, nothing important is lost.

Exercise 2: Looking for the Five Ws

Clip a news story out of today's newspaper, and tape it to a piece of paper. Label these parts of the story if the article has them: headline, byline (the reporter's name), and dateline (the place and perhaps the date of origin of the story). Now complete the chart.

Important information	**Is it in the lead? (yes/no)**
1. who: _____	_____
2. what: _____	_____
3. when: _____	_____
4. where: _____	_____
5. why: _____	_____
6. how: _____	_____

Exercise 3: Writing a Preposterous News Story

Write an imaginary news story. Make it as ridiculous as you can, but write in the objective style of a straight news article. Begin with a lead paragraph that includes the five Ws. Develop the story with invented quotations, statistics, and other "facts." Select the best ones for a classroom newspaper. Give your paper an appropriate name, such as *The Daily Nonsense* or *The Preposterous Daily News.*

Headlines

For feature stories, headline writers often try to play with the language, to insert some humor by using a pun or a figurative comparison. But for hard news stories dealing with significant local, national, and international events, the headline is likely to be more direct. It is usually a summary of the most important aspect of the story. Study the front-page headlines in a newspaper. Notice that most contain ten words or less. Writing a good headline is a challenge. Are you ready?

Exercise 4: Writing Headlines

Work in groups of 4. Each member of the group should select a recent news story, cut off and save the headline, and make three photocopies of the article. Each member of the group will then try to write a good headline (10 words or less) for each story. Allow ten minutes for the reading and headline writing for each article. Write each headline on a 3" x 5" notecard. Collect and read the student headlines for each article, decide which one best reflects the content of the story, and then compare it to the one published in the newspaper. Which one is better—yours or the original? Why?

EDITORIALS AND OPINIONS

USA SNAPSHOTS®

A look at statistics that shape the nation

Health care's big bite
Percentage of gross domestic product spent on health-care:

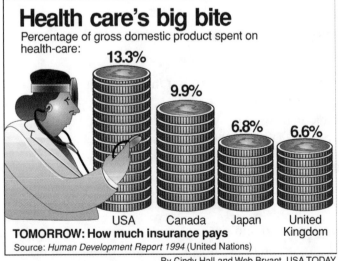

13.3% USA
9.9% Canada
6.8% Japan
6.6% United Kingdom

TOMORROW: How much insurance pays

Source: *Human Development Report 1994* (United Nations)

By Cindy Hall and Web Bryant, USA TODAY

ARTICLE 1A
High court to rule on term limits

ARTICLE 1B
Pull plug on term limits

PREVIEWING THE ARTICLES

"Experience is the best teacher" is an old saying that reflects the usual reverence for long years of training at a job. A new trend, however, indicates that longevity as a member of Congress may be a negative job qualification. Many people favor imposing limits on the number of terms Congress members may serve. They say that too many years on the job has distanced Congress members from the public they serve. Term limit supporters are proposing state laws to prevent repeat reelections.

The Constitution clearly defines the minimal qualifications for Senators and members of the House of Representatives, but it does not deal directly with the issue of limits. Does this allow individual states to set those limits? The state of Arkansas has recently passed a term limit law. The following article and the accompanying editorial explore an issue that could dramatically alter the election process in your state.

BEFORE YOU READ

1. Find the Article in the Constitution that sets the qualifications for Senators and House members. Why do you think these are so minimal? What do you think the framers of the Constitution had in mind?

2. Who are the Senators and House member from your area? How many terms have they served? A longtime member of Congress is said to enjoy "the power of incumbency." What do you think this means? What could cause an established incumbent to be defeated for reelection? Discuss these questions as a class.

AS YOU READ

As you read the following article and editorial, look for the differences between a news report and an opinion piece. In the editorial, notice how one position is portrayed more positively than the other.

High court to rule on term limits

By Tony Mauro
USA TODAY

1 The Supreme Court will decide whether voters can limit the number of terms served by members of Congress.

2 The justices Monday agreed to consider an Arkansas term limit provision—similar to those in 14 other states—that was struck down as unconstitutional by a state court.

3 "It will be a landmark case that will direct what type of government this nation will have in the 21st century," says Arkansas Attorney General Winston Bryant.

4 The Arkansas provision bars from the ballot anyone who has served two Senate terms or three House terms.

5 The court will hear arguments in the case this fall. A decision is unlikely before 1995.

6 The first term limit was enacted in Colorado in 1990. Challenges are also pending in Florida and Washington state. Nebraska's term limits were thrown out last month.

7 The Arkansas court cited a high court ruling in 1969 that said Congress could not exclude from membership any elected candidate who meets constitutional requirements.

8 Opponents say term limits go beyond that.

9 "We already have term limits. They're called elections," says Becky Cain, president of the League of Women Voters.

10 But advocates say states can design their own elections.

11 "The public's gut sense is that this is about the accountability of members of Congress to the people of their states," says Cleta Mitchell of the Term Limits Legal Institute.

Pull plug on term limits

By Tony Mauro
USA TODAY

1 In a welcome intrusion, the Supreme Court Monday waded into the spreading wallow over limiting terms for Congress. It will hear a test case this fall.

2 Not a moment too soon. A "round 'em up and move 'em out" mentality is in full swing across the USA as distrustful voters seek new ways to ride herd on their representatives. Since 1990, 15 states have enacted laws setting limits, ranging from six to 12 years, on U.S. senators and House members. Another seven states are considering similar restrictions.

3 With luck, this case will stop the stampede. Term limits offer a needlessly complicated solution to a simple problem, as the Supreme Court's new case shows.

4 In 1992, Arkansans voted to prohibit House members who have served three two-year terms or senators who've been in office 12 years from having their names on the ballot for the same offices.

5 But Arkansas' Supreme Court overruled, saying the U.S. Constitution sets no limits on congressional terms, so states cannot.

6 History agrees. The Constitutional convention toyed with the notion of restricting tenure when it created our government in 1787. But it rejected the idea as a bad one, and so it remains.

7 Arkansas term-limit advocates—trying to disguise their pig with a petticoat—contend no one is barred from Congress because incumbents can still run as write-in candidates. But if they're right and incumbents have a real chance, what's the point? Then limit backers defeat their purpose.

8 Nationally, those favoring term limits argue they're needed because incumbents enjoy unfair advantages, such as lobbyists' money and franking privileges.

9 True. But, again, why bother with convoluted and unconstitutional laws?

10 It's ridiculous to think that Congress will be made smarter or more honest simply by changing the nameplates every few years.

11 Instead, the good will be tossed out along with the bad. Voters will be barred from keeping representatives they like —no matter how rotten the other choices. Small states will no longer be able to temper large-state dominance with member seniority.

12 Here's a better idea: Trust democracy.

13 U.S. voters don't need any help "throwing the bums out." They already can and do. And states don't need to waste taxpayer time and money trying to tinker with a system that's worked for over 200 years.

14 Forced turnover is not fair play and it's not constitutional. That's a message the states need to get loud and clear from the Supreme Court.

USA SNAPSHOTS®

A look at statistics that shape the nation

How USA feels about term limits

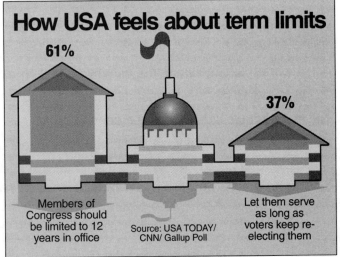

61%
Members of Congress should be limited to 12 years in office

37%
Let them serve as long as voters keep re-electing them

Source: USA TODAY/ CNN/ Gallup Poll

By Nick Galifianakis and Marty Baumann, USA TODAY

GETTING THE MESSAGE

A. Read Article 1A and fill in the blanks with the correct word or phrase.

1. The state of _____ has enacted a term limit law.

2. The provisions of the law limit Senators to _____ terms and House members to _____ terms.

3. After the law was passed, it was judged _____ by the _____ court and will be decided sometime in the future by the _____ Court.

4. _____ other states have passed similar laws.

5. Since law is based on previous decisions, the Arkansas court cited a _____ (year) ruling that stated _____ .

6. The _____ opposes term limits as unnecessary because we already have term limits in the form of _____ .

7. The _____ supports term limits so that Congress members will be _____ to the people of their state.

B. Read Article 1B and fill in the chart below by summarizing the arguments for and against term limits. Although the editorial is clearly opposed to term limits, it gives some justification for both sides of the issue.

Against term limits (paragraphs 3, 5, 6, 11, 13)	**For term limits** (paragraphs 8, 9, 10)
1. _____	1. _____
2. _____	2. _____
3. _____	3. _____
4. _____	
5. _____	

PLAYING WITH WORDS

A. Fill in each blank with the word or phrase from Article 1A that means the same as the italicized word.

1. In paragraph 2, a word that means *stipulation:* _____

2. In paragraph 3, a word that means *an example of importance:* _____

3. In paragraph 4, a word that means *keep off:* _____

4. In paragraph 5, a phrase that means *to present a case before a judge:*

    _____

5. In paragraph 7, a word that means *referred to in a court of law:* _____

B. Match the words from Article 1B with their definitions. The paragraph where the word can be found is indicated in parentheses.

_____ 1. prohibit (4)

_____ 2. toyed (6)

_____ 3. advocates (7)

_____ 4. incumbents (7)

_____ 5. dominance (11)

a. tried out

b. power

c. those who are currently holding elective office

d. prevent

e. those who support an idea

DIGGING BENEATH THE SURFACE

How a writer uses words often sets the tone for an editorial. Find three examples of word play in Article 1B. One is done for you. You may find word play in such paragraphs as 1, 2, 3, and 7.

	Word play	Location	Type and effect
1.	Pull the plug	headline	uses a cliché, alliteration, adds humor
2.			
3.			
4.			

GOING BEYOND THE TEXT

A. *Learning Together*

At some time in the near future there will probably be an election in your school, state, or local area. Find out all you can about an issue on the ballot or a candidate you could support. Find three or four classmates who agree with your position. Form a campaign committee. Write a list of *positive* points and design several campaign posters that highlight these issues. Try to use clever word play, but be sure the poster includes factual information and does not attack the opposition.

B. *Responding in Writing*

Write a letter to a member of Congress, the President, the Governor, or a state legislator asking for information about his or her position on an issue that interests you. Keep your letter specific to one issue and include your feelings about the issue. In several weeks, you will probably receive a reply. Share your letters and results with other members of the class.

One of the strongest features of our form of government is the input that average citizens are supposed to have about the issues that concern them. The connection between the people and their representatives is essential. Lately, some people seem to have lost faith that their representatives are actually responding to their concerns. That is the basis for this term limit debate. Review some of the articles in the "News," "Science," and "Education" sections of this book and the lead stories in a newspaper for a week. Make a list of the top five issues that seem to be on the minds of people. Then make a personal list for yourself. Share your lists with others in class and discuss how you think government could respond to these problems. Consider, also, if it is government's responsibility to respond to these issues at all.

ARTICLE 2A

Condemn caning, flogging; torture merits no applause

ARTICLE 2B

Singapore is "extreme," but the U.S. isn't?

Crime probably ranks as the number one problem in the minds of most Americans. Vandalism by juveniles, some would conclude, is epidemic. Graffiti, shoplifting, stealing cars, and muggings are all symptoms of youth who don't have a sense of values and who don't feel the consequences of their actions. Since the actions of children are society's responsibility, government searches for solutions. A simple answer, to some, is punishment that is immediate and severe.

In the summer of 1994, a news item appeared about an American teenager living in Singapore who was caught and convicted of criminal mischief. The common sentence in this small Asian country, known for its quiet, clean streets and low crime rate, is quick and severe—several lashes with a bamboo cane. Suddenly, every TV talk show, news interview, and newspaper editorial board was taking sides on the issue of corporal punishment.

The following two opinion pieces are against caning. While one is a traditional editorial, the other uses the incident to form a logical argument against a far more serious subject.

BEFORE YOU READ

1. On a map, find Singapore, Iran, Saudi Arabia, and the United Arab Emirates.

2. Before reading the articles, discuss your current feelings about spanking, rapping on knuckles, and so on as a punishment. Is physical punishment ever justified? Is there a difference between a parent using physical punishment and an institution such as a school or government using it? (Note: Many state governments allow school authorities to paddle students.)

AS YOU READ

1. As you read, pay special attention to how the writers develop logical arguments in favor of their opinions. See if you can find flaws in the arguments.

2. Compare the presentation of the two articles. See if the "objective facts" are the same in both articles.

Condemn caning, flogging; torture merits no applause

Singapore's harsh ways are too high a price to pay for safe streets, here or abroad.

1 Singapore keeps ugly company, and Iran proves it. The same day American teen-ager Michael Fay was caned for vandalism in Singapore, officials in Tehran announced an American woman had been given 80 lashes for drunkenness.

2 The woman's confession—that "her job was corrupting young Iranians"— sounds coerced, which further strengthens the Iran-Singapore bond. Fay claims, with considerable supporting evidence, that his confession was forced, too.

3 Coerced confessions are not unusual in either nation, and predictably so. Legal systems that permit human beings to be flayed for drinking or vandalism usually have few compunctions about forcing the necessary statements of guilt first. The Inquisition operated in much the same way.

4 Yet, astoundingly, nearly half of all Americans think Singapore's canings show the way to improve security here.

5 They most emphatically do not.

6 True, Singapore's streets are famously clean and safe. But that's not just because the law allows experts in the martial arts to wound and scar those who behave in anti-social ways. They are clean and safe because Singaporeans tolerate a widespread loss of rights. Speech freedoms are restricted. Political independence is discouraged. Criminal suspects have no right to silence, no automatic right to trial.

7 Many nations have crime rates we would envy. But only 16 resort to canings or floggings. They include:

▶ Saudi Arabia, where a woman received 200 lashes for simply being *accused* of adultery;

▶ And the United Arab Emirates, where a 16-year-old got 550 lashes, meted out over three months, for drinking alcohol.

8 Lucky Michael Fay. Singapore reduced his punishment from six strokes to four in response to protests from Washington. But Fay's parents rightly point out that four scarring strokes is still torture. The milder sentence does nothing to mitigate Singapore's rejection of international conventions against torture.

9 When it comes to travel, you pay your money and take your chances. Local law is local law. But regardless of where it takes place, statutory corporal punishment—floggings or beatings or amputations and castrations—merits loud condemnation, not wishful applause.

10 You can pretend that justice with a stick is the same as a parent with a switch. But it's no coincidence that court-ordered corporal punishment is usually associated with truncated human and civil rights.

11 In Singapore, the streets are safe because some people are afraid to act out, and because everybody has been forced to compromise important rights and freedoms.

12 In the United States, Americans have every right to openly regret that surrender elsewhere in the world, and every obligation to fight a similar surrender here.

Singapore is "extreme," but the U.S. isn't?

By DeWayne Wickham

How hypocritical to condemn caning but expand death penalty.

1 For weeks, U.S. diplomats—largely inept at solving the real crises of our times—have tried mightily to save an American teen-ager from being spanked with a bamboo cane.

2 Sentenced to receive six lashes by a court in Singapore after he was found guilty of committing 16 acts of vandalism during a 10-day crime spree, the 18-year-old boy has become a minor *cause celebre* for the Clinton administration.

3 President Clinton has asked Singapore to spare the rod. Others in his government threaten a sharp reaction if the sentence is carried out.

4 The punishment, Clinton says, is just too "extreme."

5 This week, the House Rules Committee is expected to consider a bill that contains 66 new death penalties, at least two of which would be imposed in cases that do not involve murder. The Senate has already passed its version of the bill, with 52 new death penalties.

6 The president finds nothing extreme about either.

7 Despite mounting evidence that race continues to play a major role in determining who is charged with capital crimes in our legal system—and who actually gets sentenced to death—the Clinton administration hasn't been heard to utter a single word of complaint about Congress' frantic push for more capital punishment.

8 As a result, people in and out of Congress who consider the death penalty even more "extreme" than being beaten with a bamboo cane are scrambling to blunt the fatal blows supporters of these crime bills seek to deliver.

9 They pushed for—and won—passage in the Judiciary Committee of amendments providing for: (1) nearly $7 billion to attack the causes of crime, (2) a remedy for racial discrimination in murder cases and (3) an adequate federal court review of death penalty convictions and sentences.

10 But holding these victories won't be easy in this election year when many in Congress pander to voters' fear of crime.

11 So far, Clinton has shied away from publicly supporting any of these amendments. Without his backing, the House leadership may not give them the procedural protection that's needed to survive the challenges they will face when the crime bill comes up for a final vote later this month.

12 But if the bill Clinton ultimately signs does not include these safeguards against abuse, he'll have to shoulder most of the blame for the fate—far more extreme than a caning—that his lack of support will heap upon untold numbers of Americans right here at home.

GETTING THE MESSAGE

Scan Article 2A for the information you need to answer the following questions.

1. What are the four countries mentioned where lashing or caning is punishment for certain crimes?

2. According to the writer, a country that would punish by lashing or caning would not hesitate to do what else?

3. The author believes that caning is not the key issue about justice in Singapore. Using paragraphs 6 and 12, summarize this more significant main issue.

PLAYING WITH WORDS

Find the following words in Article 2B and match them to their definitions. Use context clues or the dictionary to assist you. The number in parentheses refers to the paragraph where you will find the word.

_____ 1. inept (1)   a. turbulent

_____ 2. sentenced (2)   b. directed

_____ 3. major (7)   c. bumbling

_____ 4. imposed (5)   d. accommodate

_____ 5. frantic (7)   e. given a jail term

_____ 6. pander (10)   f. important

DIGGING BENEATH THE SURFACE

A special feature of most newspapers is a commentary by columnists. They reflect on how individual news events fit into the "big picture" of our lives. In Article 2B, DeWayne Wickham reviews the events of the Singapore caning and relates it to the issue of the death penalty being discussed in a crime bill before the United States Congress. The organization of his writing reveals the logic of his argument. Regardless of whether you agree or disagree with his position, recognize the precision of his writing.

A. Separate the twelve paragraphs into four sections and fill in the chart below.

Sections	Summary of the information
Paragraphs 1 through 3	_____
Paragraphs 4 through 7	_____
Paragraphs 8 through 11	_____
Paragraph 12	_____

B. Follow the logic of the writer's opinion by choosing the best word in each statement.

1. Caning is (less serious) (more serious) than extension of the death penalty.
2. Supporters of (more death penalty cases) (fewer death penalty cases) won amendments in the Judiciary Committee.
3. (More) (Fewer) racial minorities are charged with capital crimes.
4. The Clinton administration (has) (hasn't) complained about the extremes of the death penalty.
5. Wickham wants (more) (less) review of death penalty convictions.

GOING BEYOND THE TEXT

A. *Learning Together*

One of the best ways for any problem to be solved is for people of good will to work together. Form a problem-solving team of four or five members and choose a problem that concerns your group. It can be a "big" issue, such as preventing vandalism against cars, or a more local issue, such as improving attendance at school dances. Use the following three-step process for solving problems.

1. **Define the problem:** Spend ten minutes carefully summarizing the problem and all of its implications. The more specific you can be about the problem, the better the process will unfold.

2. **Brainstorm:** Spend fifteen minutes on this part. All members of the team should participate actively in suggesting ideas for solutions. Solutions should be as far-ranging and creative as possible. During brainstorming, no criticism or evaluation is allowed. The goal is to suggest as many solutions as possible.

3. **Evaluate:** Spend twenty to thirty minutes on this section. Summarize briefly all solutions offered. Make a list of four or five criteria for evaluation before you begin evaluating any solution. Judge every solution against these criteria. During this part of the process you may want to combine parts of solutions. You may also flesh out details of a solution. After each solution has been considered, choose the two or three best and write a summary of how they may be able to solve the problem.

B. *Responding in Writing*

Choose a local problem that you think will interest a number of people. Briefly interview five people and write a short summary of their opinions. Many newspapers have a section called "Opinions of the People" or a similar title. Often they include a picture and a short excerpt from an interview. If you have a camera available, take pictures of the people you interview and display them with their short quotes.

MAKING CONNECTIONS

In the "Money" section of this book, there are several articles that relate to this editorial. One article is about the generation gap between employers and employees in terms of skills. Do you think this generation gap exists in terms of attitudes about punishment of teenagers?

ARTICLE 3A
Don't give up on health care for everyone

ARTICLE 3B
Health crisis? Don't ask

What is on the minds of most Americans? It depends largely on what their personal situations are. If one is out of work, then unemployment is a priority. If a family member is in the hospital, the health-care issue is of utmost importance. If someone you know has recently been a victim of a mugging, then the crime problem is important. Each President's administration must assess what Americans are concerned about and formulate policy accordingly. When President Clinton was on the campaign trail, he heard repeatedly about the public's concern about health care. Those who had it were afraid of losing it, and those who had none were afraid of becoming sick. And everyone was upset about the high cost of doctor, hospital, and prescription bills. As soon as he was in office, President Clinton called the problem a health-care crisis. In the spring and summer of 1994, the newspapers were filled with information about specific proposals winding their way through Congress.

The following articles look at the interplay of government and health care. The first focuses on the issue of universal coverage. The second looks at the polling process that seems so important to defining issues in the political arena.

BEFORE YOU READ

1. Look in a history book or ask you social studies teacher to review how a bill becomes a law in Congress. Discuss whether you think the process is a complicated one and whether this insures full discussion of complex issues.

2. Discuss your experience with doctors and hospitals. If possible, look at a bill for a hospital stay and the cost for items such as ordinary aspirin, tissue, and lotion. Why do you think medical costs are skyrocketing?

AS YOU READ

As you read, look for the difference between factual information and opinions. Because an editorial is not meant to be objective, the two are often intertwined.

Don't give up on health care for everyone

1 The White House ought to be kicking and screaming over the prospect that Congress will reject employer mandates, and thus any chance of universal health care. Yet this week, it has accepted that possibility with barely a murmur or moan.

2 For many Americans, it's a puzzling retreat. Poll after poll shows that most of us support comprehensive health reform and think employers should help pay for it. In one recent USA TODAY/CNN/Gallup Poll, 90% of those surveyed said employers should pay for all or part of the cost of their employees' health insurance.

3 And why not? An employer-based network of providers is in place and working well. Indeed, almost 60% of the population gets health insurance through the workplace. Using employer mandates to expand that network to the millions of workers who cannot get health insurance is just common good sense.

4 Still, the mandate is on the ropes. In Congress, many Republicans and moderate Democrats are fighting it as if it were a tax. And they're winning. Sens. Daniel Moynihan and Bob Packwood of the powerful Senate Finance Committee visited the White House this week to tell Clinton face to face that the mandate won't fly.

5 A major reason is the opposition of lawmakers like Bob Dole, the Senate minority leader, who has flatly said that mandates are unacceptable. Given his preposterous January declaration that there is no health-care crisis, his opposition to mandates—and reform in general—is no surprise.

6 Other senators at least are looking at alternatives. Packwood and Sen. John Breaux have offered compromises that employ "triggers" to force additional action if lesser reforms fail to achieve specific results by a specific date.

7 Trouble is: Trigger-based reforms do not—cannot —assure universal coverage. To the contrary, they allow lawmakers to avoid making the necessary commitments.

8 Congress is fast approaching legislative lockup over comprehensive health reforms, and the public has failed to rally 'round. Momentum is melting like a Popsicle in the sweltering Washington summer.

9 Plainly, the time has come for voters to defend their interests more loudly.

10 Likewise, the White House should stay cool and fight hard for its central principles—including health care with every job and universal coverage for all. And if it is forced to accept an inadequate, trigger-based deal, it should make certain that, this fall, voters know who was responsible for the sabotage of true and comprehensive health reform.

Health crisis? Don't ask

Public opinion depends on how polling questions are framed.

1 On Jan. 9, Democratic Sen. Daniel Patrick Moynihan of New York opined, "We don't have a health-care crisis in this country. We do have a welfare crisis."

2 With that, he temporarily emboldened the Republican Party to attack the Clinton administration's attempts to address health care by enlarging the government and taking over about 14% of the economy.

3 But scared off by polls showing over four out of five Americans believed there *was* a health-care crisis, the GOP quickly retreated and began crafting a safer counterattack of compromise and accommodation.

4 But what do Americans really believe?

5 In June 1991, Gallup asked: "In your opinion, is there a health-care crisis in this country today, or not?" In response, 91% said "yes."

6 Gallup asked it again in May of 1993. Same results.

7 In early January when the question was asked yet again, 84% still said "yes."

8 But this got pollsters wondering if results would differ if people were given an alternative.

9 So in late January Gallup asked, "Which of these statements do you agree with more—the country has a health-care crisis, or the country has health-care problems but no health-care crisis?"

10 Bingo. Only 57% said there's a crisis.

11 In early February, a *Time*/CNN poll offered even more choices. It asked whether the health-care system was in a crisis; having major problems, but not in a crisis; having problems, but not major ones; or no problems. Only 22% said the system is in crisis.

12 Attitudes about health care had not changed. The fact is, people don't have a solid opinion about it, and their response varies wildly with how the question is asked.

13 During the same period that *Time*/CNN was polling, Harris asked the question in the original form, "Do you agree or disagree that there is a health-care crisis?" By failing to offer alternatives, again they got the 84% "yes" response.

14 Just how fickle is the public on this issue?

15 In April, Gallup experimented with the "crisis vs. major problem" question and discovered that simply by changing the order in which the choice was offered, there were big differences in the response.

16 If you mention crisis first, 42% agree there's a crisis. Mention it last, and 61% think there's a crisis.

17 Opinions do not change that radically when people truly believe something.

18 For instance, you can ask: Does Clinton make firm decisions and stand behind them? Or waver on important issues?

19 It doesn't matter which you ask first or second, because nearly three out of four people will always choose "waver."

20 That's what they really believe about the guy, and they believe it firmly.

21 The reason they believe this is because the folks in the White House, like the GOP, are too busy running around testing public opinion before they decide what they believe and what their policy is going to be.

22 Clinton spends some $2 million a year (more than double what his predecessors spent) having his pollsters check the political winds. It doesn't matter if the question is Bosnia intervention, Haitian rescue, crime, assault weapons or the economy.

23 Moynihan was wrong.

24 We don't have a health-care crisis—we have a leadership crisis.

GETTING THE MESSAGE

A. After reading Article 3A, mark each of the following statements true or false.

_____ 1. Congress will probably reject universal health care.

_____ 2. The polls show that most Americans are against health-care reform.

_____ 3. More than three-quarters of Americans get coverage through the workplace.

_____ 4. Republicans and moderate Democrats have joined forces to oppose universal coverage.

_____ 5. Bob Dole supports the idea that the health-care system is in crisis.

_____ 6. Bob Packwood and John Breaux are trying to block any compromise.

_____ 7. The editorial encourages the President to fight for the principle of universal coverage.

B. Article 3B is a commentary by columnist Joe Urschel. Read the article and summarize the four main parts.

1. The main idea of paragraphs 1 through 3: _____

2. The main idea of paragraphs 8 through 12: _____

3. The main idea of paragraphs 14 through 16: _____

4. The main idea of paragraphs 17 through 20: _____

PLAYING WITH WORDS

A. Use context clues to match the words from Article 3A with their definitions. The paragraph where the word is found is in parentheses.

_____ 1. *mandates* (1)   a. change from a stated position

_____ 2. *retreat* (2)   b. absurd, not believable

_____ 3. *comprehensive* (2)   c. requirements

_____ 4. *network* (3)   d. connections between different groups

_____ 5. *preposterous* (5)   e. complete in all areas

_____ 6. *universal* (7)   f. obstruct

_____ 7. *momentum* (8)   g. including everyone

_____ 8. *sabotage* (10)   h. the build-up of action

B. Describe how these words or phrases are used in colorful ways to add interest in Article 3A.

1. *White House* (1) _____

2. *on the ropes* (4) _____

3. *triggers* (6) _____

4. *lockup* (8) _____

5. *rally 'round* (8) _____

A. Distinguish between fact and opinion in these paragraphs from Article 3A. Find at least one fact and one opinion in each. Remember, a fact is something that can be verified as true or untrue, while an opinion is based on personal feelings.

	Fact	Opinion
1. paragraph 2		
2. paragraph 3		
3. paragraph 4		
4. paragraph 8		

B. A *figure of speech* is the use of symbolic language to make writing more interesting. Article 3A contains a figure of speech called a *simile*, which compares one quality of two otherwise unlike objects. A simile usually has the word *like* or *as* in the comparison. An example of a simile is, "The crowd was as silent as the stillness of a winter's night." Read the simile in paragraph 8 and answer the following questions.

1. What are the two parts of the comparison?

2. What quality is being compared?

3. Summarize the meaning of the simile.

4. Write a simile for the following ideas:

   a. You are angry at a friend for deceiving you.

   b. You feel sad after reading about a tragic accident.

   c. You want to describe the slow pace of a boring baseball game.

   d. You want to describe your favorite sports hero's abilities.

A. *Learning Together*

Test Joe Urschel's theory about poll taking. In a group of four or five students, write three versions of the same poll question. One should be focused on a word with powerful meaning, such as *crisis*; one should offer alternative responses; and one should change the order of the choices. Survey twenty people using each variety of the question, and compare the results.

B. *Responding in Writing*

Choose an issue that clearly has two valid points of view. You may want to scan the editorial pages of a newspaper to help you find a topic. Be sure you have researched at least five facts you can use. Write an editorial from both points of view. Try to sound as if you believe in each viewpoint. Use some of the same facts in each version, with different opinions about what they mean.

MAKING CONNECTIONS

Americans thrive on the exchange of viewpoints on issues they care about. Review all the articles in this book and see how many show a difference of opinion about ideas. Consider how compromise is reached when people of goodwill hold different opinions.

ARTICLE 4
Hike gas tax; deficit-cut choices are running low

PREVIEWING THE ARTICLE

Taxes, budget deficit, national debt—are these just boring topics of United States politics? Perhaps, until a President suggests a fuel tax to remedy economic problems. That sets everyone's pocket change jingling. After all, nearly everyone drives or rides in a car. Next to food, gasoline is the most regular purchase made by Americans.

A generational difference can be measured by those who remember gasoline rationing during World War II and those who assume fuel is as available as white bread. Except for a brief period in the early 1970s, long gas lines are not a reality or a fear for most of us. President Clinton opened a Pandora's box when he tapped into gasoline as a means of reducing the enormous national debt.

Around the world, high gas taxes are used for government funding and to reduce gasoline consumption. While Europe and Japan were promoting small, gas-efficient cars in the '60s and '70s, American manufacturers were still building heavy, gas-guzzling automobiles. The U.S. car industry experienced a rude awakening when sales declined. Gas efficiency finally became a goal of American car manufacturers. Government mandates promoting fuel efficiency also became a reality during the 1980s. By the 1990s, however, gasoline complacency was back.

The Clinton administration began its tenure with a dialogue about increasing gas taxes. Legislators were quick to take sides as the public railed against any increase in the price of gasoline. Article 4 and the accompanying graphs support an increase in the gas tax and show a worldwide comparison of gasoline prices.

BEFORE YOU READ

1. Do you ever worry about the availability of gas? Discuss the current price of gasoline in your area. Figure out how much gas the average family car uses in a year and how much that costs each year based on the current price.

2. Assume that there was a world crisis, and oil for gasoline suddenly became scarce. What measures would you institute to curb gas consumption? What actions would you mandate? Which would you encourage to be voluntary?

AS YOU READ

1. Pay special attention to the points made in support of a hike in the gas tax. Imagine how you could use the information to write an editorial from the other point of view.

2. Study the bar graphs that compare costs over several years. Prices are "adjusted for inflation" so you can compare actual changes.

Hike gas tax; deficit-cut choices are running low

OUR VIEW A gas-tax boost can throttle down the nation's staggering deficit without hurting the economy

1 Tax writers for House Democrats want to pump some life into deficit reduction. But President Clinton and some nervous senators are slapping them down.

2 They're rebuffing a proposal to hike the gas tax 9 cents a gallon to raise $9 billion a year, indicating it's "high."

3 High to whom?

4 Clinton's own defunct energy-tax proposal, aimed at raising $22 billion a year for deficit reduction by 1998, would have increased gas taxes 7.5 cents. Another cent and a half won't kill anyone.

5 Even if oil and gasoline prices remained unchanged, the average household would pay only $8 a month more to cover a 9-cent higher tax.

6 That's about a fifth of the monthly savings the average homeowner might gain if deficit reduction knocks another point off mortgage rates.

7 Meanwhile, oil and gasoline prices are falling. In May, the Senate could have imposed its proposed 4.3 cents-a-gallon tax increase, and motorists wouldn't have felt a thing; gas prices dropped that much. Indeed, after accounting for inflation, gasoline prices today are at their lowest level since World War II.

8 That's led to Americans losing the conservation habit. Surveys of new car buyers show, for example, that fuel efficiency is only their sixth priority.

9 Other major nations are much more forceful in encouraging conservation. Gas taxes in Japan and Europe are 10 times the levels here. Even Canada and Mexico, despite more ample energy supplies, tax gas more than the USA does.

10 So, the House's proposed 9 cents-a-gallon increase is hardly "high." What's high is a federal deficit that now equals $3,000 per household a year. And higher gas taxes are vital to bringing that down.

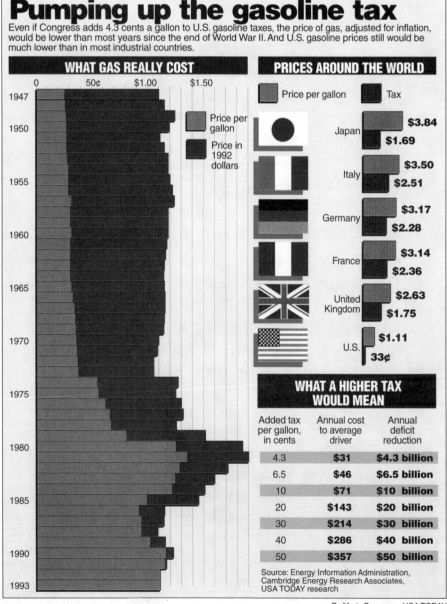

Gas prices in other nations

Prices per gallon of gasoline, including taxes:

Mexico*: $1.52
Canada: 1.64
Britain: 2.91
Germany: 3.71
France: 3.73
Italy: 3.94
Japan: 4.12

*1992

Source: Energy Information Administration

Pumping up the gasoline tax

Even if Congress adds 4.3 cents a gallon to U.S. gasoline taxes, the price of gas, adjusted for inflation, would be lower than most years since the end of World War II. And U.S. gasoline prices still would be much lower than in most industrial countries.

WHAT GAS REALLY COST

Price per gallon
Price in 1992 dollars

PRICES AROUND THE WORLD

Price per gallon — Tax

	Price per gallon	Tax
Japan	$3.84	$1.69
Italy	$3.50	$2.51
Germany	$3.17	$2.28
France	$3.14	$2.36
United Kingdom	$2.63	$1.75
U.S.	$1.11	33¢

WHAT A HIGHER TAX WOULD MEAN

Added tax per gallon, in cents	Annual cost to average driver	Annual deficit reduction
4.3	$31	$4.3 billion
6.5	$46	$6.5 billion
10	$71	$10 billion
20	$143	$20 billion
30	$214	$30 billion
40	$286	$40 billion
50	$357	$50 billion

Source: Energy Information Administration, Cambridge Energy Research Associates, USA TODAY research

By Marty Baumann, USA TODAY

GETTING THE MESSAGE

Scan Article 4 and answer the following questions.

1. Who is promoting the idea of a tax hike in gasoline? _____

2. What is President Clinton's position on the tax hike? _____

3. What is the estimated monthly increase in cost to consumers of a nine cent rise in the price? _____

4. What is the predicted benefit of the increase? _____

5. What is the cost of gasoline today, compared to 1946, when adjusted for inflation? _____

6. What has led to Americans losing their sense of priority for fuel efficiency in automobiles? _____

7. How do other countries enforce fuel conservation? _____

8. What does the federal deficit cost each household every year? _____

PLAYING WITH WORDS

A. Several words in this article are related to economics. Look these up in a dictionary or other resource and write the definition that fits the context. The numbers in parentheses refer to the paragraphs where the words are found.

1. *deficit (1)* _____

2. *deficit reduction (1)* _____

3. *energy tax (4)* _____

4. *mortgage rates (6)* _____

5. *inflation (7)* _____

B. Circle the best definition for these words from Article 4. The numbers in parentheses refer to the paragraphs where the words are found.

1. *rebuffing* (2) a. rejecting
                    b. waxing to a shine

2. *defunct* (4)   a. no longer working
                    b. popular

3. *accounting* (7) a. adding up figures
                    b. considering

4. *conservation* (8) a. use of less of a commodity in order to save it
                      b. meeting

5. *ample* (9)   a. abundant
                    b. not enough

6. *vital* (10)   a. living
                    b. important

A. The concept of adjusting for inflation is important for comparing prices in different years. If a loaf of bread cost 20 cents in 1947 and inflation has increased five times by 1992, then the adjusted price is one dollar in 1992. Use the "What gas really cost" bar graph to answer the following questions.

1. The actual cost of gasoline in the U.S. stayed at about 25 cents from _____ to _____ .

2. Adjusted for 1992 dollars, the two years that gas prices fell below 1947 prices were _____ and _____ .

3. Two of the years the adjusted price was over $1.50 were _____ and _____ .

4. The adjusted price has actually _____ since 1947 except for a small increase in 1990.

B. Look at the "Prices around the world" graph and answer the following questions.

1. Name two countries where the tax is more than 50 percent of the total price of gasoline. _____ _____

2. What percent of the total cost of gas is the 33 cent tax in the U.S.? _____

3. Which country pays the least part of the cost of gas in taxes? _____

4. Which country pays the most part of the cost of gas in taxes? _____

C. Use the graph "What a higher tax would mean" and information in the article to complete the following statements.

1. The graph supposes that the average American driver will use _____ gallons of gas a year.

2. The graph shows clearly that for every 1 cent of added gas tax, the deficit will be reduced by _____ .

3. If the tax that the editorial supports is enacted, the deficit would be reduced by _____ .

A. *Learning Together*

This editorial and the accompanying graphs used percentages to calculate taxes. Math plays an important role in analyzing information. A fun way to practice calculations of percentages is by ordering from a restaurant menu.

Form a small group of four or five. Each person should visit a favorite restaurant and ask for a copy of their menu for a school project. Many restaurants have take-out copies they will readily give to the public. Work together to order a meal from each restaurant. Order several courses. Then add up the bill, including your local tax, and add a 15 percent tip. Finally, figure out how much each person would pay if the bill were split evenly.

B. *Responding in Writing*

Article 4 promoted the positive results from increasing the gas tax. There are certainly negative consequences from such a tax. Pretend you are the owner of a trucking company or the driver of a long-haul produce truck. Write a list of all the reasons you would be opposed to a gas tax hike. Consider some of the following questions. Would it increase the cost of doing business? Would it affect your wages? Would it increase the cost of food to everyone? How would it affect poor people? Since the purpose of the tax is to reduce the deficit, are there other ways besides the gas tax?

Write an editorial of at least five paragraphs. Be sure to express a clear viewpoint. Use colorful adjectives and factual information that supports your position.

MAKING CONNECTIONS

According to Article 1 in the "Money" section ("Pace could mean gains or portend slide"), the state of the economy has a great impact on the stock market. What do you think the impact on the stock market might be to news of potential tax hikes?

EDITORIALS AND OPINIONS

Analyzing Editorials, Political Cartoons, and Letters to the Editor

News stories are supposed to be objective, to tell a story without expressing a particular viewpoint. Most newspapers have special pages or sections reserved for commentary and opinions on important issues. There are several types of articles you will find in the editorial or opinion section of a newspaper.

Editorial articles contain the views of an editorial board that represents the newspaper. They often meet to discuss political candidates, legislation that is pending in local or national government, social issues, and so on. After they decide on their viewpoint, one person writes the article. Sometimes an opposing view or commentary also appears to show that there are various viewpoints on an issue.

Letters to the editor are submitted by readers who state their views on issues of the day or responses to previous editorials.

Political cartoons are a special art form where an artist uses pictures and a few words to illustrate a point of view about a topic in the news. Often, pictures are used symbolically and require interpretation by the viewer. While political cartoons are often amusing, some are very serious in tone. One of the most famous political cartoons pictured the statue of President Abraham Lincoln at the Lincoln Memorial in Washington, D.C., with his head bowed, in tears. It appeared after the assassination of President Kennedy. Using no words, it expressed the sorrow of a nation grieving for its fallen leader.

Exercise 1: Facts or Opinion

In the news section, a headline might read "U.S. Mints New Coins," while an editorial could appear as "Is the Penny an Obsolete Coin?" Find three news articles, read them, and cut out their headlines. Write an original title for an editorial that could be written about the same subject as the news article.

Exercise 2: Your View or Mine

Choose an editorial about an issue that interests you. Answer the following questions by listing the main points of the issue. You may agree with some points and disagree with others. Be prepared to discuss your article and your viewpoint.

1. What is the headline of the editorial? _____

2. What are some key words which show the writer's feelings on the issue?_____

   _____

3. Summarize the main issue of the editorial. _____

4. List five ideas the writer uses to support his or her view.

a. _____

b. _____

c. _____

d. _____

e. _____

Exercise 3: A Picture Is Worth a Thousand Words

A. Find a political cartoon about a current issue in the news.

1. Who is the artist? _____

2. Describe the picture. _____

3. If there are words in the cartoon, explain their use. _____

4. What is the issue presented in the cartoon? _____

5. What viewpoint does the cartoon take about the issue? _____

6. Is the tone of the cartoon humorous or serious? Explain your answer. _____

B. Now you try one. Choose an issue that interests you. Draw a political cartoon that expresses your viewpoint.

Exercise 4: People Are Talking

1. Read some letters to the editor for several days. List three issues that currently are on the minds of people, judging from your review. _____

2. Write a letter to the editor about an issue in the news that you have an opinion about. Be sure to express a clear point of view and include supporting details.

MONEY

USA SNAPSHOTS®

A look at statistics that shape the nation

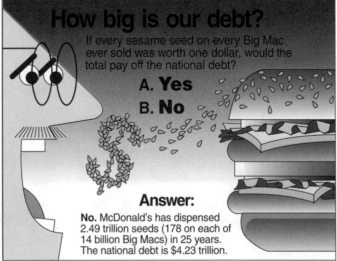

How big is our debt?

If every sesame seed on every Big Mac ever sold was worth one dollar, would the total pay off the national debt?

A. **Yes**
B. **No**

Answer:

No. McDonald's has dispensed 2.49 trillion seeds (178 on each of 14 billion Big Macs) in 25 years. The national debt is $4.23 trillion.

Source: McDonald's, OMB   By Sam Ward, USA TODAY

ARTICLE 1
Pace could mean gains or portend slide

PREVIEWING THE ARTICLE

On any given workday in America, the New York Stock Exchange experiences the buying and selling of millions of shares of stocks in hundreds of companies. The stock market is a buying and selling forum for companies that issue shares of stock at a set price to individuals who then own a portion of the value of that company. A company originally sells stocks in order to raise capital, or operating money, for expansion and development. Once the stock is sold, its value rises or falls in reaction to a combination of many factors, some related to the company's success or failure, but some related to political conditions, as well as economic conditions in general. For example, if the unemployment rate goes up, the stock market could take a dive; if an international peace treaty is signed, the market could soar fifty points.

There are currently over 138 stock markets in the world. The oldest stock exchange is in Amsterdam, Holland, founded in 1602. The New York Stock Exchange dates back to 1896.

One way to judge the highs and lows of the billions of shares traded is with an index. One such index is the Dow Jones Industrial Average, a measure of stock-market prices based on thirty leading manufacturing companies listed on the New York Stock Exchange.

Every day, the newspaper reports individual stock prices along with the daily Dow Jones Average. Behind these numbers is an exciting world of people and money. You may not actually own stock, but if you buy products from a company that issues stock, if you have a bank account, if your family pays utility bills, then you, too, play a role in this vast world of the stock market. This article discusses one day in the life of the stock market when the Dow Jones broke a psychological barrier.

A word about math and reading. It is essential to understand how to read and interpret graphs and charts and to be able to work some math calculations in order to participate in your own economic future.

BEFORE YOU READ

Look at the business or money section of any daily newspaper. Check the format for the stock-market listings in the New York Stock Exchange (NYSE). There are other markets listed, such as the NASDAQ, but this article will discuss only the NYSE.

AS YOU READ

As you read this article, look for differing views on the outlook for the economy and the predicted effect on the rise or fall of the stock market.

Pace could mean gains or portend slide

By Eric D. Randall
USA TODAY

1 Ever dream that you're running, but each step gets harder until you're barely moving?

2 Maybe you've been dreaming about the stock market. It's been moving forward and setting records, but it's looking mighty sluggish.

3 Wednesday, the Dow Jones industrial average, the closely watched measure of 30 big-company stocks, rose 18 points to 3605, breaking the 3600 mark and setting its 17th record this year. Many other stock indexes also set records.

4 That might sound impressive. But by historic standards, the pace of the market's advance is slow.

5 In the average bull market, the Dow jumps about 36% a year, according to a study done by brokerage First Albany for USA TODAY. The current bull market, which began in October 1990 when the Dow was 2365, is pushing the Dow up at half that pace: 18% a year. There have been 21 bull markets since 1890, First Albany says. Seventeen of them have been faster than the current one in terms of the Dow's percentage gain each year.

6 "Slow would be one way to describe this market," says Hugh Johnson, First Albany's research chief. "Painful is another. Or difficult."

7 But a slow rally may be just what the stock market needs most. Some stock watchers believe that because stock indexes are rising relatively slowly, there's less chance of a sudden correction—a sharp 10% or 15% across-the-board drop in stock prices—or a bear market anytime soon. A slow rally means everything is under control. Investors are being logical—pushing stocks up slowly because the economic recovery is progressing slowly. It's rational to expect the market to remain in low gear until corporations report stronger earnings growth, says Kevin Bannon, chief investment officer of the Bank of New York.

8 Not everyone is so optimistic about this gradual rally. "Eventually you're going to have more volatility, a correction and a bear market, which we haven't had since 1981 or 1982," says Joseph McAlinden, stock market strategist at investment bank Dillon Read. He doesn't count the crash of '87 and the Dow's 21% fall July through October 1990 as bear markets because those slumps didn't last long enough.

9 Apprehension is high even among bullish stock analysts. Wall Street has had little experience recently with long, slow rallies. The four rallies the past 100 years slower than this one started in 1893, 1910, 1960 and 1966. Even the most recent is more than 25 years ago. More common are raging bull markets like the Dow's 81% rise January 1986 through August 1987. Such rallies typically end in corrections. Sometimes the rallies end more dramatically: Oct. 19, 1987, the Dow plummeted 23%.

10 Fear of a big correction is common on Wall Street. Four of 10 portfolio managers surveyed by *Barron's* in June said they think there is at least a 50-50 chance that there will be a "major market collapse" within 12 months.

11 The conventional wisdom is that a correction is inevitable because the market is "high." Analysts say a market is high when the price of stocks in the Standard & Poor's 500 index seems out of whack with the annual earnings per share reported by those companies.

12 What's tricky is that some analysts look at the price relative to the past 12 months' earnings, and others compare the price with their estimates of the coming 12 months' earnings.

13 The people who look back are worriers. The past 12 months, companies in the S&P 500 index had earnings per share of $19.84—adjusted to account for each company's weighting in the index. At Wednesday's close of 456, that means the index is selling for 23 times those earnings. The past 67 years, that price-earnings ratio has averaged

How the 30 Dow stocks have fared

How the 30 stocks in the Dow Jones industrial average performed while the Dow rose 20% since first closing above 3000:

Stock	Price April 17, 1991	Price Wed., Aug. 18, 1993	Change
Goodyear	$11⁵/₁₆	$41³/₈	+266%
Allied Signal	$30	$72³/₄	+143%
Caterpillar	$49¹/₈	$81¹/₄	+64%
AT&T	$37⁷/₈	$59⁵/₈	+57%
McDonald's	$35³/₈	$54⁵/₈	+54%
Coca-Cola	$28	$42³/₄	+53%
Sears	$37³/₈	$53¹/₄	+42%
Eastman Kodak	$42⁷/₈	$60³/₈	+41%
J.P. Morgan	$54	$74³/₈	+38%
General Electric	$75¹/₄	$97¹/₈	
Disney	$30¹/₄	$38⁷/₈	
United Technologies	$45⁵/₈	$58³/₄	
DuPont	$40¹/₈	$49¹/₄	
3M	$89¹/₄	$108	+21%
General Motors	$38⁷/₈	$44³/₈	+14%
American Express	$29⁷/₈	$33⁵/₈	+13%
Chevron	$79³/₈	$88⁷/₈	+12%
Alcoa	$68	$74¹/₂	+10%
Procter & Gamble	$44³/₄	$49¹/₈	+10%
Exxon	$60¹/₈	$64¹/₈	+7%
International Paper	$64⁷/₈	$66	+2%
Union Carbide[1]	$18³/₈	$18	−2%
Bethlehem Steel	$13³/₄	$13³/₈	−3%
Texaco	$68⁷/₈	$63¹/₄	
Merck	$38¹/₄	$32¹/₂	−15%
Boeing	$47	$39	
Woolworth	$32³/₄	$25	
Philip Morris	$70⁵/₈	$50¹/₈	−29%
Westinghouse	$29¹/₈	$15³/₈	−47%
IBM	$109⁷/₈	$42³/₄	−61%

14.2, Lipper Analytical Services says.

14 People who look forward tend to be more optimistic. Stock analysts expect the S&P 500 index earnings to be more than $26 this year, says Zacks Investment Research. Earnings are expected to jump that much because many companies took big charges against earnings late last year to cover changes in the way they account for retiree health-care benefits, among other things. By the end of this year, those charges won't be included in the past 12 months' earnings anymore. So the S&P 500 is selling for 17.5 times estimated earnings. "I don't think the market's overvalued," Johnson says. "I think it's undervalued."

15 But McAlinden of Dillon Read says earnings gains will be too little, too late to save the market from a correction. The key is not really earnings but expectations of earnings, he says. And the nation's economic growth prospects are so lackluster that a cloud will hang over companies, he says. "I think that before rising earnings expectations have a chance to work their magic, we're going to have a major correction of six to nine months," McAlinden says.

16 His reasoning: "In contrast to previous cycles, the market will be quite vulnerable to rising interest rates." McAlinden says that as interest rates rise, investors will pull their money out of the stock market and put it into interest-bearing investments like bank certificates of deposit. That would unravel the market's 2½-year rally, which is attributed by many to investors abandoning interest-bearing investments to buy stocks and stock mutual funds as interest rates have fallen. The yield on 1-year CDs has fallen from more than 8% three years ago to 3.1% now.

17 Investors have been pouring about $10 billion a month into mutual funds this year, the Investment Company Institute says. "Clearly, people are coming out of CDs looking for higher returns," says Garrett Nagle, a Boston money manager.

18 People have been coming into stocks gradually as their CDs expire. But if

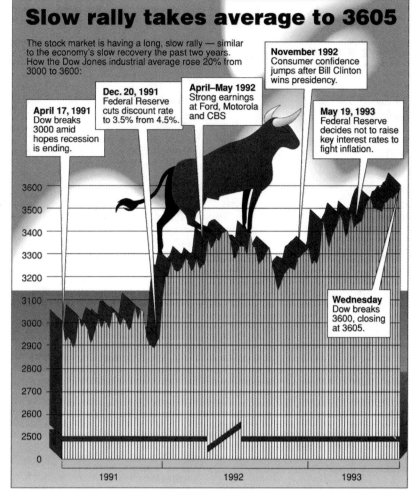

Slow rally takes average to 3605

The stock market is having a long, slow rally — similar to the economy's slow recovery the past two years. How the Dow Jones industrial average rose 20% from 3000 to 3600:

April 17, 1991 Dow breaks 3000 amid hopes recession is ending.

Dec. 20, 1991 Federal Reserve cuts discount rate to 3.5% from 4.5%.

April–May 1992 Strong earnings at Ford, Motorola and CBS

November 1992 Consumer confidence jumps after Bill Clinton wins presidency.

May 19, 1993 Federal Reserve decides not to raise key interest rates to fight inflation.

Wednesday Dow breaks 3600, closing at 3605.

Source: USA TODAY research

By Sam Ward, USA TODAY

interest rates go up quickly, they might all want to leave at once.

19 But Bank of New York's Bannon says he isn't worried. "We're out of the boom-and-bust mentality," he says.

20 Fundamentally, conditions are good, he says. The weak economy has forced companies to cut costs. Inflation seems under control. The weakening of the European Monetary System frees those nations to cut interest rates and stimulate their economies, which should mean consumers there will buy more U.S. goods. And anxiety over the Clinton administration's health-care package will dissipate much like anxiety over the energy tax and deficit-reduction package, Bannon says.

21 "This administration knows that to get re-elected they have to create a lot of jobs," Bannon says. He's looking for a continuation of gradual economic growth, continued low interest rates and investor thirst for high single-digit or double-digit returns that only stocks can provide as long as interest rates remain low. "My read on this is demand for stock will outstrip supply."

A. Choose the best answer.

1. In this article, the major stock market event is that _____ .
   a. the Dow Jones announced that thirty new companies were formed.
   b. the Dow Jones broke the 3600 mark.
   c. the S & P 500 had earnings per share of $19.84.
   d. the Dow plummeted 23 percent.

2. The stock market of 1993 was considered sluggish by some because _____ .
   a. the current market was decreasing.
   b. the market was increasing too rapidly.
   c. the market was increasing but at a slower pace.
   d. the reported rate of increase was 36 percent, half what it had been in the past.

3. The four stock markets in the years 1893, 1910, 1960, and 1966 had the following in common: _____ .
   a. they were all losing years.
   b. they were all rally years slower than 1993.
   c. they were all rally years faster than 1993.
   d. they all had major corrections in market prices.

4. The crash of 1987 and the Dow's 21 percent fall in 1990 did not count as bear markets, according to some analysts, because _____ .
   a. those slumps didn't last long enough.
   b. the market was undervalued.
   c. investors had been pouring about $10 billion a month into mutual funds.
   d. the economy was too strong.

B. After reading the article, mark the following statements true or false.

_____ 1. Fear of a big correction is common on Wall Street.

_____ 2. A market is considered low when the price of stocks in the Standard and Poor's 500 index seems out of whack with the annual earnings per share reported by those companies.

_____ 3. The earnings on a one-year CD fell from 8 percent in 1990 to 3.1 percent in 1993.

_____ 4. Stock market analysts who look at the price of stocks relative to the past twelve months' earnings tend to be optimistic about the market's performance.

_____ 5. Stock market analysts who look forward in analyzing the S & P 500 tend to be pessimists about the market's performance.

_____ 6. Investors often come to the stock market when CD returns are high.

_____ 7. The outlook by most analysts is that inflation seems under control.

_____ 8. A market "correction" is expected when the market is viewed as "high."

—— 9. There is agreement by most optimistic analysts that the market is under-valued.

—— 10. Investors have put about $120 billion into mutual funds this year.

PLAYING WITH WORDS

Many professions use a special vocabulary, sometimes called *jargon,* that is understood by those working in the field. Using a dictionary or other reference source and context clues from the article, write a specific definition for the following terms used in the world of finance. The paragraph where the word is used is indicated in parentheses.

1. *Dow Jones* (3) _____

2. *bull market* (5) _____

3. *rally* (7) _____

4. *volatility* (8) _____

5. *bear market* (8) _____

6. *Wall Street* (10) _____

7. *mutual fund* (16) _____

8. *yield* (16) _____

9. *deficit-reduction* (20) _____

10. *double-digit returns* (21) _____

DIGGING BENEATH THE SURFACE

A. Below are several quotes from the article that use idiomatic expressions. An *idiom* is a word or phrase that is understood by native speakers of a language, but may not have an exact literal meaning. Write the meaning of the following expressions as they are used in this article. The paragraph in which the quote appears is indicated in parentheses.

1. "across-the-board drop in stock prices" (7) _____

2. "major market collapse" (10) _____

3. "have a chance to work their magic" (15) _____

4. "the boom-and-bust mentality" (19) _____

5. "the demand for stock will outstrip supply" (21) _____

B. Use the line graph to help you interpret information in order to answer these questions.

1. What has been the general trend of the Dow average since April 1991?

2. What three events seemed to have had a positive effect on the Dow's rise?

3. How does the line graph show that the Dow rose 20 percent from 1991 to 1993?

4. Why is the bull an appropriate animal symbol for the actions of the Stock Market in the last two years?

5. What periods of time show the greatest changes over the two-year period, and what events may account for the unsteady growth?

C. Using the chart that lists the Dow Jones thirty stocks, answer these questions.

1. The column "change" actually lists the percent of increase or decrease between the April 1991 price and the August 1993 price. Review how these percents were calculated using a calculator or manual math method.

   Note: the fraction actually refers to 3/8 of a dollar, or 5/16 of a dollar, and can be changed to a decimal such as $3/8 = .375$ or $5/16 = .3125$. Thus $41\,3/8 = 41.375$ and means 41 dollars and 38 cents (rounded).

   The formula for percent of increase or decrease is {difference of new and old, divided by old then multiplied by 100}. Here is a sample for the Goodyear company:

   $$\frac{41\,3/8 - 11\,5/16}{11\,5/16} \times 100 = +266\%\ \text{(Goodyear's change, a rise in value)}$$

   Here is a sample for Westinghouse:

   $$\frac{15\,3/8 - 29\,1/8}{29\,1/8} \times 100 = -47\%\ \text{(Westinghouse's change, a decrease in value)}$$

2. Find the change for the following companies:
   a. General Electric _____
   b. Disney _____
   c. United Technologies _____
   d. DuPont _____
   e. Texaco _____
   f. Boeing _____
   g. Woolworth _____

GOING BEYOND THE TEXT

A. *Learning Together*

The Dow Jones stocks represent a variety of types of companies. Research one company to learn what it manufactures or sells. The entire class should share the information. Then, with a partner, divide the thirty companies into at least three different categories, but not more than six categories. Give a title to the category that describes the connection between those companies included in the group and list the related companies under that title. Each pair of students should publish their groupings and explain their criteria for the categories.

B. *Responding in Writing*

Form a group of students into an "investment club." Give your group $10,000 to spend on buying shares of stocks in companies listed on the New York Stock Exchange. Choose a period of time in which to trade, at least several weeks in duration. Before you begin trading, investigate several companies whose stocks you might buy. Check out the popular products and industries in your area. At least once a week, get together with your group and decide what stocks you will buy or sell. Use the information in the newspaper to determine the buy or sell price. Most papers also print information about the success or failure of many industries.

You should read the business section of the paper regularly while you are playing the stock market.

Keep a journal of your trades, including the buy and sell prices and decisions of the group. Each week, a new member of the group should keep the records, so everyone has a chance to experiment with the trading experience. After a set number of weeks (five or ten is a manageable number), each group should add up its net worth by selling off all of its stock. Groups should chart and share their results.

MAKING CONNECTIONS

Several news articles in this book could have influences on the stock market. One article is about Brazil and its laws regulating car phones ("News" Article 2D). Which types of stocks do you think could be affected by this news? What effect do you think this news will have on these stocks?

For several days, compare national and international events in the news and the ups and downs of the stock market and review the connections.

ARTICLE 2
Underlings' skill can give them an edge

Can you imagine this scene in ancient China 3,000 years ago? A young Chinese assistant quickly adds the totals for the month's silk trade on the newest technology, an abacus, while his senior boss calculates using the "old-fashioned method," pebbles and parchment. The abacus could be considered the forerunner of the modern computer, the first mechanical device designed to perform a task in a speedier manner than human tabulation.

The earliest computers were designed to solve complex problems. One version, Jacquard's loom, tabulated on punch cards in order to assist in weaving complex patterns. Another, Hollerith's machine, assisted in the 1900 census count for the United States. The computers of the 1940s and 1950s, ENIAC and MANIAC, filled giant rooms with tubes that could do thousands of calculations in a minute. But, for most people, early computers were a complex hodgepodge of strange language and more confusing manuals.

In the late 1980s, computer technology became user-friendly. It entered the everyday world of cash registers, bank money machines, telephones, and VCRs. The younger generation faced computers without fear as a part of everyday life. Almost every school district hired or trained a "technology coordinator" to bring teachers and students alike into the computer generation.

This first generation of computer literates is now in the job market, using their skills on a daily basis. In the meantime, the bosses that hire them still have their VCRs flashing 12:00. This article discusses this new "generation gap" between executives who are computer illiterate, or at least suffering from computer discomfort, and their underlings who have an edge on an important tool of business.

1. Discuss the many ways you use computer technology every day, in school and out. What technological skills do you have that your parents may not? Do you feel uncomfortable when you are faced with a new technology, or do you just begin to experiment without fear?

2. Answer the following question for yourself, then poll your classmates and parents. When faced with a new piece of technology—for example, a new CD player or a programmable coffee maker—do you immediately start to experiment with its operation or do you start to read the instruction manual?

Consider carefully the attitudes expressed by the business leaders. Think about your comfort level in using computers.

Underlings' skill can give them an edge

By Julia Lawlor
USA TODAY

1   Howard Jonas runs his $20 million high-tech company using a phone and a legal pad.

2   While his twentysomething staff drag-races daily on the information superhighway, Jonas is stalled in first.

3   At home, he has a rotary phone, a watch he winds and old-fashioned knobs on his stereo. His latest innovation at work: a service to computer-illiterate execs that converts their e-mail into paper faxes.

4   "I hate technology," says Jonas, 37, chief executive of IDT, a telephone company in Hackensack, N.J. "I don't want a computer on my desk. It's a waste of time."

5   For every Howard Jonas, there are hundreds of closet technophobes in the workplace hiding a dog-eared copy of *DOS for Dummies* in their desk drawer. They dread having to record a message on the office voice-mail system.

6   They disappear when the copier needs refilling, throw up their hands when the laser printer breaks down. To them, RAM is still a male sheep.

7   Ironically, many of these technologically impaired people occupy positions of power in the corporate world.

8   Often born on the far side of the baby boom, they find themselves managing twentysomethings who were raised on video games and have little patience for the old ways.

9   Phil Knight, 55, CEO of athletic shoe maker Nike, was dragged "kicking and screaming" into interfacing with his Mac, which he now claims he couldn't live without. "I am a Ticonderoga 2 $1/2$ (pencil) in a WordPerfect world," he says.

10   In the new book *Just Do It,* author Donald Katz says Knight has trouble using the company's voice mail system, needs instructions for operating the company garage opener taped to his rear-view mirror and used to compose letters on a laptop computer, which he then handed over to an assistant to hit the necessary buttons. "I am suspicious of technology," Knight says. "I know it's important but I resist it emotionally."

11   Despite the presence of 34 million computers in U.S. workplaces, technology is the Achilles' heel of many managers.

12   No wonder, then, that some twentysomethings use their superior abilities to "create a secret world away from their bosses," says Marilyn Moats Kennedy, founder of Career Strategies, a career consulting firm in Wilmette, Ill.

13   Since they are capable of accessing databases, the Internet and other sources of information the boss can't, underlings can now "manipulate you . . . and you'd never know it," she says.

14   People who work alongside technological dinosaurs are getting more exasperated by the minute.

15   "With older people, you have to slow down," says Helen Stephens, 27, a logistics analyst for Purolator Products in Fayetteville, N.C. Stephens works with older male engineers who until recently kept all their data in paper files.

16   She says she was "force-fed" computers in college. "Someone will ask me, 'What do I do when it says hit the F2 key?' And I say, 'Well, you hit the F2 key.' Real basic stuff."

17   Linda Belton, fortysomething office manager for Ernst & Young in Los Angeles, is amazed at how quickly recent grads catch on. In "three to six months, they teach me. They read the manual, they know it. Computers are an enigma to me."

18   But don't think for a moment that being technically inept means unintelligent. Technical aptitude is like the ability to learn a foreign language. Some people have it, some don't. And it's always more difficult to acquire the older you get.

19   "When you take adults into the world of electronics, they're learning a whole new language," says Ira Chaleff, president of the Institute for Business Technology, a Washington, D.C., consulting company that helps white-collar workers cope with their electronic and paper workload.

20   There are other barriers. Computers require users to type. Many older managers never learned: they had secretaries.

21   Then there's the issue of time. Mastering a PC takes hours.

22   "It's like asking a pilot flying a plane through a storm, 'Would you mind if we installed a new instrument panel?' It's adding another layer of stress," Chaleff says.

23   Ultimately, when communication is done almost exclusively on e-mail, a manager caves in or risks being ostracized. "When everyone knows if they want to get a message through to Joe they have to take a yellow sticky and put it on his computer screen, he is seen as slowing down the team," Chaleff says.

24   Indeed, the tide has turned against those who resist technology. "Now you're a geek if you *don't* use a computer," says Bernadette Grey, editor of *Home Office Computing* magazine.

25   Arthur Mirante, 50, CEO of New York real estate firm Cushman & Wakefield, was shamed into using a computer by a client. While checking out a headquarters site with Pete Hart, former president of MasterCard, "he told me what an imbecile I was for living in the Dark Ages," Mirante recalls. "He said, 'You can't possibly function as CEO of a major company today without being computer literate.'"

26   Mirante promptly got a PC, had the company's systems person train him and now uses the "hunt and peck" system to communicate by e-mail with the firm's foreign offices.

27   Techno-dolts increasingly are at a disadvantage in social situations, since conversations about computers go over their heads. Jonas was snubbed during a recent telecommunications convention when a software company executive asked for his e-mail address. "I said I didn't have one, and he walked away."

28   But Robert Bittlestone, head of consulting and software company Metapraxis, argues CEOs shouldn't be faulted for not being technically up to speed. "There are very few useful things they can do with a computer," he says.

29   Except for e-mail, he says, most everything else can and should be delegated. A recent survey of Fortune 1000 CEOs by *Chief Executive* magazine supports his contention: 80% of CEOs use a computer every day, primarily for e-mail.

30   This may be one of the few times in history that twentysomethings have so easily intimidated their superiors. At Ernst & Young, the firm's partners take classes separate from the younger staff. "They don't want to look silly," says Belton.

31   Howard Jonas gets résumés all the time from recent graduates that make him cringe. One candidate seeking a sales job listed 18 programs under "Skills," including Windows, Excel, Word, Powerpoint, Lotus 1-2-3, Quatro Pro, M-Track, LAN, D-Base and WordPerfect. Nowhere did he mention a quality that would help him in sales—such as being good with people.

32   Jonas says a 23-year-old staffer recently told him that in time "there will be no more English language. People will communicate only by computer icons."

33   Jonas rolls his eyes but keeps installing computers and hiring people to run them. He has no choice. "People with computers have taken control of everything," he says. "It's a plot."

The statements below refer to information in the article. Write true or false in the space provided. If false, rewrite the statement so that it truthfully reflects the information provided in the article.

_____ 1. Howard Jonas prefers to operate his business and personal life in a nontechnological world.

_____ 2. Many corporate executives disagree with Jonas and are eager to institute computer technology in their businesses.

_____ 3. Helen Stephens represents workers in their twenties who still do not know how to use computers.

_____ 4. According to Ira Chaleff, two barriers to using new technology are time and the ability to read instruction manuals.

_____ 5. Arthur Mirante is an example of a business executive who was shamed into learning to use computers.

_____ 6. Some executives set up separate computer classes for themselves to avoid embarrassment.

_____ 7. Howard Jonas is pleased with job applicants who emphasize their computer skills over people skills.

PLAYING WITH WORDS

A. Write the word or phrase in the paragraph indicated in parentheses that has the same meaning as the italicized word or phrase below.

1. he has a *dial* phone (3) _____

2. there are hundreds of *hidden people who fear computers* (5) _____

3. hiding a *well-read* copy (5) _____

4. computers are *confusing and not understood* by me (17) _____

5. a manager risks being *made an outsider* to his or her peers (23) _____

6. *people who don't understand computers* increasingly are at a disadvantage (27)

_____

B. Use a dictionary, encyclopedia, or computer reference book to explain each of the technical terms or abbreviations used in the article. The numbers in parentheses refer to the paragraphs where the word are found.

1. *e-mail* (3) _____

2. *DOS* (5) _____

3. *CEO* (9) _____

4. *Mac* (9) _____

5. *interfacing* (9) _____

6. *databases* (13) _____

7. *Windows* (31) _____

8. *icons* (32) _____

The statements below can be inferred from the article. Some are fact and others refer to opinions. Check the best column for each statement.

	Fact	Opinion
1. The response to computers of major business executives like Phil Knight and Howard Jonas is due to emotional fears of technology based on their discomfort.	_____	_____
2. Job seekers in their twenties and those in the future will have had training in computers in grammar school or college.	_____	_____
3. Younger job applicants feel that computer skills are very important to their successful employment.	_____	_____
4. The primary use of computers for business managers is for e-mail.	_____	_____
5. Managers often become computer literate because they are concerned about their image to clients and employees.	_____	_____
6. There are at least eighteen computer programs that are used in business, including Quatro Pro and LAN.	_____	_____

GOING BEYOND THE TEXT

A. *Learning Together*
With a partner, choose a want ad from the job market section of a local newspaper. Role play a five- to ten-minute job interview. The employer should write down at least five questions to ask the prospective employee. The sixth question should be, "What skills and personal qualities will you bring to this job?" The interviewee should prepare a list of positive personal qualities and job skills he or she possesses.

B. *Responding in Writing*
On the following page is a format for a résumé. A résumé is a general information packet that is sent to prospective employers. Choose a want ad from the job section of the newspaper and send a résumé. You may invent educational and related background that is necessary for that job.

```
┌─────────────────────────────────┐
│            ┌─────────┐           │
│            │ Résumé  │           │
│            └─────────┘           │
│                                  │
│   Name                           │
│   Position desired               │
│   Education background           │
│   _____  │
│                                  │
│   Salary desired                 │
│   Previous work experience       │
│   _____  │
│                                  │
│   Technological experience       │
│   _____  │
│                                  │
│   Write one or two paragraphs describing │
│   what you could contribute to a company if │
│   you were hired.                │
│   _____  │
│                                  │
│   _____  │
└─────────────────────────────────┘
```

MAKING CONNECTIONS

Sociologists believe that in the future people may change careers several times in their working lives due to improved technology. Also, many jobs will allow employees to work in their homes and check into an office via e-mail and fax machines. Read the money or business section of a newspaper for a week and discuss what jobs could be done at home with advanced technologies. Make a list of five careers that do not exist now but might in the year 2050.

ARTICLE 3
Chunnel is no tunnel of love

Jean-Marie Saletti, a French soldier, escaped from a British prison ship and swam across it to Bologne in 1815. British merchant navy captain Matthew Webb swam across its twenty-one miles in 1875. The famed American swimmer Gertrude Ederle was the first woman to swim across it in 1915. The oldest crosser was fifty-five, the youngest was thirteen. For thousands of years, the English Channel has been a challenging barrier separating the continent of Europe from England.

Throughout history, this geographic waterway has served as a physical and psychological barrier. It protected England from the onslaught of Hitler's army in World War II until the Allies could mount the D-Day invasion on June 6, 1944. Until 1994, the only way to cross the Channel, other than swimming, was by airplane, ferry, or hovercraft, an airboat that travels on a cushion of air trapped between the hull and the surface of the water.

The following article tells of the completion of an underwater rail system linking France and England. The Chunnel, as it is called, is meant to be an economic aid to the trade of many European countries, as the Channel is one of the world's busiest shipping lanes. The article discusses the details of this engineering achievement and the effects it might have on the relationships between the people it connects.

BEFORE YOU READ

1. Look at a map showing the main continent of Europe and the British Isles. Using the scale of miles, estimate the distance between them at the narrowest and widest points.

2. Imagine you are traveling across the English Channel. What method of travel would you choose: train, plane, or ship? Discuss the advantages and disadvantages of each. After reading the article, return to this discussion, and see if you have changed your mind.

AS YOU READ

As you read, look for examples of negative attitudes about the Chunnel based on a historic lack of affection between the British and the French.

Chunnel is no tunnel of love

By Del Jones
USA TODAY

1 FOLKESTONE, England—Queen Elizabeth and French President Francois Mitterrand will hop a train through the $15 billion Channel Tunnel today, crossing the English Channel by land for the first time since it was a marsh 8,000 years ago.

2 Commoners still have to fly, float by ferry or hovercraft, or grease bodies and swim.

3 Though today is being billed as the official opening, the most enormous privately funded construction project ever still isn't open. Not to shareholders, the officers of 220 banks that floated history's biggest loan, or 3,000 surface-locked journalists trying to imagine three parallel tunnels beneath 100 feet of water and 130 feet of fossil-filled clay.

4 When it really opens, probably in October, the 31-mile Channel Tunnel (nicknamed the Chunnel) will be 15 months behind schedule and $7 billion over a budget set in 1987.

5 That's when 1,000-ton machines began removing their weight in clay every half hour as they bored between here and Coquelles, France.

6 The main causes of recent delays have been linking two very different rail systems. And security: how to make a bull's-eye of terrorism terrorist proof. Officials won't disclose the time at which the queen and president make their trip.

7 People on both sides of the English Channel are proud of the engineering feat. But most wonder if it's worth it given their historic lack of affection for each other.

8 "If they had linked us to Spain, that would have been more use to us now, wouldn't it?" says Peter Lingley, a London visitor to The Chunnel Exhibition Center. Spain is a favorite vacation destination for the British. He laughs when the narrator of a film about the Chunnel said it will make the British feel more European.

9 "Propaganda. A sales pitch," Lingley says. "The British will never feel European."

10 England has been trying to conquer, or defend itself from, Europe for 1,000 years. If not for the channel moat, England or France surely would have swallowed the other.

11 "The remains of a generation still remember when only 21 miles stood between Hitler and the conquest of England," says James Cockburn, an English history professor at the University of Maryland and a native of England. "It is ironic that the opening is coming at the same time as (the 50th anniversary of) D-Day."

12 There is little intermarrying, or even travel between Britain and France. Many British make day trips to France to eat a good meal and skirt high British taxes on beer.

13 Some French come the other way for discount clothing; not the food. But the French take vacations along their own Mediterranean coast and the British, increasingly in Miami.

14 The French remain paranoid that their language will become extinct. The British think a sick animal will drag itself through the tunnel and introduce the

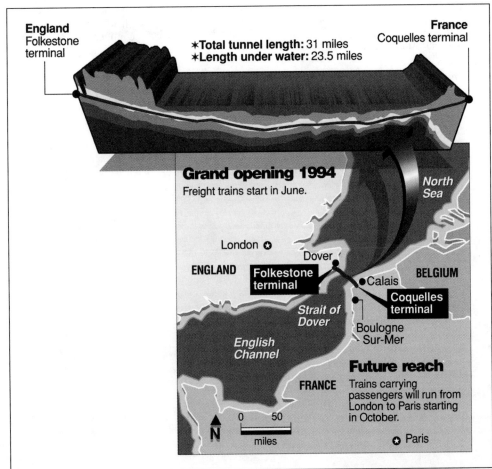

England
Folkestone terminal

France
Coquelles terminal

∗**Total tunnel length:** 31 miles
∗**Length under water:** 23.5 miles

Grand opening 1994
Freight trains start in June.

London ⊙
Dover
ENGLAND
Folkestone terminal
● Calais
BELGIUM
● Coquelles terminal
North Sea
Strait of Dover
Boulogne Sur-Mer
English Channel
FRANCE

Future reach
Trains carrying passengers will run from London to Paris starting in October.

0   50
miles
N

⊙ Paris

By Stephen Conley, USA TODAY

island nation to rabies.

15 "It is a bit of a scare even if it is psychological," says Rosie Norman, a tourist from London at the Exhibition Center. What do the French think about the Chunnel? "We don't know any French."

16 Gerome Camilotto, a 10-year-old from Paris on a field trip to Britain, says his mother visited Britain as a child. His father never has.

17 The differences go on.

18 Upon leaving Paris, trains will zip 186 mph until they get to the Chunnel, but will chug as slow as 50 mph behind commuter trains the last 68 miles to London. Britain won't upgrade its system until after 2000, spurring Mitterrand to quip that passengers will have "plenty of time to enjoy the British countryside."

19 Time across the channel: 35 minutes vs. 90 minutes by sea. Total travel time, including getting on and off the rail cars: 1 hour, 35 minutes.

20 The idea of tunneling beneath the channel goes back to 1802 when an engineer suggested it to Napolean as a horse-and-buggy route. Wooden chimneys to the sea surface would provide air. Napolean was too busy and dozens of other efforts were abandoned including serious ones in 1884, 1923, and 1974. The British were too worried about invasion.

21 The Chunnel will transport about 7 million passengers a year. Among them

By Stephen Conley,
USA TODAY

will be those who would have flown between London and Paris. If you take the Chunnel, it's about the same time as flying: three hours. It now takes more than six hours by rail and hovercraft.

22 Trains won't be delayed by weather. Fares have not been set, but they're expected to be about the same as ferry and airline service.

23 Economists say airlines will be big losers. The Chunnel could set off a U.S.-style fare war in Europe. London-Paris is by far the busiest international airline route in the world. More than 3 million people fly between the cities yearly, vs. 2.2 million between London and New York.

24 Rail freight will begin quietly in June. Eventually, the equivalent of 700,000 truckloads a year will be transported through the Chunnel.

25 One thing the British hope will be left behind is terrorism.

26 In March, an unexploded Irish Republican Army bomb was found on the commuter railroad tracks between London and the Chunnel. *The Daily Telegraph* reported that Chunnel delays have been the result of faulty alarms, ventilators and only "partially successful" evacuation procedures. The London *Mail* reported a major security failure last year.

27 Eurotunnel, the company that operates the Chunnel, issues press releases saying newspaper reports are inaccurate. But they provide no details about the state of security.

28 The key to an evacuation is the smaller inner tunnel that runs between the two train tunnels. Portals connect the train tunnels to the service tunnel every quarter mile and provide escape routes.

29 Each train has two electric-powered engines in case one fails. A $3.6 million police station will be staffed with high-tech equipment and 99 officers.

30 Engineers say a movie-like disaster is unlikely in the Chunnel because it wouldn't be flooded by a bomb. The tunnel is too far beneath the sea floor.

31 But that doesn't satisfy some who believe it should never have been built.

32 "It's just a matter of time before someone takes a crack at it, isn't it?" says Robert Lees of Canterbury, England. "We'll no longer be tied to the continent. A rather normal state of affairs."

A. Fill in the blanks with the correct factual information from the article.

The Chunnel will be _____ miles long, connecting the cities of
_____ , England, and _____ , France. The final cost of the
project will be about _____ billion dollars, although the original budget
was _____ billion. The Chunnel will actually be three _____ tunnels,
a total of _____ feet beneath water and clay. It is expected that about
_____ passengers and the equivalent of _____ truckloads
a year will be carried in the tunnel. To cross the Channel by sea currently takes
_____ minutes, compared with _____ minutes by Chunnel.
The actual travel time including boarding and unloading is _____ .

B. Put the following historical facts in correct chronological order as explained in the article.
Number the event that happened earliest as 1, and next 2, and so on.

_____ The English Channel was a marsh not completely separating England and France.

_____ Queen Elizabeth and French President Francois Mitterrand rode a train through the Chunnel.

_____ The Chunnel opened to passengers.

_____ The budget and schedule was set for the current Chunnel project.

_____ D-Day, the invasion of France in World War II from across the Channel from England, occurred.

_____ An engineer suggested to Napoleon that a tunnel under the Channel would be a good horse-and-buggy route.

_____ A serious effort was made to build a tunnel in the nineteenth century.

_____ An effort to build the tunnel in the last half of the twentieth century was abandoned.

_____ Rail traffic in the Chunnel began.

_____ An unexploded bomb threatened the extension tracks from the Chunnel to London.

A. Use context clues to determine the meaning of each italicized word found in the paragraph indicated in parentheses. Circle the best definition.

1. *hop* (1)
   a. jump on one foot
   b. board a bus or train

2. *commoners* (2)
   a. not from the royal family
   b. very ordinary in appearance

3. *feat* (7)
    a. a trick performed by circus acts
    b. an achievement by skilled professionals

4. *intermarrying* (12)
    a. marriage between people of different cultures, races, or faiths
    b. exchange of ideas and culture

5. *skirt* (12)
    a. woman's apparel
    b. avoid

6. *set* (22)
    a. established
    b. placed

7. *fare war* (23)
    a. battle under international rules
    b. price competition for travel

8. *key* (28)
    a. tool to open locks
    b. main idea or concept

B. Below are five synonyms for the word *says* and five quotations. First, look up each word in the dictionary to find its exact meaning. Next, find the quotation from the article and replace *says* with the synonym that fits the attitude presented. The paragraph in which the quote appears is indicated in parentheses.

a. warns

b. asserts

c. rants

d. reminisces

e. quips

_____ 1. says Peter Lingley (8)

_____ 2. Lingley says (9)

_____ 3. says James Cockburn (11)

_____ 4. says Rosie Norman (15)

_____ 5. says Robert Lees (32)

DIGGING BENEATH THE SURFACE

This article contains both facts and emotional attitudes about the Chunnel. Fill in the following chart based on information in the article.

Factual reasons supporting the Chunnel

1. _____

2. _____

3. _____

Emotional attitudes against the Chunnel

1. _____

2. _____

3. _____

A. *Learning Together*

The purpose of the Chunnel is to connect European countries that possess a variety of languages, currencies, and cultures. Working in small groups, choose a European country and research information about its currency and other facts. Check with a current newspaper and find the "exchange rate" between that currency and the American dollar. Cut out several ads and show the dollar amount converted to that currency. Find a picture of your country's flag. Place all your information on a poster and share with other groups in the class.

B. *Responding in Writing.* Choose one of the following writing projects.

1. Interview a travel agent or someone who has traveled to England or France. Ask about the most interesting sites to visit. Take notes or tape the interview. Then write your own travel article about a planned tour.

2. Check the "Editorial" section of this book and examine several sample editorials to understand the tone and style of a written editorial. Pretend that the Chunnel has not been built yet and that you are in favor of spending billions of dollars to build such a rail tunnel. Be sure to include specific factual details about the advantages of such a project. Or choose the position that a Channel tunnel is unneeded, unwanted, and may be dangerous. Write an editorial expressing that viewpoint using information provided in the article.

MAKING CONNECTIONS

The English Channel is today a major trade and passenger route, but it has great historical significance as well. You can read about the D-Day invasion across the Channel in the "News" section of this book.

ARTICLE 4
Lovers still passionate about roses

PREVIEWING THE ARTICLE

Shakespeare wrote in *Romeo and Juliet,* "a rose by any other name would smell as sweet." Throughout history, the rose has been associated with sentiments such as love, peace, war, and loyalty. This article shows, however, that roses are really big business in America. Over one billion roses were sold in 1993 for birthdays, graduations, anniversaries, and proposals. But the biggest rose day in the year is Valentine's Day. Over 10 percent of all rose sales occur on that one day.

Like any business, the rose business must adapt to changing conditions in the marketplace in order to succeed. In the past, a florist was most likely a local, independently owned business that bought roses from a wholesaler, or middle person, who purchased them from a grower. For Valentine's Day, the cost of a dozen roses rose twofold or more as a result of high demand. Cost for a dozen delivered roses could be $150 or more. Today, suppliers of roses include large supermarket chains, wholesalers who sell directly at many locations, and direct telephone marketers who don't even have to have a storefront. Add to this the price competition of imported roses grown in countries with low labor costs on the equator, and the romance of roses is replaced by economic realities.

This article explores the financial aspects of the rose business and the business approach of three different companies who peddle petals.

BEFORE YOU READ

1. Have you ever sent or received flowers for a special occasion? How did you feel when you received flowers? Discuss the occasions that are traditional for sending flowers in general or roses in particular.

2. Different flowers symbolize different feelings. Discuss the emotions or ideas associated with different flowers, such as daisies, lilies, roses (red, white, yellow, and pink), crocuses, and violets. Are there other flowers that hold special meaning?

AS YOU READ

As you read, look for information about the different aspects of the rose business. What roles do growing, selling, pricing, and marketing play? Pay attention to the line graphs that accompany the article. They give you information about the topic in a visual format.

Lovers still passionate about roses

By Rhonda Richards
USA TODAY

1 NEW YORK—She is gorgeous. Still, Lorena won't be on the minds of most male customers today at this Roses Only store here.

2 Lorena is a rose, the color of pale pink. Too bad. As always on Valentine's Day, more than 80% of the USA's lovers will opt for red, red, passionate red.

3 This will be the day for sexy Nicole, blushing Jacaranda, and fiery Carambole.

4 Nothing says love like a dozen long-stemmed roses on Valentine's Day. More than 80 million roses will be sold today, the biggest day of the year for the nation's rose industry. For rose growers, distributors and sellers, this year's anticipated 7% increase in sales will be sweeter than a 5-pound box of chocolate butter creams.

5 "Red roses say 'I love You,'" says Gerald Celente, executive director of the Trends Research Institute. "It's going to remain the most popular flower because love never goes out of style."

6 Yes, a rose is a rose is a rose. But selling them is no longer a rose garden for full-service florists. Supermarkets and toll-free 800 lines now offer convenience to the harried lovestruck. And discount rose shops help the hopelessly infatuated save a buck.

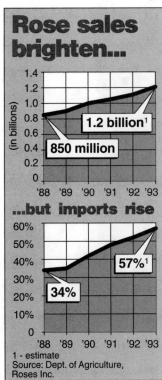

Rose sales brighten...

1.2 billion[1]

850 million

(in billions)

'88 '89 '90 '91 '92 '93

...but imports rise

57%[1]

34%

'88 '89 '90 '91 '92 '93

1 - estimate
Source: Dept. of Agriculture, Roses Inc.

By Stephen Conley, USA TODAY

7 Roses Only is a good example of discount rose retailing in the '90s. Except today, prices range from $6 for a dozen short-stems to $19 for a dozen of its longest stems.

8 The company has three stores in New York, one in Toronto and five in Spain. It plans to expand to Philadelphia, Washington and Boston this year and in 1995. And the company is considering selling partnerships to small florists.

9 Inside this store, on Sixth Avenue near 40th Street, a contemporary white decor and wall-to-wall mirrors give it an upscale look. Customers —some dressed in work clothes, some in expensive suits and overcoats —gawk at shelf after shelf of roses in more than 50 colors. Some customers say the high quality of the roses makes them look as if they spent a fortune. The best part is that their sweeties are never the wiser.

10 "I spent $20 but (they) looked like I had paid 60 or 70 bucks," says David Treadwell, a travel guide publisher in Manhattan.

11 National studies show more people are buying roses in ones, twos and threes these days. In fact, more than half of all roses are sold in numbers fewer than a dozen, says the Floral Index, a private firm that researches the florist industry. But Roses Only's prices encourage splurges. Even on Valentine's Day, when the price of a dozen roses and delivery can soar as high as $150, 12 of Roses Only's most expensive stems sell for just $35.

12 "If we can make someone's day brighter for $35 instead of $65, then they'll have enough money left over for candy *and* dinner," says Carl Hanson, general manager of Roses Only's New York stores.

13 Hans Maarschalk, a Netherlands entrepreneur who began the chain in 1989, holds prices down by controlling every link in the rose chain.

14 He grows his own roses on farms in the Andes Mountains near the Ecuadorian capital, Quito. Fresh roses are flown to his stores three times a week. His New York stores sell about 45,000 stems a week, along with an assortment of vases, balloons and stuffed animals. Roses Only can arrange delivery by Federal Express to anywhere in the country.

15 While discount rose retailers watch their business bloom, U.S. rose growers are wilting in the heat of foreign competition. Sales of U.S.-grown roses have declined from 565 million in 1988 to an estimated 520 million in 1993, says Roses Inc., a trade group for rose growers.

16 In 1988, imports accounted for 34% of roses sold here. Today, more than 57% of roses sold in the USA are grown in 19 other countries. The biggest foreign producers are Colombia and Ecuador, which accounted for almost 90% of the more than 692 million roses imported last year. Imported roses are sold by everyone from big flower-shop operators to street-corner peddlers.

17 The trend has hurt domestic rose growers such as Kitayama Bros. in Union City, Calif., considered to be this country's largest producer.

18 "The rose industry in this country is going down," says Ted Kitayama, the company's secretary. "Our profits have dropped substantially."

19 Kitayama, 64, is one of four brothers who founded the company after their release from World War II internment camps in 1948. Second-generation family members and in-laws now help run greenhouses in California and Colorado. Kitayama won't give specifics, but he says the company sells "several million roses" a year.

20 What's happening to domestic rose growers is a familiar experience for Kitayama. Until the 1960s, the Kitayamas grew nothing but carnations. Then the "offshore people" jumped into carnations, he says, and virtually ran U.S. carnation growers out of business.

21 The volume of rose imports has already crushed some domestic growers. Now, instead of fighting overseas competitors, the Kitayamas are trying to work with them.

22 "We have a few wholesale houses where we sell some imported roses," Kitayama says. "We may go more into the service areas and be a middleman for the overseas flower producers."

23 To offset lost rose sales, the Kitayamas and other growers also are planting Dutch flower crops, such as lilies, tulips and snapdragons.

24 U.S. growers got a break this Valentine's Day. A recent frost killed 25% of Colombia's rose crop. The loss could

mean sharp rose shortages in some parts of the country today. But next year, the weather may not be on their side.

25 "It's hard to operate a business on someone else's handicap or disaster. This way we're not controlling our own destiny," Kitayama says.

26 The rose business is big, but it attracts its share of small entrepreneurs.

27 Two couples in Pigeon Forge, Tenn., Robert and Shelly Shuler and Morris and Eve Spiegel, all in their late forties, launched 1-800-23-ROSES last year with less than $500.

28 The couples, who have been friends for 10 years, came up with the idea after brainstorming ways to boost the Shulers' small florist business. They decided on roses.

29 "It is the Mercedes-Benz of the florist industry," Morris Spiegel says. "By specializing in that item alone, you're creating the impression that you have the highest quality."

30 The couples take turns taking orders out of a small office. At night, they have calls transferred to their homes. Callers place orders using American Express, Visa and Discover credit cards. Orders are then dispatched to one of 52,000 florist shops in the company's network. They make their money from a $5 processing fee charged to the customer. A box of a dozen roses ordered today from 800-23-ROSES costs $60 to $100, depending on the city.

31 So far, business has been slow because of a lack of advertising. To launch a national advertising campaign, the couples would need at least $150,000, Spiegel says.

32 All the changes are making some in the rose business yearn for the good old days, when neighborhood florists arranged and delivered every Valentine's Day bouquet.

33 "It's the mystique," says rose grower Joel Effron, owner of Hillcrest Gardens in Petaluma, Calif. "Somebody shows up at work and puts them on a desk. Then everybody oohs and aahs and wonders who sent them to her."

34 And today, some will wonder whether they cost $10 or $100.

By Acey Harper

EVERYTHING'S COMING UP ROSES: The company run by the Kitayama family, including, (front to back) Ted, Ray, Robert and Dave, is considered the nation's biggest rose producer.

A. Read the information in the top graph.

1. The amount of rose sales is measured in billions (along the left side of the graph). Write the numerical value of 1.2 billion.

_____

2. What is the percent of increase in rose sales from 1988 to 1993? (The formula for percent of increase or decrease is: difference of new and old, divided by old, then multiplied by 100.)

_____

B. Read the information in the bottom graph.

1. What year showed almost no increase in imported roses?

_____

2. What two years showed about a 10 percent increase in imports?

_____

C. After reading the article, answer the following questions. Be sure to answer in complete sentences.

1. What do Nicole, Jacaranda, and Carambole have in common?

_____

2. How is Lorena different from the others, and why is she unsuitable for 80 percent of the buyers on Valentine's Day?

_____

3. What were the projected sales of roses for Valentine's Day in 1994?

_____

4. What is the main advantage to the buyer of the "discount" rose seller over the traditional florist shop?

_____

5. Since 1988, what has changed in the rose-growing business?

_____

6. What happened to improve the position of U.S. rose growers in 1994?

_____

7. What is the price for the most expensive roses from Roses Only as compared to the higher prices charged by retail florists?

_____

8. What is Joel Effron's theory on why roses are so popular?

_____

This article uses many technical business terms. Below is a list of words used in the article. Fill in the blanks with the best choice of words.

soars	discount
distributors	domestically
full-service	entrepreneur
imported	volume
competition	

1. A flower shop that is _____ offers special courtesies, such as potting plants, wrapping gifts, and gardening advice, but a _____ florist charges less and is more limited in its offerings.

2. On Valentine's Day, the price of roses _____ because of the great _____ of sales.

3. A farsighted _____ could start a new business with one good idea, such as sending roses by phone.

4. American rose growers are being hurt by roses that are _____ from the Andes mountains rather than being grown _____ .

5. The Kitayama family were _____ of carnations grown in California but were in _____ with off-shore people, so they switched to rose growing.

DIGGING BENEATH THE SURFACE

Each of the following rose businesses approaches the industry differently. After reading the article, summarize the business strategy for each one. Be sure to include specific details.

1. Roses Only

_____

2. Kitayama Brothers

_____

3. 1-800-23-ROSES

_____

GOING BEYOND THE TEXT

A. *Learning Together*

Discuss with the class how "new" products are often improvements or adaptations of other products. Some typical adaptations include making a product smaller, making a product larger, combining features of different products, simplifying a product, elaborating on an idea, providing a new service, and so on.

Choose a partner or form a small group of three or four. First choose a common product that you will adapt. Any useful product will do. Brainstorm for at least twenty minutes about what adaptations you could use. One member of the group should act as recorder of ideas during the session. After brainstorming, discuss which adaptation would have the best chance for financial success in the market.

Design a picture that shows the new product your group has created. Be sure the picture is detailed and colorful. Give your new product a name. Share your idea with other groups.

B. *Responding in Writing*

Business products offer an opportunity for creative writing using illustrations. Collect several product-name logos from advertisements or actual products. Some examples could be detergent boxes, candy wrappers, chewing gum, or cereals. Design a Valentine's Day card to accompany a dozen roses using the collected product pictures. An example (without pictures) follows:

> The *Tide* may come and go
>
> From *Mars* to the next *Era*
>
> But you will always be my *Dove*
>
> And I will be your *Life Saver*
>
> on Valentine's Day

MAKING CONNECTIONS

New business ideas can be found everywhere. Several news articles in this book suggest financial opportunities for entrepreneurs. What kinds of business opportunities are suggested by the articles in the "News" section on the fiftieth anniversary of D-Day or the end of apartheid in South Africa?

ARTICLE 5
Drug changes shorten heart patients' stay

The cost of medical care in this country is skyrocketing. Major hospitals spend hundreds of thousands of dollars on CAT scanners, MRI machines, and other expensive technology. The cost of a hospital stay increases as expensive procedures are developed to treat life-threatening conditions. All patients pay a share of the cost for medical care for the poor. In order to make effective cost-cutting changes, an entire team of problem-solvers must work together. An annual award was created in 1992 and is given jointly by *USA TODAY* and the Rochester Institute of Technology's College of Business to reward efforts in money management. In this article, the 1994 Quality Cup Award for a nonprofit organization was announced.

BEFORE YOU READ

Discuss the concept of cost-cutting. What measures could your family take to budget more carefully? Which items could be eliminated completely from your budget, and which could change slightly with minimum effect on the quality of life?

AS YOU READ

This article discusses the difficulty in solving a problem that involves many different people. As you read, pay special attention to the needs of each group and how each contributes a part to the total solution. The team solution saves several thousands of dollars for each patient. Think about how this affects the cost of medical care over a long period of time.

Drug changes shorten heart patients' stay

By Del Jones
USA TODAY

1 BURLINGTON, Vt.—Open-heart surgery at the Medical Center Hospital of Vermont used to cost patients an average $26,300. Today it's $3,000 less.

2 Also saved: patients' discomfort. They used to suffer for about 37 hours after surgery on average with a plastic tube as thick as a thumb running through their mouth or nose and down 11 inches of windpipe. The tube assists breathing, but patients say it's like a "hot poker" through their vocal cords and hurts more than having their chest sawed open.

3 Two years ago, a 15-member team at the 115-year-old teaching hospital, under pressure to cut costs from a health maintenance organization, was empowered by the hospital's chief administrator to find a way to get the tube removed sooner. That would ease the pain and help the hospital transfer patients from intensive care—an area that charges patients or their insurance company $1,600 a day—sooner. The hospital was facing an expensive expansion because of a chronic shortage of beds in intensive care. Transferring patients sooner would eliminate the need for additional beds.

4 Until recently, many hospitals would have resisted steps that moved patients out of intensive care and into a room that costs $800 a day. But the national effort to slash health care costs has dramatically changed the way hospitals think. Insurance companies and HMOs increasingly are paying hospitals a set amount for each patient, regardless of how long they stay. One HMO was threatening to move its heart-surgery patients from Medical Center Hospital of Vermont to Albany, Vt., if the hospital didn't get its costs down.

5 The team—six doctors, three nurses, three respiratory therapists, two pharmacists and an administrator—studied the situation and came up with improvements that earned the team the 1994 Quality Cup in the not-for-profit category.

6 Thanks to the team, the hospital stay of an open-heart surgery patient dropped from an average nine days to seven days. Some leave in just five days. Patients typically have the tubes in their throats about 29 hours. And mortality rates have dipped slightly, possibly because fewer infections set in once any foreign object is removed.

7 Early on, the team used the quality-improvement concept known as benchmarking—adopting the best methods or processes used by other companies. The members borrowed a seven-step problem-solving process from Florida Power & Light. Each meeting focused on one step. First, they tried to understand what was wrong with the process. At the second, they set a target for improvement.

8 Team members also studied the medical literature and interviewed new employees who had worked at other hospitals. They discovered some hospitals were removing the tube much faster. The hospitals had cut way back on hefty doses of morphine during and after surgery that were given primarily to control blood pressure, not pain.

9 "This was a story about results," says Cup judge Derek Brink, European marketing manager for Transarc. "They have given themselves more flexibility to respond to impending health care reform."

10 By using narcotics that wear off quickly and an Advil-like medicine, patients weren't "whacked" into long slumber and could breathe on their own sooner. They suffered no additional pain, awoke more alert, and the tube was removed quickly—sometimes six hours after surgery.

11 The team, led by Joan Blondin, supervisor of respiratory care, dubbed the process "surgery light" because patients are kept just barely asleep rather than out cold. Nurses had a pleasant surprise: Because patients weren't so heavily drugged, they became lucid soon after entering intensive care. The staff still refers to patients as "fresh hearts" because they arrive cold and colorless from surgery. But because patients no longer remain sleeping slabs, nurses got to know them sooner and helped them recover, says team-member Wendy LaCaunce, a respiratory therapist. "That's nice."

12 Although team members knew almost from the start that reducing narcotics was the answer, they also faced entrenched resistance. They spent six weeks educating everyone about the changes and winning the cooperation of surgeons, anesthesiologists, nurses and respiratory therapists—all of whom had grown comfortable with the old procedure.

13 When team member Dr. Brian Calhoun gave lectures to his fellow anesthesiologists, he called it a "new technique." About 10 of the 40 anesthesiologists balked. He learned to call it a "suggested technique" because people "don't like to be told what to do. It wouldn't have worked if we tried to ram this down."

A. Answer the following questions.

1. What was the problem the Medical Center Hospital of Vermont was trying to solve?

2. What are the two reasons the Center won the Quality Cup?

3. How would the early transfer of patients from intensive care save money?

4. According to paragraph 4, why are hospitals changing their thinking about moving patients from high-cost intensive care to cheaper rooms?

5. Explain the "benchmark" concept (see paragraph 7).

B. From each of these paragraphs, explain one of the specific changes the team made in hospital procedures.

1. paragraph 7 _____

2. paragraph 8 _____

3. paragraph 10 _____

4. paragraph 12 _____

PLAYING WITH WORDS

A. Circle the best definition for the following words from the article. The numbers in parentheses refer to the paragraph in the article where the word is used.

1. *empowered* (3)
    a. authorized
    b. not allowed

2. *chronic* (3)
    a. occurring once
    b. frequently recurring

3. *respiratory* (5)
    a. related to breathing
    b. related to inspiration

4. *mortality* (6)
    a. life
    b. death

5. *lucid* (11)
    a. unclear
    b. clear

6. *entrenched* (12)
    a. set firmly
    b. loose and pliable

7. *balked* (13)
    a. resisted
    b. accepted

B. Several words in the article are specifically related to jargon used in hospitals. Use context clues to define the meaning of the following.

1. *intensive care* (3) _____

2. *surgery light* (11) _____

3. *fresh hearts* (11) _____

4. *sleeping slabs* (11) _____

DIGGING BENEATH THE SURFACE

Below are some statements that might have been made by members of the cost-cutting team. Using the italicized words as clues, write the code letters for that team member. The team members are: hospital administrator—HA; respiratory therapist—RT; nurse—N; pharmacist—P; surgeon—S.

1. The *medication* needs to be adjusted so they get less *morphine* and less *sleep-inducing drugs,* causing less pain and early alertness.

2. Here are the *statistics of patient cost* per stay and details of mortality rates in this hospital.

3. Patients suffer from *large tubes,* so we have to examine how we can assist *breathing* within a shorter time span.

4. My *colleagues* in the *operating room* may have a problem with this new technique, so I'll discuss the benefits to patients and stress that they practice this "improvement."

5. We like the results when patients recover more quickly. We can *assist the doctors* more efficiently.

GOING BEYOND THE TEXT

A. *Learning Together*

Form a problem-solving team of four or five students. Choose one of the roles below and stay in character. Imagine how that person might see the situation and what special knowledge that person brings to the team. Here are the members of the team: the principal of the school, a well-liked teacher, a popular student, a parent of a chronic troublemaker, the custodian of the school. (You may have more team members if needed.)

Here is the problem: Students want to be able to chew gum and candy during the school day. In the past, gum and candy wrappers have been a major problem in classrooms and hallways. Gum has even been found in books and desks. It has cost the school district extra salary for custodians to clean it up. Parents are particularly upset because they want more nutritious snacks. Some parents have complained that punishment for students caught chewing gum has been too harsh. What can the school do to solve this problem?

Use the following steps in your problem-solving. One member of the team will need to take notes about all the ideas.

1. Each team member states the problem from his or her point of view.

2. Each member makes suggestions about possible solutions. While the group is brainstorming for solutions, no one's ideas should be judged negatively.

3. All possible solutions should be evaluated for positive and negative aspects.

4. Try combining the best parts of suggestions to form a solution that each team member can live with.

5. Write up a plan for implementation.

B. *Responding in Writing*

Interview someone in the medical profession: a nurse, doctor, pharmacist, or hospital administrator. Find out what specific role the person plays in the total care of a patient. Ask about his or her educational background and what he or she likes or dislikes about the profession.

Being prepared for an interview is very important. Write out five questions you plan to ask before you actually do the interview. Be sure to take notes during the interview. When you have finished, write up a report using some direct and some indirect quotes.

MAKING CONNECTIONS

In the "Editorials and Opinions" section, review the articles on health-care reform. Several views on health care are given, but all agree health-care cost is a major problem. How could the approach of the team in this article be used to solve other problems, such as the high cost of emergency room care, the problem of uninsured children, the dilemma of expensive research and development of new drugs with high risk of law suits for phamaceutical companies, and so on?

MONEY

Surveying Types of Money Articles; Relating to General News

The money or business section of a newspaper focuses on information about the economic lives of people. Individuals with money to invest can find a reliable daily report of the activities of stocks, bonds, and currencies. But there is a wealth of other information in this section:

- articles reporting the financial situation of companies;
- articles reporting new products and technology;
- articles about trends in the United States and world economy;
- information on the stock markets and currency;
- graphs and charts that support all types of articles; and
- commentaries and opinions on money trends.

Exercise 1: What Business Is It of Yours?

Work with a small group and arrange a display of the different types of money or business articles. Use the list above to label the articles.

Exercise 2: The Language of Business

Read the articles from Exercise 1 and list ten vocabulary words that are special to this section of the paper.

Word	Specialized meaning
1. _____	_____
2. _____	_____
3. _____	_____
4. _____	_____
5. _____	_____
6. _____	_____
7. _____	_____
8. _____	_____
9. _____	_____
10. _____	_____

Exercise 3: Up Front with Money News

Read the front page of the news section of the paper for several days. Choose three articles that relate to economics. Write the headline and describe the possible effect of the news on such areas as international trade, employment trends, a particular industry, stock market trends, and so on.

Exercise 4: The Ups and Downs of Stocks

Newspapers run lists of stock and bond prices for several stock exchanges. Investors who own stocks can follow the changing prices daily. Read your newspaper's explanation of stock listings and practice following a stock for two weeks. Imagine that you buy one hundred shares on your start date, record at least four stock prices within the time period, and sell the stock at the end of two weeks. Record your profit or loss. Choose a company whose product you are familiar with, such as a popular clothing store, an auto company, a food manufacturer, or a utility. Use the form below to keep track of your stock.

Name of company ——————————— Newspaper symbol ———————————

Date of purchase ——————————— Price per share ———————————

Date ——————————— Closing price ———————————

Date ——————————— Closing price ———————————

Date ——————————— Closing price ———————————

Date ——————————— Closing price ———————————

Profit or loss on one hundred shares ———————————————————————

SPORTS

USA SNAPSHOTS®

A look at statistics that shape the sports world

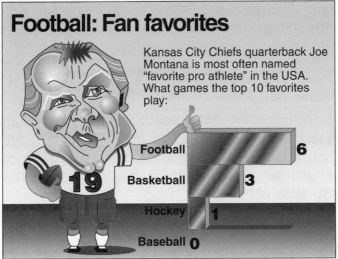

Football: Fan favorites

Kansas City Chiefs quarterback Joe Montana is most often named "favorite pro athlete" in the USA. What games the top 10 favorites play:

Football **6**

Basketball **3**

Hockey **1**

Baseball **0**

Source: ESPN Chilton Sports Poll   By John Riley and Marcia Staimer, USA TODAY

ARTICLE 1
Aaron paid a price for beating Ruth

PREVIEWING THE ARTICLES

Ask one hundred people who the home-run king of baseball was and odds are they will mention Babe Ruth. The Babe is a legend in sports history. During his lifetime, abundant press coverage promoted his enormous talent. Every fan knows the story of how Babe pointed to the outfield and called home runs to fulfill a promise to a sick child in the hospital. After two movies, one years ago with Bill Bendix and one recently starring John Goodman, Babe Ruth has been immortalized in the annals of baseball history.

Although Ruth's home-run record lasted for thirty-nine years, it was broken in 1974 by Henry Louis Aaron, known as Hank. The year Aaron beat the Babe's record, there were few accolades and no great cheers from fans. Instead, as this article relates, Aaron received death threats and boos. Could it be that racism reared its ugly head at America's beloved summer game? In this article, Hank Aaron discusses the twentieth anniversary of his amazing achievement.

BEFORE YOU READ

Use an encyclopedia to research Jackie Robinson, the first African American to play major league baseball, in 1947. Read about his struggles to integrate the game.

AS YOU READ

Today Hank Aaron is an accomplished business executive who merchandises sports memorabilia. Consider his reactions twenty years ago and now. Some of the direct quotes in the article indicate that much anger remains over the lack of public recognition for his accomplishments. Consider whether you agree with him that racism is the reason he was ignored as a baseball legend in favor of Ruth.

Aaron paid a price for beating Ruth

By Chuck Johnson
USA TODAY

By Joe Marquette, AP

Aaron: "My life has never been better"

1 Hank Aaron keeps The Ball in a bank vault in Atlanta.

2 He tries to keep the memories locked away, too. But on today's 20th anniversary of surpassing Babe Ruth as baseball's all-time home run leader, his recollections come rushing back—as ugly now as when he lived through them.

3 Death threats. Hate mail. Federal protection for his daughter. So imprisoned in his hotel room that a teammate had to bring his meals.

4 "It was a very sad time," Aaron says. "I don't think about it much because of all the things I had to go through. My kids had to suffer. My daughter was in college and wasn't able to do everything she wanted to do. That period left some very bad and deep scars on me."

5 After Ruth retired in 1935, his 714 home runs were revered as the record that would never be broken. Aaron changed that April 8, 1974, hitting home run No. 715 over the left-centerfield fence at Atlanta-Fulton County Stadium.

6 For shattering a myth, Aaron was vilified by some who saw his feat as a slap to Ruth's legend. Volumes of hate mail dripped with resentment that a black player now held baseball's most coveted record.

7 "It was pure racism, that's the only way you can look at it," Aaron says. "I can recall when Pete Rose had his hitting streak. He said it was probably one of the greatest thrills he had and one of the greatest times. I can't say the same."

8 Major league baseball has dedicated the week of April 8-15 to Aaron. Each home team will mark the anniversary before today's game. In addition, the Atlanta Braves will honor him Wednesday, the night after their home opener.

9 Aaron will celebrate with his wife, Billye, and family. But he says any celebration by baseball seems too little, too late.

10 "Here it is 20 years later. Why should I be excited now?," he says. "When I hit it nothing happened. It's done with. It was accomplished and maybe someday it will be appreciated."

11 Al Downing, now 52, was the Los Angeles Dodgers' left-hander who gave up Aaron's 715th homer. He agrees not enough has been done to honor Aaron's record.

12 "It is one of the best-kept secrets in baseball," Downing says. "In my 17 years in baseball, it was the most significant thing to happen, yet baseball doesn't even commemorate it."

13 Jim Small, spokesman for major league baseball, disagrees: "You celebrate records on anniversaries, and that's what we are doing this year. No doubt he is the most prestigious hitter in all of baseball, and we salute him whenever we can."

14 Aaron didn't feel appreciated as he neared the record. The media kept constant watch, but few knew his private agony.

15 Despite constant threats against him and his family, Aaron went about business as usual at the ballpark. But nowhere did he feel safe. He encountered his scariest moment in Montreal: "I was standing in the outfield and somebody set off about 15 firecrackers. I thought for sure somebody had been killed."

16 Aaron says he owes a lot to Paul Casanova, a Cuban-born catcher who became his closest friend during the chase.

17 "He was the one who stuck by me," Aaron says. "I couldn't go out of my room, so he would get my meals and anything else I needed. I don't know what I would have done without him."

18 Aaron says he was wise to take every threat seriously. "People said I shouldn't pay it any attention. But that one letter might be the one you shouldn't have ignored. Look at what happened to Monica Seles and that skater," Nancy Kerrigan.

19 Aaron keeps the vile and threatening letters, occasionally re-reading them. "They will never be burned. They show just how ignorant some people can be. People need to be reminded about things like that or the past will keep repeating itself."

20 Aaron, 60, is a senior vice president and assistant to the president of the Atlanta Braves, and vice president of business development for the Airport Channel, a subsidiary of Turner Broadcasting System, which also owns the Braves.

21 His company, Henry Aaron, Inc., is licensed to produce apparel commemorating the anniversary. He is also a licensee to produce merchandise for the '96 Summer Olympics in Atlanta.

22 "I'm in part two of my life. My (five) kids are out of school and doing well. I have two grandchildren. I don't have to think about home runs or anything pertaining to baseball anymore except for my merchandise. I've never been more busy. My life has never been better."

23 Aaron will be promoting his merchandise tonight on QVC, the TV shopping channel, from 9 p.m. to midnight ET.

24 Aaron considers himself fortunate to be working for a team owner like Ted Turner: "He's someone who thinks about you as a human being and not just someone who's a token."

25 Although his situation is secure, Aaron remains vocal about injustices he sees in baseball. He feels the game still is dragging its feet on hiring minorities in decision-making positions.

26 "Some people may hold that against me, but I'm going to continue to voice my opinion. . . . I'm speaking because it's something that needs to be said."

27 Aaron, a native of Mobile, Ala., started pro baseball at 18. He joined the Braves in 1952 after they bought his contract from the Indianapolis Clowns of the Negro American League.

28 He played for the Braves—in Milwaukee and Atlanta—for all but two seasons of his 23-year major league career and still holds more batting records than anyone in history.

29 He has the most runs batted in (2,297), most extra-base hits (1,477) and most total bases (6,856). After two seasons with the Milwaukee Brewers, he retired in 1976 with 755 home runs.

30 Even now he senses some would like to see an asterisk by his record. "All you hear about is Babe Ruth," he says. "It's like he still holds the record. At one point, it used to bother me. Now I don't have time to worry about it. No matter how they choose to observe it, when you look at the home run leaders, there's my 755 on top and then there's Babe Ruth."

31 Aaron, whose highest salary was the $225,000 he made each year with the Brewers, says players today "deserve every nickel." But he finds it hard to compare generations.

32 "Guys like Willie Mays, Ernie Banks, Ted Williams, Mickey Mantle, myself and Juan Marichal, did it year in and out. Not for two years, but for seven, eight and nine years. The only player I see that can come close to that today is Barry Bonds."

33 Aaron expects his home run mark to last longer than Ruth's 39 years. Again, it seems the record never will be broken. "Not taking away anything from the athletes, but when you make so much money, you still have to have the initiative and drive."

34 He believes his home run mark helped pave the way for today's black stars. "It relieved pressure from the standpoint that it had been just a few years since blacks were admitted into baseball. It proved that if given the opportunity, we could do everything and probably more than a lot of players.

35 "I clipped the home run title. Lou Brock passed Ty Cobb in base-stealing. It makes you think about what would have happened if blacks had been let into baseball before Jackie Robinson (in 1947). It's just a shame that Americans were deprived of seeing so many great ballplayers."

GETTING THE MESSAGE

A. Below are several statements about three baseball greats. On the space provided, write the name each statement refers to: Babe Ruth, Hank Aaron, or Lou Brock.

_____ 1. held the title of home-run king for thirty-nine years

_____ 2. career total of 755 home runs

_____ 3. retired from baseball in 1935

_____ 4. hit 714 home runs in his career

_____ 5. broke Ty Cobb's base-stealing record

_____ 6. hit his record home run off Al Downing

_____ 7. week of April 15, 1994, is dedicated to him

B. Identify these important dates in baseball history as related in the article.

1. 1935 _____

2. 1947 _____

3. 1952 _____

4. 1974 _____

5. 1976 _____

6. 1994 _____

PLAYING WITH WORDS

Use context clues to determine the meaning of each word from the article. The paragraph in which each word is used is indicated in parentheses. Match each word in the first column with its meaning in the second column by writing the letter on the blank lines.

_____ 1. *vilified* (6)   a. remember

_____ 2. *dripped* (6)   b. famous

_____ 3. *coveted* (6)   c. desired

_____ 4. *commemorate* (12)   d. condemned

_____ 5. *prestigious* (13)   e. part of a larger group

_____ 6. *subsidiary* (20)   f. were filled with

_____ 7. *initiative* (33)   g. energy

_____ 8. *drive* (33)   h. lacking

_____ 9. *deprived* (35)   i. ambition

DIGGING BENEATH THE SURFACE

A. Make a list of three negative consequences of Aaron's accomplishments in 1974.

  1. _____

  2. _____

  3. _____

B. Compare how Aaron handled setting the record in 1974 to how he deals with it now.

C. Discuss two examples that would support Aaron's belief that his record was not appreciated as much as Babe Ruth's because of racism.

D. As a class, discuss the feelings expressed by Al Downing and Jim Small.

E. Summarize in writing Aaron's feelings about the state of baseball today in regard to racism.

GOING BEYOND THE TEXT

A. *Learning Together*

Work in a group of three or four to complete the following chart using an encyclopedia or sports almanac. Use several different reference books to compare the type of information given in each. You may add other sports to the chart as well as those given.

Sport	Name of record	Record holder	Year record made
1. Football	_____	_____	_____
2. Baseball	_____	_____	_____
3. Tennis	_____	_____	_____
4. Soccer	_____	_____	_____
5. Basketball	_____	_____	_____

B. *Responding in Writing*

Read a biography of a famous minority person who achieved greatness in the field of sports, music, science, entertainment, medicine, or politics. Design a timeline for the biography you read. Choose ten to fifteen important events in his or her life and summarize them next to the dates of their occurrence. Lay out the dates across the timeline from birth to death or from birth to current times if the person is still living. You may have to use a reference source such as *Current Biographies* or an almanac to update a living person. You may enhance the timeline with pictures.

MAKING CONNECTIONS

Review the articles in the "News" section on South Africa and the problems of dismantling apartheid. Compare Hank Aaron's experience and feelings with the future problems facing blacks in South Africa. Keep in mind that American baseball was integrated in 1947, yet Aaron still feels the pangs of discrimination.

ARTICLE 2A
Female golfers still face boys club attitudes

ARTICLE 2B
Gold medalist mom leaves big skates for daughter to fill

ARTICLE 2C
Granato wouldn't be cowed into quitting

PREVIEWING THE ARTICLES

Imagine watching Monday Night Football and hearing this announcement about the lead quarterback: "Number 44, Mary Smith, for the Chicago Bears." How do you feel about women playing professional sports that were previously considered "all male"? Is your attitude that women should play if they are good enough? Or should they be kept from participating on men's teams? Along with women's integration into other traditionally male occupations, such as construction, law enforcement, fire fighting, medicine, and engineering, has come women's desire to compete in all areas of sports.

The role of women in sports has been limited to "girls' teams" until recently. There was much more funding for male teams at high schools and colleges. Big-money professional sports like basketball, football, and hockey were male-dominated, and the money for endorsements followed the pattern. Today, federal law, Title IX, guarantees certain rights to women in sports in public schools and colleges. These articles examine the struggles of women in the sports of golf, speedskating, and hockey.

BEFORE YOU READ

1. Look at the sports pages of a newspaper and scan for the number of articles dealing with males and females in sports. Discuss the results of your investigation.

2. Survey your classmates and parents to determine if they read the sports section of the newspaper regularly. Be sure to keep track of male and female responses. Discuss the possible reasons for any differences you find.

AS YOU READ

As you read these three articles, look for specific examples of how women are discouraged from participating in certain sports. Pay special attention to the persistence of these women in pursuit of their sports dreams.

Female golfers still face boys club attitudes

By Rachel Shuster
USA TODAY

1 The winds of change barely ripple across the fairways for women seeking equal standing in golf.

2 Or would Ice Age be a better reference point?

3 "It's pretty glacial change, it seems, from the phone calls we get," says Kathryn Reith at the Women's Sports Foundation.

4 Why wouldn't '90s women recoil at the '50s notion that membership to golf clubs often remains open only to men?

5 Or that the prime tee times remain reserved for men only.

6 Or that the sanctity of the men's grill must not be violated by the presence of ladies.

7 Sounds pretty silly, doesn't it? Especially three years after Shoal Creek founder Hall Thompson unwittingly exposed the inequity of golf membership for anyone other than white males.

8 But those attitudes still circumscribe the boundaries for many women who dare to take up golf and become addicted to it as much as men.

9 "The attitudes for change perhaps are in the works, but the mechanics are taking a little longer," says Judy Thompson, who tracks trends and the numbers at the National Golf Foundation.

10 One of the surprising numbers is that women's golf leveled off in 1992 after years of being hailed as the fastest-growing group. About a 2% dip.

11 Perhaps that's because of the uncertain economy—golf is not an inexpensive sport—although equipment/clothing sales still are booming.

12 And no doubt women can find golf a frustrating game.

13 But it's also true that when the welcome mat never appears, the new arrival gets the message: Stay out of the way.

14 Even women who have played for a while get that feeling, and not only at the fancy clubs where membership is exclusive in both the figurative and literal senses.

15 I joined a threesome of women at a public course this summer and found them unnerved by what the starter said: "You ladies are standing too near the first tee, and you're talking too loud."

16 Thing is, they weren't that loud, and they were a decent distance back off the tee. They weren't angry, though. "That's the way we're always treated," the ladies said.

17 The same week I went to one of the huge golf discounters in the Washington, D.C., area, hoping to find a 5-wood. When I asked where the ladies' woods were, the clerk replied, "In with the left-handed clubs." I found exactly two, while men had about 200 to inspect.

18 When I asked where the ladies' irons were, the clerk, exasperated, said in hostile tones, "What is it that you want?" I only wanted to browse through the single irons the way the men were doing.

19 Nancy Oliver, in the golf industry for 13 years, has had the same experience shopping for clubs and being taken seriously as a golfer.

20 That's why she founded the Executive Women's Golf League two years ago, with chapters forming around the country to educate women about the game and to provide golfing opportunities.

21 Oliver had 650 women join the first year, "And now we're averaging 600 a month."

22 Yet even Oliver acknowledges the women often are naive about the golf environment.

23 "It isn't until they polish their game enough that they say, 'Gee, I think I'm going to invest in joining a club.' And all of a sudden they find out they can't. They'll call me and say, 'Did you know this happens? I'm appalled this would be the case in the '90s.' "

24 "So how will the attitudes change so the policies change?

25 "When the wife of a member is restricted, that's one thing," Oliver says. "But when a man's daughter who he's put through law school is told she can't play, that's when you hit a nerve."

26 Still, that's relying on men to pave the way.

27 Women must be bold and insistent, which is tough in the conservative atmosphere of most clubs. But that's how the winds of change become more than a ripple.

Gold medalist mom leaves big skates for daughter to fill

By Steve Woodward
USA TODAY

By Porter Binks, USA TODAY

COACH MOM: Speedskating coach Dianne Holum, who won Olympic medals in '68 and '72, now coaches her daughter.

1   SAN ANTONIO—After a speed-skating gold medal at the 1972 Olympics, Dianne Holum awaited her post-athletic future with uncertainty.

2   "I was happy with what I had accomplished," says Holum, who also won a bronze in '72 and a silver and a bronze in '68 when she was 16. "I knew there wasn't much life after skating in my sport."

3   Holum has been surprised by the inaccuracy of that statement ever since. She was lured into coaching in Madison, Wis., where she soon met a 13-year-old named Eric Heiden. By 1980, Heiden was the USA's premier speed-skater, winning five gold medals at the Winter Games in Lake Placid, N.Y. Holum was his coach.

4   Now Holum has another 13-year-old on her hands—U.S. Olympic Festival participant Kirstin Holum, her daughter.

5   "(Kirstin) is one of the group, and I have to keep her one of the group," says Holum, who coaches about 35 skaters at a West Allis, Wis., club. "If I start to single her out, it becomes a mom thing.

6   "She's 13 and starting to feel some independence. That's the age where kids start letting the parents know they can do it their own way."

7   Kirstin's first Festival competition proved that genetics don't guarantee instant success. She was fifth in the short-track 1,500-meter final Monday but fell short of the finals in Tuesday's 1,000 meters and 3,000 meters.

8   "Last year, I didn't even want to be a speedskater anymore," says Kirstin, raised in a single-parent environment. "I decided I wanted to be a swimmer because I wanted to be with my friends. But after this past year, I was convinced I would be able to do (speedskating)."

9   With doubts behind her, Kirstin is working toward December, when she attempts to qualify for the Junior Short Track World Championships.

10   "I think she's still at the age," Dianne says, "that when she's on the (starting) line she wants to win, but off the line she doesn't think about it. That's coming, though."

11   Both mom and daughter agree that their dual relationship on and off the ice can have some drawbacks.

12   Says Kirstin: "When your parent is your coach, you see them all the time. They're always there."

By Porter Binks, USA TODAY

GOLDEN GENES: Kirstin Holum, 13, daughter of Olympic gold medalist Dianne Holum, is competing in San Antonio.

13   Says Dianne: "Sometimes I wish I could find a really good coach for her to go to, someone who I'd feel good enough about to say, 'Here, you take her.'"

Granato wouldn't be cowed into quitting

By Steve Woodward
USA TODAY

1 SAN ANTONIO—Cammi Granato's experiences while trying to develop her ice hockey talents raise doubts about whether we live in an enlightened society.

2 The resistance Granato often encountered as a girl playing among boys was not always verbal.

3 "I had a couple of threats, even from coaches," says Granato, 22, recalling her days in youth hockey tournaments. "I dealt with it, though. When I was 13, I ended up with a concussion during a tournament in Kansas City. Some guy just plowed into me from the side."

4 Granato refused to yield, however. She enrolled at Providence College, one of the few schools offering women's hockey scholarships in the late 1980s, and went on to become a three-time Eastern Collegiate Athletic Conference player of the year.

5 The 5-7, 140-pound forward from Downers Grove, Ill., also helped Team USA win a silver medal in the inaugural women's world championship in 1990. She made the world team again last year as Team USA again finished second to Canada. She'll play with a U.S. squad against Canada at the Olympic Festival beginning Friday night.

6 This summer, she is the only woman on a Wisconsin club team.

7 As a kid, there was only one choice. "I had my mind set," she says. "My brothers were all older than me, so I wanted to do whatever they did."

8 Tony Granato, a 1988 Olympian, plays for the Los Angeles Kings. Brother Don led Wisconsin to an NCAA title in 1990. Youngest brother Rob plays for Wisconsin now.

9 "Hockey was always part of our

By Robert Hanashiro, USA TODAY

FAMILY TIES: Cammi Granato, left, sister of the Kings' Tony Granato, grew up leaving her skates on with brothers for dinner.

lives," says Cammi, who graduated last spring with a social sciences degree. "We'd come home from the pond across the street from our house, leave our skates on for dinner and then go back out to the pond."

GETTING THE MESSAGE

A. Fill in the blanks to complete the sentences according to the information provided in Article 2A.

1. Women today find the golf world still _____ .

2. One example was the author's experience buying a club, where she found

   _____ .

3. The purpose of the Executive Women's Golf League is to _____

   _____ .

4. The author suggests that to stop discrimination in golf, women should _____

   _____ .

B. After reading Article 2B, determine if the following statements are true or false.

_____ 1. Dianne Holum thought that her career in speedskating was over after her 1968 and 1972 medal wins.

_____ 2. Dianne believes that her daughter is at the top of the group she coaches and needs special treatment.

_____ 3. Kirstin's skating success was immediate as she won her early races.

_____ 4. Kirstin's desire for success is consistent on the track and off.

_____ 5. Both mother and daughter agree their dual relationship as mother/daughter and coach/team member can have problems.

C. Choose the best answer to complete each sentence after reading Article 2C.

1. Cammi Granato probably learned to love hockey because _____ .

   a. her father was a championship player

   b. as an only child, her parents encouraged her love of any sport

   c. she joined her brothers skating for fun when they were young

   d. she had no other skills to make a living with

2. Cammi has found that in the world of skating _____ .

   a. she has been welcomed as a talented team member

   b. although there are a few obstacles to overcome, her talent has been recognized

   c. it has been a constant struggle to achieve recognition for her talent

3. Cammi has played on _____ .

   a. only women's teams

   b. only men's teams

   c. both women's and men's teams

PLAYING WITH WORDS

A. Prefixes add meaning to root words. Below are a few prefixes used in Article 2A. Find the word in the article that uses one of the prefixes and fits the meaning given. The numbers in parentheses refer to paragraphs in the article.

re: go backward	*ex*: out of
un, in: not	*dis*: take away

1. to jump backward (4) _____
2. not equal (7) _____
3. not costly (11) _____
4. keeping people out (14) _____
5. not have control of feelings, upset (15) _____
6. take away some of the cost (17) _____
7. out of control with anger or frustration (18) _____

B. In Article 2A, Rachel Shuster uses language in combinations of images in order to give her views strength and power. Discuss how the following image words are used effectively. Tell how they make the rest of the paragraphs more meaningful.

1. paragraph 2 and 3, *Ice Age/glacial change*
2. paragraph 6, *sanctity/violated*
3. paragraph 27, *winds/ripple*

DIGGING BENEATH THE SURFACE

The three articles in this section are tied together by their common theme. Each explores the role of women in today's world of sports. In each article, there is evidence to support the idea that women are making inroads in terms of participation and recognition, but each article also shows that problems still exist.

1. Choose one example from each article that shows discrimination toward women in sports.

    Article 2A _____

    Article 2B _____

    Article 2C _____

2. Choose one example from each article that shows a positive accomplishment of women in sports.

    Article 2A _____

    Article 2B _____

    Article 2C _____

A. *Learning Together*

Use your creativity to invent a new sport. Bring into class an array of sports equipment from a variety of sports, such as baseballs, football helmets, roller skates, fielders' mitts, croquet wickets, jump ropes, and so on, and place them in a large carton. Form teams of four or five people. Each person picks one item from the sports carton without looking. Using the selected items chosen by the members of your group, design a new game. Be sure to design a playing field and create rules. Be clear about the object of the game. Concentrate on skills rather than on violent contact. If a gymnasium is available, try out your new game and improve it, if need be. Design a uniform for your team. As a group project, write a report on your game and put all the reports on new games into a sports booklet.

B. *Responding in Writing*

Both Articles 2B and 2C deal with young female athletes who had families involved in sports. Write a five- to seven-sentence paragraph comparing the role that each girl's family played in her pursuit of sports. Include the attitudes of Kirstin Holum (Article 2B) and Cammi Granato (Article 2C) about their families' influence on their achievements. Follow these steps:

1. State the common idea in both articles.

2. Give several examples of how the articles show likenesses.

3. Give several examples of how the articles show differences.

4. State a conclusion about the experiences of both athletes.

5. Be sure to use transition words such as *but, while, therefore, since, more than,* and so on.

MAKING CONNECTIONS

The experiences of Hank Aaron are detailed in Article 1 in this section. Aaron discusses the struggle of minorities in sports. These articles about women in sports suggest that they, too, struggle for recognition. Discuss whether these two groups share common experiences.

ARTICLE 3
Fireworks set off new string of theories

PREVIEWING THE ARTICLE

Start with a cork center, surround it with three layers of wool yarn, cover the yarn with cowhide, sew by hand 108 red stitches, send the sphere to a rolling machine to provide universal height, and the product is the perfect baseball. Regulation balls must be almost identical—their weight between 5 and 5¼ ounces and their circumference between 9 and 9¼ inches. The major baseball supplier to the major leagues is a company called Rawlings, which provides 750,000 balls a season to twenty-eight teams. Rawlings goes to extreme lengths to ensure reliability and standardization of baseballs.

But every few decades a "juice" controversy arises. In 1920, the "kangaroo theory" emerged—that balls were being hit farther because they were wound with a new Australian yarn. In 1965, there were claims that the Chicago White Sox tried freezing baseballs in order to improve hitting distance. Richard Larsen, a physicist, actually proved that heating a baseball in an oven helps it gain distance. In 1987, the major leagues asked for independent testing. A team of professors at the University of Missouri at Rolla did air-cannon tests but found the baseballs all within the standard range. Today, the major leagues have strict safeguards against tampering. Five-dozen baseballs, each in a sealed package, must be given to the umpires an hour before each game.

This article looks at the juice controversy of 1994. Even though the manufacturing process assures that baseballs are strictly uniform, theories abound from managers, players, and fans alike that baseballs are being doctored to fly farther.

BEFORE YOU READ

Before you read, define the word *rumor*. Rumors about "juiced baseballs" have created theories that are not based on any factual information. Are rumors usually correct? How do you think they get started? Discuss how rumors about people or ideas can be damaging. Consider why people seem to want to believe rumors rather than scientific facts.

AS YOU READ

In this article, several people give theories to explain some facts about the 1994 baseball season. As you read, decide which theories seem reasonable and which sound too far-fetched to be taken seriously.

Fireworks set off new string of theories

By Mike Dodd
USA TODAY

1 St. Louis' Ray Lankford—the first batter of the first game—started it all when he led off the season with a home run.

2 Now, major league teams are on pace for more runs a game (10.4 through April) than any year since 1930 (11.09) and more homers a game than ever.

3 The increase is sudden and significant. April '94 batting statistics are significantly higher than numbers from the first month of the last several seasons:

▶ The last seven years (including the Big Bang year of 1987) major league teams averaged 1.57 home runs a game in April. This year, it's 2.22—a 41% increase.

▶ Opposite-field homers are up 63% from the previous six years. The 121 opposite-field homers this year are more than double the April total for any of the other years.

▶ Saves are being blown at a record pace. Closers are successful in only 61% of their save opportunities—12% lower than the average of 1988–93.

4 "I've never seen anything like it," says Oakland reliever Dennis Eckersley, in his 20th year in the big leagues. "It's pretty glaring what the hitters are doing."

5 Players, coaches and managers summon as many theories as pitching changes.

6 Many pitchers say the ball is livelier and strike zone smaller. Hitters say they're just stronger and better.

7 Coaching staffs and front-office execs offer several explanations, including the lack of quality pitching.

8 "All you've got to do is look at the replays on ESPN and watch the pitches that are getting hit," says Texas pitching coach Claude Osteen. "They're bad pitches; they're pitches that are up in the strike zone or in the middle of the plate. For 100 years in this game, you couldn't get away with that, and you can't get away with it today."

9 California's Buck Rodgers, Minnesota's Tom Kelly and St. Louis' Joe Torre are among managers who think the ball is different.

10 "The balls are harder," says Torre. "The seams are higher, which adds to the rotation and the ball stays in the air longer."

11 Cards pitcher Rick Sutcliffe agrees: "Most of the times when a pitcher throws the ball back, it's because it is too hard. This year, you could go through a whole box before you found a soft one."

12 Colorado manager Don Baylor recently took a baseball and unwound it, layer by layer. With each layer, he'd bounce it. "It's a superball. They're rabbit balls," he says.

13 Cubs pitcher Dan Plesac says if you watch tapes of 15 or 20 years ago, you'll notice a different strike zone.

14 "You see Bob Gibson, Don Drysdale and you see the low strikes and high strikes they got," he says.

15 Counters retired National League umpire Dutch Rennert: "Sure, blame it on the umpires. . . . It's the umps' fault they're hitting all those home runs."

16 Rennert says his strike zone didn't change in 19 years in the majors. He thinks it's the ball: "Either that or they're using illegal bats again. The solution is to make the balls in the U.S." Rawlings Sporting Goods Co., which supplies all major league baseballs, manufactures them in Costa Rica.

17 Hitters say they're not being given credit where it's due.

18 "I just think players are stronger than they were in the past," says Expos outfielder Moises Alou. "Everybody works out."

19 Adds Cubs coach Billy Williams: "The ball could be juiced up a little bit, but I think the players are just bigger, stronger, quicker. . . . If you look in the weightroom every day, you see guys pumping weights."

20 Don Sutton, a 300-game winner and now analyst on TBS, says the best athletes used to become pitchers and short-stops, but now they play other positions. "Good athletes are more offensive-minded because that's what we're glamorizing, and that's where the money is," he says.

21 Also, he says, high school and college pitchers learn their trade against competition using aluminum bats, which propel a ball farther than a wooden bat. As a result, they pitch scared—trying to trick hitters instead of relying on a fastball in at the hands.

22 Eckersley says hitters are smarter: "They're studying pitchers much more . . . and getting better plate coverage."

23 Many hitters stride over the plate to reach the pitch on the outside corner. "And everybody (gets upset) when you come inside," he says.

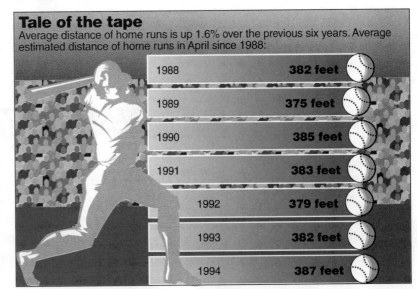

Tale of the tape
Average distance of home runs is up 1.6% over the previous six years. Average estimated distance of home runs in April since 1988:

1988	382 feet
1989	375 feet
1990	385 feet
1991	383 feet
1992	379 feet
1993	382 feet
1994	387 feet

Source: *The Physics of Baseball*, STATS, Inc., USA TODAY research

GETTING THE MESSAGE

Scan the article for the information needed to complete the following sentences.

1. The 1994 baseball season began when _____ hit a _____ .

2. The pace for runs in a game at the time of this article was _____ per game.

3. The year of 1987 was called the _____ with an average of _____ home runs per game. But in 1994, there was an average of _____ home runs per game.

4. Since 1988, opposite-field home runs have increased _____ percent.

5. From 1988 to1993, saves have decreased by _____ percent.

PLAYING WITH WORDS

Baseball is famous for its "jargon"—vocabulary unique to that game. Use your own knowledge or a sports reference book to find the baseball meaning for the following words. The paragraph in which the term is used is indicated in parentheses.

1. *led off* (1) _____

2. *runs* (2) _____

3. *opposite-field* (3) _____

4. *saves* (3) _____

5. *strike zone* (6) _____

6. *plate* (8) _____

DIGGING BENEATH THE SURFACE

A. Discuss the different theories proposed in this article about why balls are flying farther.

B. Write a summary of the opinions of various hitters about the increased numbers of multiple-base hits.

GOING BEYOND THE TEXT

A. *Learning Together*
Form science teams of three to four students to design an experiment on baseballs. Start by measuring the weight, circumference, and number of stitches of several baseballs. Ask your science teacher about possible experiments you could safely conduct on the baseball, such as bounce tests. You might try heating and then cooling baseballs and then observing any changes in their measurements. Remember to keep accurate records and compare information with other groups.

B. *Responding in Writing*

Check the current (or most recent) statistics for home runs, compare them with the information in this article, and write a summary of your conclusions about whether baseballs are, or ever were, juiced.

MAKING CONNECTIONS

The final paragraphs of the article entitled "Look who's talking to themselves: Just about everyone" in the "Science, Health, and Behavior" section relate to the mental attitudes of coaches and players. How are athletes in general improving their mental and physical health?

ARTICLE 4
For complex times, simple footwear

PREVIEWING THE ARTICLE

Imagine that you are in any city or state in America (or, for that matter, almost anywhere in the world), standing on a street corner and looking down. The odds are that you will soon forget local tradition, custom, and dress and, instead, focus on the universal footwear—the sneaker. The gym shoe moved out of the gymnasium in the 1970s and onto the fashion pages of the finest magazines in the 1980s. In the '90s, sneakers are popular with all age groups. The baby shops offer a selection for crawlers and toddlers. Whole stores, shelves filled with hundreds of styles, cater to teens. Health-club shops cater to members of Generation X and baby boomers. The mid-life crowd and the gray generation haunt established department stores insisting on comfort and walkability. No other product, except perhaps jeans, has such broad multi-generational appeal.

This article examines the latest trend in sneaker fashion's seventy-seven year history—520 million pairs sold and still going strong.

BEFORE YOU READ

Discuss the current fashion trends at your school. If your school has a prescribed school uniform, explain your feelings about wearing it. Would you rather wear fashionable clothing or do you like wearing your uniform? If your school does not have a prescribed uniform, would you like one?

AS YOU READ

This article begins with a list of high-tech trends in society. As you read, look for fashion trends that have been influenced by the '90s computer age.

For complex times, simple footwear

By Elizabeth Snead
USA TODAY

1 Wasn't it nice when there weren't as many annoying bells and whistles?

2 Harken back to the calmer era before microwaves, interactive TVs, surround-sound stereos, phone mail, fax machines, cyberspace and Internet.

3 Remember when your sneakers didn't blink, glow in the dark, pump up or fasten with Velcro?

4 Those were the days. And those were the shoes.

5 Now, reflecting the 1990s' back-to-basic dream of returning to uncomplicated times, those lazy, low-tech, do-nothing sneakers are back in vogue.

6 Tonight, classic sneakers are getting a special award for their impact on global fashion from the Council of Fashion Designers of America. The top five players honored will be adidas, Converse, Keds, Nike and Reebok. The award recognizes trends, from Harley-Davidson biker panache to the red AIDS ribbon, that have had an impact on fashion but are off the beaten track. "The sneaker defines the year," says Fern Mallis of the council.

7 So turn off your LED heel lights. And for heaven's sake, stop inflating that silly pump! Generation X-ers and hip boomers alike are downscaling with down-to-earth antique sneaks—Pro Keds, Converse One Stars and Dr. J's, adidas Gazelles and Puma Suedes.

8 "We're all teched-out," explains Haysun Hahn of Promostyl, an international fashion forecasting agency. "The retro look in sneakers is a logical rebellion against complicated technology. It shows we want to stay human."

9 Meg Whitman, a Keds vice president, says the movement stems from a desire for authenticity: "Things are so complicated now. People are naturally looking back."

10 Peter Moore, CEO and creative director of adidas America, credits the '90s sensibility with being . . . sensible.

11 "It's the direction the whole world is going," Moore says. "Even new cars are getting simpler. That's why honest, no-frills shoes are popular."

By Matt Mendelsohn, USA TODAY

COMFORT IS SUPREME: Sneakers are getting a special award for their impact on global fashion from the Council of Fashion Designers of America tonight. Among hot styles: Mossimo's Urban Smile, left, Pro Keds, Mossimo high tops, adidas Gazelles, Chanel's high heels, Reebok's classic.

12 No frills. No kidding. According to Karen Arena of the Federation of Swiss Watches, the Next Big Thing is plain-faced watches that don't do a darn thing but tell time. "Today, function creates the fashion," adds Spencer White of Reebok.

13 As always, this trend has trickled up, not down. The high-fashion presence of the lowly sneaker is made possible in most part by your local colleges and high schools.

14 Generation X-ers prefer to sport the "athe-leisure" laid-back look that complements their active computer-klatch and coffeehouse lifestyles.

15 Trade mag *Footwear Plus* fashion editor Adrienne Weinfeld-Berg chose classics such as adidas Gazelles and Puma Suedes in recent fashion shoots as alternatives to clunky Doc Martens: "They're major cool. They're a spinoff, the alternative to the big, black, ugly shoe."

16 "It's all coming from the street," Weinfeld-Berg says. "What's helped bring back old-fashioned sneakers is the vintage fashion craze."

17 There's definitely a fashion link. Converse's renewed classic Jack Purcell sneaker got four pages of editorial play in a recent *Vogue,* worn by supermodel Linda Evangelista.

18 Tennis shoe trend watchers are keen for "street potential" and closely monitor the alternative music scene. Adidas' Moore says grunge had a tremendous influence on the sneaker market. And it's *not* dead yet. "Grunge continues to evolve and be redefined and restyled," Moore says. "Young people today are incredibly influenced by music."

19 No wonder grungers Nirvana and rap group Cypress Hill adore One Stars. Sonic Youth's lead singer Kim Gordon lives in Puma Suedes.

20 Even actress Winona Ryder, who dates Dave Pirner from Soul Asylum, swears by One Stars. The Ramones stick with Converse All Stars.

21 Baysie Whightman, Converse's creative director, says alternative music groups call to borrow the latest sneakers for music videos: "It helps them and it helps us."

22 It's been a long and winding road from the do-nothing sneaker to rock star music videos and high fashion spreads.

23 Sneakers were born in the late 1800s, when Charles Goodyear invented vulcanization, the process that bonds canvas shoes to rubber soles. Converse first introduced the currently hip All Star back in 1917. Since then, it has sold, gulp, an estimated 520 million pairs. Keds were the first shoes to use Goodyear's process and have been "the sneaker America grew up in" for 78 years. Keds still bear that charmingly anachronistic Good Housekeeping Seal of Approval.

24 America's fondness for sneakers grew in the athletic '80s as modern technology lifted them to frightening heights of performance.

25 But today's high fashion sneaker appeal is far from high-tech. Young kids don't wear them to "work out." They wear them to work, then to trance dance at all-night raves.

26 So Converse is responding by bringing back models from its '70s catalogs, including a suede oxford, the One Star and a basic transportation model Pro Leather (worn by Julius Erving in the mid-'70s).

27 Also back: the Jack Purcell, originally a badminton shoe and then chic for tennis players in the '60s. Back then, it was a top-of-the-line sports performance shoe; now it's strictly fashion-forward.

28 Seeing how hot the old shoes have become, fashion designers like Donna Karan are doing faux retro lines. Chanel and Jean-Paul Gaultier are making high-heeled sneakers (Chanel's cost a mere $640). And New York designer Nicole Miller now designs platform tennis shoes.

29 Cult California sportswear designer Mossimo has gone retro with his new unisex sneaks, which bear his signature on the sole: Urban Smile, with a rubber toe cap that looks like a smile, and Tez, a classic '70s-style running shoe with an M logo that resembles adidas' triple stripe design.

30 In fact, Portland, Ore.-based adidas America's triple stripe design can now be seen imitated on everything from sportswear to evening dresses. For the hipper-than-thou, it has replaced Chanel's double C as *the* must-wear logo.

31 Meanwhile, the old reliable tennis shoe companies, sensing an untapped fashion-conscious market, are taking a walk on the wild side.

32 Converse is already doing platform, velvet and plaid high tops. This fall it'll introduce a sweatshirt fleece sneak with a deconstructed inside-out look.

33 Also new: high-heeled, corduroy and brocade All Stars and beefier sneakers with hiking boot lug soles à la Doc Martens.

34 L.A. Gear is doing glow-in-the-dark sneakers that gleam like Donna Karan's reflective spring '94 clothes. Shoe-biz folks say changing footwear is easier than changing clothes.

35 "Your feet don't gain weight. You can wear hip and trendy footwear long after you can wear hip and trendy clothes," says Moore of adidas.

36 But where will all this stylish activity lead?

37 Won't making the sneaker trendy with new fabrics, thicker soles and hip colorations destroy the authentic appeal? Maybe.

38 But twenty years from now, kids will be dying for those plaid '90s grunge sneakers.

A. Choose the best answer to complete the following sentences.

1. The Council of Fashion Designers of America will give an award to five major sneaker companies because _____ .

   a. they have sold more shoes than any other style

   b. they have donated money to AIDS research

   c. they have had an impact on setting trends in fashion

2. The latest style in sneakers will probably be _____ .

   a. simplicity, because the fashion trend is against high-technology

   b. simplicity, because it lowers the price of production

   c. high-tech, because the market demands it

   d. high-tech, because of new discoveries in improving athletic ability

3. Trends in gym shoe fashion are set _____ .

   a. by magazines such as *Vogue* and *Footwear Plus*

   b. by local college and high school students

   c. by music stars like Kim Gordon and Cypress Hill

4. High-fashion designers like Donna Karan and Chanel _____ .

   a. are also designing simple sneakers

   b. are designing retro lines with platform heels

   c. are lowering prices to compete with Adidas, Converse, and Nike

B. Discuss the answers to the following questions.

1. How was the first sneaker developed and what was the first commercial company?

2. What was the reason for the growth of sneaker popularity in the 1980s?

PLAYING WITH WORDS

Find the word in the article that means the opposite of the word or phrase given. The paragraph in which the word is used is indicated in parentheses. Use a dictionary for help, if necessary.

1. *act alone* (2) _____

2. *quite involved* (5) _____

3. *letting out the air* (7) _____

4. *modern* (7) _____

5. *phoniness* (9) _____

6. *does not enhance or make complete* (14) _____

7. *modern period* (16) _____

DIGGING BENEATH THE SURFACE

A. The traditional shoe companies seem to be trying two contradictory strategies in marketing. Review the strategies mentioned in paragraphs 13 through 17 and paragraphs 31 through 34 and discuss their differences. Be sure to explain how they can successfully exist at the same time.

B. At the end of the article, an explanation is given for the advantage of designer footwear over clothing. Write a summary of this explanation. Write a paragraph about what other reasons there are for the strong and lasting popularity of sneakers.

GOING BEYOND THE TEXT

A. *Learning Together*

This article talks about one fashion trend in clothing. Trends and fads have a strong impact on the American economy. Work with a partner to play the following game against other pairs of students:

1. Choose one of the following categories—current trends among teens, trends that have come and gone, the latest toys for kids, food fads, "in" spots for travel, or fashion trends. Add other appropriate categories.

2. Set a timer for ten minutes and write down as many responses as you can that fit the category chosen. Responses in the category for trends that have come and gone might include hula hoops, soda fountains, and pet rocks.

3. Compare your list of responses with other teams. Points are scored only for responses that other teams do not have. (In other words, you must be the only team to have that response to score a point.)

4. The team with the most points wins that round. Continue with other topics.

B. *Responding in Writing*

1. Ad writing requires fluency and creativity with language. Many ads rely on basic techniques that have had long-standing appeal to the public. First, design a new sneaker or adapt an old style. Then, design two different ads using two of the techniques listed below.

   a. famous endorsement

   b. bandwagon

   c. scientific information

   d. snob appeal

2. Write a letter to a sneaker company promoting your new shoe design; use at least five of the following words taken from the article:

classic	back-to-basic	low-tech
high-tech	panache	downscaling
down-to-earth	sensible	no-frills
high-fashion	generation-X	athe-leisure
spinoff	supermodel	grunge
do-nothing	basic transportation	retro
lifestyle	must-wear	logo

MAKING CONNECTIONS

1. The article entitled "Underlings' skill can give them an edge" in the "Money" section emphasizes the differences in how age groups relate to computers. This article, however, shows that sneakers have popularity across age groups. Discuss other trends that are shared by different generations and those that are not.

2. Another article in the "Money" section of this book that is linked to this article is "Pace could mean gains or portend slide," which is about the stock market. Find L.A. Gear (LA Gr) and Nike (Nike) in the listings on the New York Stock Exchange. Follow their stock value on a regular basis for several months and evaluate whether the rise or fall in the companies' stock relates to the fashion trends you observe during the same time.

SPORTS

Surveying Types of Sports Articles; Exploring Sports Jargon

Who won yesterday's game? What's the latest sports equipment? Who signed for the most money for a gym shoe endorsement? And why isn't the local football coach making the right decisions? Most newspapers have a sports section that summarizes daily sports activities and analyzes the effect of sports on society. There are several types of sports articles.

Some sports articles report on **daily results** of seasonal teams. A yearly cycle of baseball, football, hockey, and basketball articles takes up much of the section's news. They are often accompanied by charts and graphs of statistics relating to players and teams. During special events periods, such as the winter and summer Olympics or World Cup soccer, these reports feature international coverage of people and events.

A second type of article is a **sports feature** that focuses on a sports personality, a major issue in the sports world, or a commemoration of a famous event in sports history.

Another type of article is a **commentary, opinion,** or **analysis.** These can often be spotted because the article is accompanied by a picture of the writer or a special byline. The feature writer may have a column that appears on a recurring basis. It may even have a regular position on the sports pages.

Exercise 1: Who Won the Game?

Find several articles that report daily results and then answer the following questions. Be sure at least one of the articles includes a chart or graph.

1. What sport is the subject of the article?
2. What is the headline? What key words drew your attention to the article?
3. What is the important factual information of the event reported on?
4. Summarize the information in the chart or graph. How does this information add to the meaning of the article?

Exercise 2: Who's Who and What's What?

Choose several articles that are sports features. Be sure one profiles a sports personality and one deals with an issue that includes sports combined with another field, such as business, finances, or health. Answer the following questions:

1. For the person article, why did the newspaper feature that person at that time?
2. Did the feature portray the person or event in a positive or negative light? What words or phrases support your choice?
3. For the issue article, what concern does the article address other than sports? How is this issue relevant in the sports world?

Exercise 3: I Say This About That!

Choose several articles of the opinion type. Find those that appear on a regular basis or are accompanied by a picture. Answer the following questions:

1. Whose byline is used? Tell how frequently that columnist appears and his or her location in the paper.

2. What are the main points of the article?

3. Describe the tone or style of the writer. Is he or she sarcastic and critical, analytical but neutral, supportive and positive? Choose several words or phrases that support your description.

LIFESTYLES

USA SNAPSHOTS®

A look at statistics that shape our lives

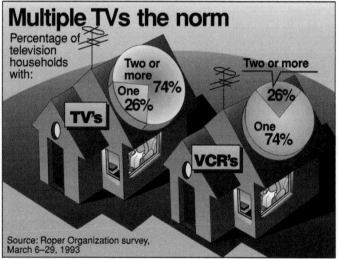

Multiple TVs the norm

Percentage of television households with:

TV's — Two or more 74%, One 26%

VCR's — Two or more 26%, One 74%

Source: Roper Organization survey, March 6–29, 1993

By Cindy Hall and Web Bryant, USA TODAY

ARTICLE 1A
Cleaning up after a million guests at Mount Vernon

ARTICLE 1B
A clean face for "Mona Lisa"?

PREVIEWING THE ARTICLES

Many Americans optimistically equate change with progress. Still, change means that the best of the past disappears; so most people have a natural desire to maintain, untarnished, a bit of the past.

Most people dwell on the past occasionally. They may experience that bittersweet feeling known as nostalgia when, while cleaning a drawer, they come across an old report card or their first valentine. But for some folks, keeping the past alive is a career.

Article 1A introduces readers to the conservator in charge of preserving one of the nation's most famous homes—George Washington's beloved Mount Vernon. After reading this article, you may feel that this kind of devotion to authenticity is excessive and perhaps even obsessive. But this conservator takes his work very seriously.

Article 1B deals with an international treasure and a debate about how best to preserve it. How often should a face in a painting be cleaned? If the face in question belongs to the *Mona Lisa,* the answer is "rarely." After all, some argue, every cleansing may remove not only dirt but also some of the portrait's authenticity.

BEFORE YOU READ

1. If you have toured Mount Vernon, tell your classmates about what you saw there. What did the home and grounds reveal about Washington's life and times?
2. The *Mona Lisa* hangs in the Louvre, a famous art museum in Paris, France. Share what you know about the Louvre and about Leonardo da Vinci, the famous artist who painted this unforgettable portrait.

AS YOU READ

Compare and contrast the forces attacking these two treasures from past centuries. What common enemy do they have? What additional destructive forces is Mount Vernon threatened by?

Cleaning up after a million guests at Mount Vernon

By Gene Sloan
USA TODAY

1 MOUNT VERNON, Va.—Imagine throwing a party and having a million people show up. Trampling the floors. Touching the furniture. *Leaning* on things.

2 Not so farfetched, really. Marc LeFrancois, the conservator here at George Washington's historic home overlooking the Potomac River, thinks about it all the time—but particularly now, Mount Vernon's busiest month.

3 "It's the little stuff. People pick at the plaster, touch the walls, play with the shutter hooks," he says. "It seems harmless. But multiply it by a million and pretty soon . . ."

4 That's how many people come through in a typical year: a million. Summer brings as many as 10,000 a day—making Mount Vernon second only to the White House as the most visited home in America.

5 And for LeFrancois—with the assistance of four carpenters, four painters and a small army of maintenance people who often work even as visitors scurry around them—that means fighting a battle that never ends. A battle against wear and tear.

6 "People just can't resist touching. They want to feel the wall for themselves. They want a piece of history to take home," he says, poking at gaps in the white paint near the front door that have been picked off by visitors.

7 In fact, the paint job was just redone two years ago. But never underestimate the power of a million people with a million pairs of curious hands, he says. Some spots are worn down to the bare, 200-year-old wood.

8 "It'll have to be fixed," he shrugs. "It's always having to be fixed."

9 Almost everything within reach of visitors, who are carefully corralled behind ropes, has been bumped, brushed or touched enough to leave marks. The blue paint on the doorway into Washington's bedroom, for example, is worn down to the wood from visitors leaning in to get a better look.

10 "We can't keep up. We paint it. Then we'll come back after one busy weekend and it's worn down again," says painting foreman Joseph Sliger.

11 Throughout the house, grayish-brown industrial carpet protects the wood floors. It's the highest-grade made, designed for airports, where it'll last a decade. Here, it lasts a year. Maybe two.

12 LeFrancois and the staff can easily fix most of this. They repaint parts of the exterior almost every year. Inside, they retouch worn doorways, repair nicks on the walls every month.

13 But as at other historic homes, the constant wear and tear of opening Mount Vernon to the public spurs debate among preservationists.

14 How much should visitors be allowed to see and touch? Should areas be closed off, preserved for later generations?

15 "We agonize over what is the best way to protect it. The furniture, for example, is irreplaceable," says curator Christine Meadows. "This *is* George Washington's home. There's only one like it."

16 One-fourth of the furniture in the house—Washington's bed, for in-

By Tim Dillon, USA TODAY

NICKS AND CRANNIES: Marc LeFrancois, conservator at Mount Vernon, stands at the doorway of the Washingtons' bedroom.

stance—actually belonged to George and Martha. The rest are period antiques from that era. All is roped off, but it still suffers from dirt and dust, she says.

17 Closing the house to the public, the best solution to preserving it, isn't an option, however. To maintain the home, its owners—the Mount Vernon Ladies' Association, a private non-profit organization founded in 1853 to save the house—need the revenue from visitors.

18 Just keeping Mount Vernon ship-shape costs $10 million a year. The home is financed entirely from private donations and the $7 admission price. It takes no government money.

19 "We know the best way to preserve (Mount Vernon) is to close it to the public and shut off the furniture in perfect, climate-controlled rooms," Meadows says.

20 "But then you wouldn't be seeing George and Martha Washington's home . . . then what's the point?"

Proper steps for repair

1 When Mount Vernon develops a structural problem, fixing it is much more complicated than just calling in the local contractor.

2 Take the stairs. When the support beams started to collapse three years ago, conservator Marc LeFrancois had to build a more elaborate support system.

3 Hitch A: Supports had to be unseen by visitors.

4 Hitch B: To make sure the stairs were preserved exactly as they were, the work had to be done without touching the original wood with drills or nails.

5 "It could be that where you put that nail is the last speck of paint that will unravel the mystery of how the room looked in Washington's time," he says.

6 Indeed, a 150-year-old mystery over the original color of the trim on the third-floor cupola was solved just last year when LeFrancois found a fleck of blue paint no bigger than a nail. Only then were they able to restore the original decor.

7 Right now, LeFrancois is supervising the reroofing of the entire house.

8 To ensure authenticity, he's having craftsmen hand-hew the cypress shingles and apply them in the way they would have been applied two centuries ago.

9 To find cypress—prevalent in Washington's day but now rare—they had to scour swamps where specimens lost during logging languished for decades.

A clean face for "Mona Lisa"?

By Nanci Hellmich
USA TODAY

1 Is art's most mysterious lady in for a face lift?

2 An article on the *Mona Lisa* in the Aug. 15 *Legal Times,* out today, speculates she may be freshened up. That could ignite "the biggest art restoration controversy ever," says Murray White, who wrote the story.

3 Plans to clean the famous painting hanging in the Louvre in Paris have "apparently not only been considered but planned," says Jacques Franck, an expert on Leonardo da Vinci, who is quoted in *Legal Times.* Franck sees a restoration as foolhardy and is trying to head it off.

4 But Pierre Rosenberg, the Louvre's chief curator of paintings, says, "We are not cleaning the *Mona Lisa,* and we have no intention to do so."

5 Critics say chemicals used in cleaning would alter pigments. But others say it can be done without harm.

6 A computer-generated image of a cleaned-up *Mona Lisa* suggests restoration would remove the yellowish tint, which some think adds to its mysterious aura, White says.

7 Martin Kemp, president of the Leonardo da Vinci Society, recently had

Photo above by John Asmus

an up-close look at the painting, from the early 1500s. It is "covered with dirt, but for a panel painting of that age it's in remarkable condition. . . . I wouldn't clean it at the moment. I would simply illuminate it better."

8 But Sydney J. Freedberg, chief curator emeritus, the National Gallery of Art, Washington, D.C., tells *Legal Times* the cleaning could be done "with a very light hand. The picture would look like something infinitely more marvelous."

SHINING BEAUTY: Computer-generated picture at left shows Mona Lisa minus the yellowish tint that experts say restoration will remove from Leonardo da Vinci's painting, right. Critics argue, however, that the chemicals may alter pigments.

A. The following statements deal with Article 1A. Mark each statement true or false. The numbers in parentheses refer to the relevant paragraphs.

_____ 1. Mount Vernon has more visitors per year than the White House does. (4)

_____ 2. George Washington laid grayish-brown carpeting throughout his home to protect the wood floors. (11)

_____ 3. The furniture in Mount Vernon gets damaged by visitors who touch it and sit on it. (16)

_____ 4. The association that owns Mount Vernon uses the money from admission fees to finance the care of the house. (18)

_____ 5. Conservators are considering closing Mount Vernon to the public because visitors do so much damage to it. (17–19)

B. After reading Article 1B, answer the following questions on a separate piece of paper.

1. What controversy does the article tell about?

2. Why do some experts object to the cleaning?

3. What suggestion does the president of the Leonardo da Vinci Society make?

PLAYING WITH WORDS

A. What does each of the following words from Article 1A mean? Use context clues to help you circle the best definition. The paragraph in which each word is found is indicated in parentheses.

1. *farfetched* (2)
   a. brought from a faraway place
   b. difficult to believe

2. *overlooking* (2)
   a. ignoring, not seeing
   b. within view of

3. *underestimate* (7)
   a. think something is less than it is
   b. estimate that something is under something else

4. *corralled* (9)
   a. driven into a corral
   b. kept within a certain area

5. *foreman* (10)
   a. a conservator
   b. a person in charge of a group of workers

6. *throughout* (11)
   a. discarded
   b. in every part, all over

7. *spurs* (13)
   a. stabs with a pointed device
   b. encourages

8. *preservationists* (13)
   a. senior citizens in good health
   b. people interested in protecting and saving things from the past

9. *fleck* (box, 6)   a. a small piece, a flake
                       b. a spot of dirt

10. *scour* (box, 9)   a. to search thoroughly
                       b. to scrub vigorously

B. Look up the words *conserve* and *preserve* in a dictionary. Then use the more appropriate word to complete the following sentences.

1. When there is no rain for a month, we need to _____ water.

2. She wants to _____ her wedding dress so that her daughter can wear it some day.

3. Don't run very fast at the beginning of the race. _____ your energy.

4. Photographs help people to _____ the moment.

C. Circle the best word to complete each sentence. The correct completions are all words used in Article 1B.

1. The word (*ignite, illuminate*) is usually used about the start of a fire, but in this article it refers to the beginning of a "hot" (*controversy, conservator*).

2. A professor (*on sabbatical, emeritus*) is a former college or university teacher who has retired.

3. Even if the *Mona Lisa* is not cleaned, her smile will look brighter if curators (*ignite, illuminate*) the portrait.

4. (*Pigments, Pygmies*) give paints their various colors.

5. A person in charge of an art museum is commonly called a (*critic, curator*).

6. If something is (*infinitely, apparently*) true, it seems to be true, but it is not certain.

DIGGING BENEATH THE SURFACE

A. Discuss this question about Article 1A with a partner: What are the attitudes of the Mount Vernon conservator and curator toward visitors who damage the home? Are they tolerant of visitors or resentful? Find evidence to support your answer.

B. Discuss these questions about Article 1B with a partner:

1. Perhaps the big controversy that Murray White expects will never occur. Why not?

2. Why do you think Murray White wrote his article on the *Mona Lisa*, considering Pierre Rosenberg's attitude?

3. Do experts think that da Vinci wanted the *Mona Lisa* to have a yellowish tint? Is that why some people object to the cleaning? Or is the yellowish tint simply the result of time, and does it have an effect that some viewers consider a benefit?

GOING BEYOND THE TEXT

A. *Learning Together*

1. Study a large reproduction of the *Mona Lisa*. What do you think Mona Lisa is thinking? Why is she smiling in that slight, mysterious way? That question has puzzled people for hundreds of years. Take ten minutes for everyone in the class to write down what they think Mona Lisa's thoughts are. Then appoint a committee of three or four students to select the most interesting, imaginative guesses and compile them into a booklet, with accompanying artwork, if possible.

2. Divide into groups of about four students each. Choose a well-known historical house to study and tell the class about. Bring pictures of it. Each member of the group should research and talk about one aspect of the topic (for example, the origin, location, and setting of the house; why it is considered of historical interest; some of the most interesting external features; the interior design of the house; its furnishings; and so on). Some houses are important because of who lived there., Some are important because they are outstanding examples of a particular architect's work or of a particular architectural style. If your community has houses of historical importance, consider selecting one of these and visiting it.

B. *Responding in Writing.*   Choose one of the following writing projects.

1. Find out about the oldest building in your community, and write a description of it. Compare it to more recently built structures in the area. Visit it, and photograph it, if possible.

2. Read about the home of an American president, and write a summary of what you read.

3. Read about the *Mona Lisa* or another famous work by da Vinci, and write a summary of what you read.

4. Write about an old and valued possession that belongs to you or to your family. Describe it. Tell about its original owner. Is it a family heirloom? Why is it important to your family?

MAKING CONNECTIONS

After reading Article 2 in this section ("Chapel offers simple way to say 'I do'"), compare and contrast the attitudes toward preserving the past that are suggested by the behavior of the people interviewed in these two articles.

ARTICLE 2
Chapel offers simple way to say "I do"

What is really the great American pastime today? Is it cheering the home team at the ballpark or taking a stroll around the shopping mall? True, the number of professional baseball teams has increased in recent years, but not nearly as rapidly as the number of shopping malls. When World War II ended in 1945, there were fewer than a dozen malls in the United States. By the end of the 1980s, the United States had about 35,000 shopping centers, and they handled about 55 percent of the nation's retail business (excluding auto sales).

Today, many malls are much more than just places to shop. People of all ages go to malls to browse, meet friends for lunch or dinner, hear a concert, attend a reading and book-signing party, meet a celebrity promoting a product bearing his or her name, and so on. Malls have become social gathering places and entertainment complexes. Unfortunately, they have also become hang-outs for gangs, pickpockets, and shoplifters. In an effort to curb crime and lessen the fears of customers, The Mall (one of Miami's largest shopping complexes) banned youths under eighteen from the premises before 6 p.m. on school days.

The largest mall in the world—the West Edmonton Mall—is in Alberta, Canada. It has more than 700 shops, an amusement park, aquariums, a hockey stadium, a skating rink, and a water park. The largest mall in the United States, developed by the creators of the Edmonton Mall, is quite an enterprise, too. Minnesota's Mall of America, featured in the following article, contains more than 350 stores, an eighteen-hole miniature golf course, restaurants and nightclubs, and the country's largest enclosed theme park, Knott's Camp Snoopy. The Chapel of Love, one of the Mall of America's newer attractions, opened in 1994, making the Mall of America the first mega-mall to have a wedding chapel. Here, couples can tie the knot quickly and inexpensively, thus saving their time and money for more exciting activities, such as riding the roller coaster.

1. Find Bloomington, Minnesota, on a map of the United States. What well-known twin cities is it near? Why do you think an enclosed mall would be especially welcome in this part of the country?

2. Discuss a large mall in your area. What does it offer shoppers besides merchandise? Does it contribute to the community or cause problems?

3. What is the largest or most unusual mall you have ever visited? Describe it to the class.

As you read this article, look for reasons why a couple might choose to get married at the Chapel of Love in the Mall of America.

Chapel offers simple way to say "I do"

By Katy Kelly
USA TODAY

1 BLOOMINGTON, Minn.—Friday afternoon, Pamela Martin, 33, and Jim Hafiz, 38, stood together in the Chapel of Love, before God, family and Judge Howard Albertson and promised to cherish one another into eternity.

2 It was, everyone agreed, a memorable ceremony. Under a canopy of moss-colored leaves, the couple, their 3-year-old son, Matthew, and six other children from their previous marriages listened as vocalist Mari Harris sang the *Wedding Song*. When the "I do's" were done, everyone inside the Chapel cheered the newlyweds.

3 So did many on the outside. Vicarious guests watched through glass doors and listened to the vows, via sound system. Most weren't dressed for a wedding but wore the kind of clothes one wears to go shopping, which is, in fact, what they were doing. As the Chapel of Love ad says: "You can get anything at the Mall of America. Even married."

4 And, presuming you want to be married in the mall, MaryAnne London Gears, owner of the just-opened Chapel, and her staff will get you what you want for your wedding. Even Elvis. All without ever leaving the 425-store complex.

5 The Chapel—the first such place housed inside a mega-mall—was created "for people who want something better than City Hall," Gears says. It's on the second floor of the biggest mall/entertainment complex in the USA, a couple of doors down from Kinney's shoes, perfumed by the sweet, yeasty scent pumped out by the nearby Cinnabon bakery.

6 The sanctuary has enough white pews to seat 75. The "Wedding Petite" ("One hour of wedding consultation, use of the bridal dressing room and chapel for one-half hour; taped music selections; decorated chapel; and candle-lit ceremony with officiate") is $295. The on-site photographer will produce one 8x10 and four 4 x 5's in a gift folio for $75 more. And you can charge it to Mastercard, Visa or American Express.

7 Hafiz and Martin took a pass on Elvis but happily accepted the $595 "Wedding Extraordinaire" package, gratis for them because they're the first to wed in the Chapel. It was, they say, a matter of convenience: For Hafiz, a restaurant owner, and Martin, a grocery store cashier, the responsibilities of work and of parenting ate up time they might have spent planning.

8 Convenience and price—the average cost of getting married (sans reception) is $3,088, says the Association of Bridal Consultants—are a selling point with couples. Some solve the problem by skipping off to Vegas. Storefront chapels are also popular in Detroit, where 16 do "6,000 weddings in a year," says Dean Bruza, owner of the Little Wedding Chapel, a franchised operation. Many of his clients "are tired of the hassles of church-related weddings."

9 At the Chapel of Love, your hassles are their hassles. If you want religion, they'll find you a minister or a judge who includes God in the ceremony.

10 What they don't offer the mall does. Hafiz and Martin got flowers and wedding wear on-site. "We picked out our rings at Gordon's Jewelers, we got earrings for the matron of honor, and a gift for the best man" at the Chapel, Hafiz says.

11 The one-stop shopping appealed to the couple for sentimental reasons, too. Now, "When we come to the mall we'll be able to say, 'This is where we got married!' " Martin says.

12 Wedding consultations are held in the retail part of the Chapel, a cosseting sort of room, with a tape of the "greatest moments" from *All My Children* weddings on the VCR and rosebud paper on the walls. Glass shelves hold bridal accouterments, including sequin-and-lace sneakers ($48), *Fruit de la passion* body oil ($14.95) and Chapel of Love mugs ($10.95). What you don't want to buy you can rent: a lace and Lucite mailbox to hold those cash-filled cards ($50) and silk bouquets ($15–$45). Bargain consignment gowns are available.

13 The Chapel has no reception facilities but staff can arrange one at one of the mall's 22 restaurants, including Camp Snoopy, where newlyweds can take a roller coaster ride.

14 In the hours before the Hafiz/Martin wedding the Chapel ladies pass petit fours and consult with various newly affianced couples. So far 16 weddings have been booked.

15 Judy Newell, 30, and her fiancé, Paul Musel, 29, have come to inspect the Chapel as a possible site for their August wedding. After seeing the bride's luxe dressing room, the groom's smaller changing area (complete with Excedrin and Band-Aids) and the flower-bedecked Chapel, the couple decide the Chapel is for them. "We've been to a lot of churches," Musel says. "But they're too formal, not intimate enough."

By Steve Woit

MR. & MRS.: James Hafiz and Pamela Martin take a matrimonial ride on escalator in Mall of America. "When we come (here) we'll be able to say, 'This is where we got married!"

16 Until now, the complications of wedding planning had them "overwhelmed. This is taking away a lot of stress. It's going to be so easy. We don't have to run from store to store. . . . A lot of people really like traditional weddings, but a lot of times it comes down to convenience," he says.

17 Newell admits that her intended wasn't always keen on the concept: "Paul said, 'I don't want to be walking past Kinney shoes on the way to my wedding.' " True, he says, but he now sees the upside. "A lot of my family hasn't been (to Mall of America), so it will be exciting for them."

18 It's not that they don't have another place to go: "We're very active in our church," but the architecture is too modern for their taste. Instead, the pastor will come to the mall.

19 For Jeanne Benson, the Chapel opened too late: "I had one of those big traditional weddings. I wish I would have done something like this. It was a wonderful day but it was a real hassle and a lot of expense."

20 And how would she feel about being married among the shoppers? "I love the mall so it wouldn't bother me."

21 Not everyone agrees. Says Judith Martin, of the syndicated *Miss Manners* column, "I sympathize with the motive. The wedding business has gotten away from anything that's reasonable or pleasant. For most people it has gotten to be a lavish event unrelated to the way people live."

22 And such arrangements, she says, can take the fun out of commitment. "This is the desire to run off and elope. (But) I don't suppose you have to run off to the mall." She'd prefer a return to the time when a wedding meant a sweet exchange of vows and post-nuptial party at home or church.

23 That would be a bummer for shoppers. Kurt Pelligrino and wife Connie came to the mall to take in a movie and caught the Hafiz/Martin nuptials on their way out. The movie? *"Four Weddings and a Funeral."*

24 At Mall of America, you get five for the price of four.

A. Scan the article for the information you need to answer the following questions.

1. Why is the Chapel of Love a more romantic place to get married than City Hall?

2. What are the main advantages of getting married in the Chapel of Love rather than having a church wedding followed by a fancy reception dinner?

3. Where is the Mall of America?

4. Why is it called a mega-mall? How many shops does it have?

5. What items needed for a wedding can be purchased at the Mall?

6. The Chapel of Love brings business to many shops in the Mall of America. What particular types of stores do you think benefit most?

B. After reading Article 2, mark each of the following statements true or false. For help, reread the paragraphs indicated in parentheses.

_____ 1. The "vicarious guests" at the Martin/Hafiz wedding were invited by the bride and groom. (3)

_____ 2. People who come to the Mall of America can watch and listen to the wedding ceremonies at the Chapel of Love without going inside. (3)

_____ 3. Hafiz and Martin paid $595 for their wedding in the Chapel of Love. (7)

_____ 4. Weddings at the Chapel of Love must be conducted by a judge, so they can have no religious content. (9)

_____ 5. The Chapel of Love sells wedding rings, bridal gowns, and flowers. (10)

_____ 6. Newlyweds can have their wedding reception at the Mall but not in the Chapel of Love. (13)

PLAYING WITH WORDS

A. Circle the best definition for each italicized word or phrase in the paragraph indicated. Try to determine its meaning in this article by using context clues. If you are unsure, use a dictionary for help.

1. *canopy* (2)
   a. a white carpet for the bride and groom to walk on
   b. an awning that is above the bridal couple's heads

2. *vicarious guests* (3)
   a. people the bride and groom invited to the wedding
   b. strangers who are not invited guests

3. *pews* (6)
   a. seats in a sanctuary
   b. pillars in a mall

4. *on-site* (6)
   a. visible
   b. at the location

5. *gratis* (7)
   a. free
   b. a bargain

6. *sans* (8)
   a. with
   b. without

7. *hassles* (9)
   a. difficulties, disagreements
   b. assistance

8. *accouterments* (12)
   a. accessories
   b. military equipment

9. *petit fours* (14)
   a. flowers
   b. small, frosted cakes

B. The following words about business appear in Article 2 in the paragraphs indicated. Discuss the meanings of these words with a partner. Then consult a dictionary to confirm your definitions.

1. franchised (8)

2. consultants (8)

3. consignment (12)

4. retail (12)

C. Match the following words about weddings with their definitions by writing the letters on the blank lines.

_____ 1. bouquet   a. promises

_____ 2. cherish   b. run away (especially to get married)

_____ 3. elope   c. the wedding ceremony

_____ 4. the intended   d. a bunch of flowers

_____ 5. nuptials   e. the fiancé/fiancée (the man or woman someone is engaged to marry)

_____ 6. post-nuptial   f. treat with affection; take care of

_____ 7. vows   g. after the wedding

DIGGING BENEATH THE SURFACE

From the information the author has selected to put into this article, what can you infer about her attitudes toward a wedding at the Mall? Do you think the author would agree with the following statements? Check *yes* or *no* and indicate which paragraph(s) helped you arrive at your answer.

Getting married at the Mall is	Yes	No	Paragraph(s)
1. a funny idea	_____	_____	_____
2. a ridiculous idea	_____	_____	_____
3. a break with tradition	_____	_____	_____
4. a beautiful event	_____	_____	_____
5. not worth the money it costs	_____	_____	_____

Getting married at the Mall is	Yes	No	Paragraph(s)
6. disrespectful to the institution of marriage	―――	―――	―――――――
7. in bad taste	―――	―――	―――――――
8. a practical idea	―――	―――	―――――――
9. fun	―――	―――	―――――――

GOING BEYOND THE TEXT

A. *Learning Together*

1. Do you think the author of this article would ever want to have her wedding at Mall of America? Discuss this with a partner. How would you describe the author's attitude toward the idea: disapproving, neutral, or enthusiastic? After you and your partner reach a conclusion, see if your classmates agree with you.

2. In groups of five or six, compare and contrast wedding customs of different religious and ethnic groups. Talk about the selection of a spouse, the engagement period, the traditional outfits worn by the bride and groom, the kinds of gifts commonly given, special foods eaten at a wedding, and so on. Consider the symbolism of various items used in a wedding ceremony. Look for some elements that weddings throughout the world have in common.

B. *Responding in Writing.* Choose one of the following writing projects.

1. What kind of wedding would you like to have? Describe it.

2. What was the most unusual or most beautiful wedding you ever attended? Describe it and tell how you felt about it.

3. Describe your favorite mall. Tell why you like to go there.

4. Have you ever worked in a mall? Would you like to? Describe a job you had or would like to have in a mall.

MAKING CONNECTIONS

The second article in the "Education" section deals with changing the traditional school year that allows two months off in the summer. This article deals with changing wedding traditions. Do you think anything is lost when traditions are discarded?

ARTICLE 3
More drawn to the no-frills spirituality

PREVIEWING THE ARTICLE

Founded in India about 500 B.C., Buddhism is one of the world's major religions. At various times in history, it has been a major religious and cultural influence in most of Asia. Often, Buddhism has blended with the dominant religion of an area.

Buddhism is now becoming increasingly popular in Europe and the United States. According to the following article, there are about 800,000 Buddhists in the U.S.

The following article focuses on Americans who are turning to Buddhism, specifically Zen Buddhism, as a relief from the predominant American lifestyles and values. Some people are stressed out by the hectic pace and constant change characteristic of urban life in the United States. Others are tired of the American obsession with accomplishing something measurable today and planning for even greater "successes" tomorrow. As this article shows, Buddhism offers alternative values.

The Zen Mountain Center near Los Angeles, California, is a popular place for those seeking an understanding of this East Asian form of Buddhism. Since the 1950s, Zen has been gaining popularity in the United States. In Zen, as in other Buddhist sects, meditation is the key that can open the door to enlightenment. Through meditation, a person strives to understand intuitively his or her own inner self. Zen also relies on a special teacher, called the master. You will meet one in the following article.

BEFORE YOU READ

1. Discuss the meaning of the word *nirvana*.

2. On a map of Asia, point out several countries in which Buddhism has been important. These include India, Thailand, Sri Lanka, Japan, and Tibet.

3. If you saw the movie *Little Buddha*, tell the class what you learned about Buddhism from the film. Discuss the life of the founder of this religion, as it was presented in the movie. Also, discuss the concept of reincarnation as it was explained in the film.

AS YOU READ

Look for reasons why Zen Buddhism might help a person cope with the stresses of contemporary American life.

More drawn to the no-frills spirituality

By Marco R. della Cava
USA TODAY

1 MOUNTAIN CENTER, Calif.—Pat O'Hara usually takes a road called Broadway to New York University.

2 But right now, the film school prof is trodding the Buddhist path to nirvana at the Zen Mountain Center.

3 "I find traditional practices lacking. Buddhism is about how we use our minds, and delivers fairly quickly a strong level of freedom," says O'Hara, 52, whose devotion to the religion has earned her the admiration of students who "five years ago couldn't care less," and the Buddhist middle name Enkyo. "You can find out so much by meditating 15 minutes a day and listening to your inner voice. You can't lose. Try it."

4 Many are purging fast-lane demons in the process. Stressed out? Go meditate. A shopaholic? Learn to live *with* and not for possessions. Soured on a childhood religion but crave spirituality? Buddhism welcomes all.

5 Among the new Western books on this ancient Eastern "ism" are a cross-religious tome by Rodger Kamenetz called *The Jew in the Lotus;* a posthumously published memoir by Maura "Soshin" O'Halloran called *Pure Heart, Enlightened Mind;* and a forthcoming inspirational tract by Chicago Bulls coach Phil Jackson, *Wake Up and Win.*

6 Subscriptions to *Tricycle: The Buddhist Review* have quadrupled since its 1991 debut, thanks to the fascination of non-Buddhists (now 55% of its readership). And the techno-zine *Wired* just logged in with a piece on Buddhists on the Internet.

7 Bookings are up at the bucolic Zen Mountain Center two hours east of Zen Center of L.A. headquarters, where plans to expand are going beyond blueprint stage.

8 And where once mainly Richard Gere and Tina Turner spotlighted the 2,500-year-old tradition, now a horde from Hollywood and beyond—philanthropist Laurance Rockefeller, Italian soccer star Roberto Baggio, rocker Courtney Love—are banging the Buddhist gong.

9 Are '60s sensibilities defining the '90s? Consider it a response to today's social ills, say Buddhists.

10 Will Christian and Jewish tents soon fold in deference to a USA gone Buddhist? Not a prayer, says one religion expert. "There are 800,000 Buddhists in the U.S., a very small group when considering the entire population (of 260 million)," says Seymour P. Lachman of the City University of New York, whose book *One Nation Under God* stocks religious affiliation data.

11 Lachman ascribes Buddhism's apparent growth to media hype generated by the religion's comparatively upscale members: "In terms of demographics, Buddhists rank at the top in income, education and property ownership. . . . They're a small but articulate group" whose voice easily finds mainstream pulpits.

12 OK, so the movie *Little Buddha* likely is about as close as most of us will get to seeing the religion in action. Nonetheless, a passionate minority is out there. And for them, Buddha is more than a cherubic icon, he's a way of life.

13 Buddha, actually, is not a god or a person, but a description meaning "the Awakened One." Most statues of the Buddha are derived from Buddhism founder Siddhartha Gautama.

14 The most well-known forms of Buddhism are Tibetan, Zen (Japanese), Theravada (India) and Vipassana (Southeast Asian). A keystone to any Buddhist path is meditation, often referred to as sitting. At the Zen Mountain Center, it is not uncommon to sit for 10 hours a day.

15 Finally, Buddhism's cornerstone: the Four Noble Truths.

16 "Understanding these truths represents a way out of our suffering," says Helen Tworkov, editor of *Tricycle.* "The level of trauma in this country is amazing. From battered women to children being killed by stray bullets. There is an extraordinary need for some spiritual view in our lives."

17 **First Noble Truth: Accept suffering as part of life.**

18 The chaos of hospital life still echoes in the mind of Anne Speiser. But the din in her head is much quieter now than when the nurse arrived a month ago at the pastoral 160-acre Zen Mountain Center in the San Jacinto Mountains.

19 "I saw so many people dying and thought, 'There must be something more to life,'" says Speiser, 46, from Storrs, Conn. "Our life is so focused on activity that you never get to experience just being. Have you ever just sat in a chair? No. You immediately think, I'm bored."

20 Speiser grows animated, leaning across a picnic table where a communal vegetarian lunch has just been served. "I could only be satisfied for a moment. And then the feeling would go away.

By Rob Brown, USA TODAY

ON RETREAT: Zen Master or 'roshi' Taizan Maezumi, front, of California's Zen Mountain Center, guides Darrell Hallenbrook, left, Anne Speiser and Pat O'Hara, among others, toward a more placid lifestyle.

Meditating allows me to sit, stop and feel myself."

21 So she "sits," often four times a day for up to an hour at a time. She braces for re-entry into the nursing world, where squawking machines replace singing bluebirds. "When I go back, I want to go with whatever's happening, like I did here."

22 **Second Noble Truth: Suffering is caused by desire.**

23 Darrell Hallenbrook, 25, sleeps peacefully under Ponderosa pines. May his dreams be better than a recent real-life nightmare: His parents' Malibu home burned to the ground in last year's fire. "Almost 20 years, and 99% of our stuff was gone," he says, shaking his head. "I had to take this in. I couldn't just move on."

24 So the Los Angeles stockbroker is here. Meditating. Sharing cooking duties. Thinking. Laughing. "This is a chance for me to work on the concept of impermanence," he says. "I can relax and think. In a society that's constantly selling something new to me, it's a chance to see what I really believe."

25 **Third Noble Truth: A way to nirvana, total letting go, exists.**

26 The road to nirvana, both on earth and in the afterlife, is not an expressway. If you expect quick results, "you usually don't stick around," says head monk Robert "Joshin" Althouse. Many who come to retreats, ranging from a week to three months, are "coming off of tremendous hardships and want to rearrange their priorities."

27 The religion's appeal is that it encourages adherents to plunge back into life, not recoil under its hardships, says Althouse, 45, a former computer programmer who still does some consulting via his battery-powered laptop. "I found that we rely too much on technology for some kind of answers. That came to me when the (Challenger) shuttle exploded," he says. "I then realized technology is a wonderful tool, but we have to ask ourselves, 'What are we using it for?'"

28 **"Fourth Noble Truth: The way out is the Eight-fold Path of Buddhism; right understanding, right directed thought, right speech, right action, right livelihood, right effort, right mindfulness, right concentration.**

29 Leading many down this path is the center's resident Zen Master, a *roshi*—or teacher—from L.A. via Japan named Taizan Maezumi. Many come simply to be taught by him. Marzena Maria Rey, 34, a Polish political refugee, came from Frankfurt for his advice: "Trust yourself."

30 Roshi, as he is known, is as unassuming as he is revered. At 63, his laugh resembles a child's soft giggle. His gaze is fixed. An easy smile suggests a man in no particular rush. He has conquered Buddhism's greatest and most elusive challenge: living in the moment.

31 "Why is Buddhism so popular?" Roshi lets the question hang in the air, then answers with a charming bluntness. "It's hard to say. But the number, you see, is one thing. The quality is another. Just having a bunch of people doesn't mean much."

The religion at a glance

▶ 150 million–500 million practice it worldwide.

▶ Estimated 800,000 in the USA.

▶ Buddhists can be involved in other religions.

▶ Manhattan-based *Tricycle: The Buddhist Review* has 140,000 readers.

▶ Types of Buddhism include Tibetan, Theravada, Zen.

Source: USA TODAY research

A. Scan the article for the information you need to answer the following questions.

1. What are two pieces of evidence that there is increasing interest in Buddhism in the Western world?

2. Why is Buddhism getting a lot of attention in the news media these days?

3. According to this article, what kinds of problems are newcomers to Buddhism seeking help with?

4. The name *Buddha* means the awakened one. What is Buddhism trying to awaken people to?

5. How does a person get on and stay on the "road to nirvana"?

B. Based upon the information in Article 3, mark the following statements true or false.

_____ 1. Buddhism places greater emphasis upon how a person lives while on earth and less emphasis upon the rewards of heaven after death.

_____ 2. Because Buddhism teaches that accumulating possessions is not important, the religion is attracting large numbers of poor, inner-city Americans.

_____ 3. Buddhism encourages people to quit their jobs and devote their lives to meditating.

_____ 4. Buddhists believe that desire leads to suffering.

_____ 5. According to the statistics accompanying this article, about .3 percent of the people living in the United States are Buddhists.

_____ 6. Buddhism is about a thousand years older than Christianity.

A. Find each italicized word in the paragraph indicated. Working with a partner, circle the best definition for each word from the two choices given. For some of the words, context clues will help. For others, you may need to consult a dictionary.

1. *trodding* (2)
    a. walking on
    b. studying

2. *posthumously* (5)
    a. after death
    b. in the mail

3. *bucolic* (7)
    a. rural
    b. urban

4. *philanthropist* (8)
    a. someone who donates large sums of money to good causes
    b. a Zen master

5. *articulate* (11)
    a. being a good speaker
    b. being a good listener

6. *animated* (20)　　a. a film of cartoon characters (drawings)
　　　　　　　　　　　b. lively, expressive

7. *impermanence* (24)　a. a long-lasting condition
　　　　　　　　　　　　b. a short-lived condition

8. *revered* (30)　　　a. moved backward
　　　　　　　　　　　b. highly respected

B. In paragraph 4, the word *shopaholic* is used. Discuss its meaning with a partner. Think of three other words that end with *-aholic,* and discuss their meanings. Then make up three new *-aholic* words that you think would be a useful addition to the English language. Collect the invented words from each team, compile them into a mini-dictionary, and display them in your classroom.

1. _____　　　1. _____

2. _____　　　2. _____

3. _____　　　3. _____

C. In small groups, discuss what the following phrases mean in this article. The number of the paragraph in which each is used is in parentheses.

1. *trodding the Buddhist path* (2) _____

2. *fast-lane demons* (4) _____

3. *forthcoming inspirational tract* (5) _____

4. *techno-zine* Wired (6) _____

5. *beyond blueprint stage* (7) _____

6. *banging the Buddhist gong* (8) _____

7. *not a prayer* (10) _____

8. *upscale members* (11) _____

9. *cherubic icon* (12) _____

10. *rearrange their priorities* (26) _____

DIGGING BENEATH THE SURFACE

A. The ancient Greek philosopher Plato wrote, "The life which is unexamined is not worth living." From what you learned about Buddhism in the preceding article, do you think a Buddhist would agree or disagree with Plato? Discuss this question with a partner.

B. In this article, what is the study of Buddhist philosophy compared to? (What is the metaphor that is repeated several times?) _____

Find two examples of this metaphor in the article.

_____　　　_____

What does this metaphor suggest about the study of Buddhism? _____

_____

C. Many people equate success with the accumulation of wealth and valuable possessions, and they work hard all their lives to increase their wealth. What would a Buddhist think of that way of life? Discuss this question with a partner.

D. What benefits of meditation are mentioned in this article? Anne Speiser is quoted as saying that meditation enables her to "sit, stop, and feel myself." Discuss the meaning of this quotation and others made about the effects of meditation.

GOING BEYOND THE TEXT

A. *Learning Together*
Learn more about Eastern influences upon Western culture by joining one of these classroom research groups: medicine, sports, foods, clothing, housing, technology, religion, and poetry. Each group will research its topic in the library and prepare a brief report. Visual aids (such as a karate block, a kimono, or an acupuncture chart) will add interest to the reports.

B. *Responding in Writing.* Choose one of the following writing projects.

1. In the preceding article, some of the visitors to the Zen Mountain Center spoke of their experiences with Zen Buddhism. Did any of their problems strike a chord with you? Discuss the person you most identified with, and tell why.

2. Buddhism provides very specific guidelines on the right way to live. Considering all you learned from the preceding article, class discussions, and your own reading on the subject, would you ever consider becoming a Buddhist? Tell why or why not.

3. Read about techniques of meditation, and then try meditating at home for fifteen minutes a day for one week. Then write about this experience. Tell if you plan to continue meditating regularly. Why or why not?

4. Read all or part of *The Way of Zen* by Alan Watts. Write about some of the ideas that you found most interesting.

MAKING CONNECTIONS

The preview to Article 2 in the "Science, Health, and Behavior" section tells about a study that concluded that Asian students feel less stress than American students. Do you think their beliefs could have anything to do with this? Do you think Buddhism, for example, helps people to handle stress better?

LIFESTYLES

"Life" in *USA TODAY*

The "Life" section of *USA TODAY* offers readers many types of articles on a wide range of topics. The emphasis in that section is upon new trends and leisure activities. There are news stories covering, for example, the latest high-tech journeys on the information superhighway, the latest far-out fashions, the just-discovered vacation paradise that everyone is running to, and the latest advice from experts on how to do just about anything.

Some articles are news stories containing just facts. Others offer analysis, explaining, for example, why some people must have the perfect lawn or why some "directionally challenged" folks cannot find their way back to their cars after a movie. Still other articles offer opinions that help readers decide where to spend their leisure time and entertainment dollars.

Reviews: Who Writes Them; Who Reads Them?

Reviewers or critics are supposed to be good judges of their media. Some may actually toil in the field that they critique (a novelist who reviews novels, for instance). However, in general, the movie critic is not a moviemaker, and the art critic is not an artist. Nevertheless, reviewers greatly influence public opinion. And some of them are very experienced and insightful judges of what they critique.

People read reviews for one of three reasons: (1) to decide whether or not to go to a particular movie, play, art exhibit, and so on; (2) to find out if the reviewer agreed with their evaluation of an event already seen or a book already read; or (3) to get the reviewer's explanation of a confusing movie, book, play, or whatever. Reviewers critique the performing arts, the visual arts, literary works, even restaurants. Many people count on newspapers, weekly magazines, and, to some extent, TV to provide these educated evaluations to steer them toward activities they will enjoy.

Reviewers have three main tasks: to summarize, analyze (interpret and explain), and evaluate. In order to accomplish these tasks, reviewers often compare a new work with an older, more familiar work and point out similarities and differences. Reviewers also use examples to clarify the general statements they make. Comparisons and examples help an author to clarify and to support general statements.

Exercise 1: Analyzing a Review

Find a recent review in a newspaper or magazine, and tape it onto a larger piece of paper. Then label the paragraphs either summary, analysis, or evaluation. Underline in red any sentences that use comparison or contrast. Underline in blue any sentences that give examples. Then, indicate how the reviewer rated the work being reviewed. What grade do you think he or she would give it? (Use the grading system of your school.)

Exercise 2: Comparing Two Reviews

Look in *USA TODAY* and another newspaper (or a weekly magazine) and find two reviews of the same movie, play, TV show, or art exhibit. Compare and contrast the comments of the two reviewers. Then, if you have seen the work, give your opinion.

Profiles of Celebrities

Because the "Life" section covers the arts and entertainment, this section of the paper often runs profiles of important people in the arts and entertainment industries. A profile provides a close-up, personal look at a public figure. The typical profile gives insights into the individual's formative years, summarizes past accomplishments, touches upon the subject's present personal and professional life, and tells about future plans and goals. The journalist usually interviews the subject (either in person or on the phone) and then quotes extensively from this conversation. The writer may get additional information for the article by interviewing people who know the subject and by reading other published pieces about the person.

A good profile makes readers feel as if they had actually been present during the interview. It should do more than satisfy curiosity. It should also give readers an understanding and appreciation of the subject's work.

Exercise 3: Analyzing a Profile

Find a profile in *USA TODAY* or another daily newspaper. Then answer the following questions about it.

1. Why is the newspaper running a profile on this person at this particular time?

2. Is the portrait painted of the subject flattering or unflattering? Write a brief description.

3. If you had been the journalist doing this interview, what questions would you have asked that this reporter did not ask? (List at least two.)

4. Do you think the reporter did a good job of interviewing the subject? Was the profile well-written? Tell why you liked the article or in what ways you found it lacking.

   (Hand in the profile that you cut from the newspaper along with your answers.)

EDUCATION

USA SNAPSHOTS®

A look at statistics that shape the nation

Who's best at current events

Percentage of people in eight industrial nations who were able to answer at least one of five current events questions such as "Who is the president of Russia?":

REPORT CARD

Rank		Percentage
1	Germany	**97%**
2	Italy	**82%**
3	Britain	**78%**
8	USA	**63%**

Answer:
Boris Yeltsin

Source: Times Mirror survey of media attitudes in eight nations (other countries: France, Canada, Mexico, Spain)

By Anne R. Carey and Stephen Conley, USA TODAY

ARTICLE 1A
Poverty impairs children's IQs

ARTICLE 1B
Praise from parents spurs better grades

ARTICLE 1C
Gifted kids are bored by U.S. schools

PREVIEWING THE ARTICLES

Education pays. New studies confirm what most people already assumed. The more education a person has, the higher his or her lifetime earnings will be. According to a 1994 Census Bureau report, high-school graduates can expect lifetime earnings of $821,000. For a person holding a bachelor's degree, the figure is about $1.4 million. For the holder of a professional degree, it exceeds $3 million. Another study revealed that men with high-school diplomas have incomes 13 percent higher than men with twelve years of education but no high-school degree. (For women, the difference is 5 percent.)

Higher education may be costly, but, in the long run, it is much more costly to do without it. Knowing this, parents and educators want to turn children on to learning. To do this, schools must pique children's intellectual curiosity and hold it. In addition, parents and educators must help youngsters develop the skills, mental powers, and self-confidence to grapple successfully with difficult information and sophisticated skills.

Article 1A points out that poverty lowers a child's IQ (intelligence quotient). In a way, this is good news. If IQ is not an innate, fixed quality, like the color of one's eyes, if it can be adversely affected by a deprived environment, then it can also be improved by an enriched environment. The next step is to provide the right stimulation. The research discussed in Article 1B illustrates again that it is not simply innate ability that makes a good student. Self-confidence is an important ingredient. No one denies that American schools allow many disadvantaged students to remain uneducated or undereducated. But do our schools at least meet the needs of the academically or artistically gifted? Article 1C provides a discouraging answer to that question.

BEFORE YOU READ

Imagine that you're the parent of a preschool child. What would you do to help prepare him or her for academic success?

AS YOU READ

As you read these articles, some of the conclusions will confirm your past ideas and others will contradict them. Jot down the conclusions that were a surprise to you. Later, reread the articles to decide if sufficient evidence was presented to support the conclusions that surprised you.

Poverty impairs children's IQs

By Marilyn Elias
USA TODAY

1. By age 5, kids who have always lived in poverty have IQs an average of nine points lower than those who were never poor, a new study finds—and the gap can't be chalked up to differences in mothers' education, divorce rates or race.
2. Income seems to have "the biggest effect on a child's cognitive development," says economist Greg Duncan, University of Michigan, Ann Arbor.
3. Money means the difference between "whether you can buy things or not, do things with kids or not—whether you feel hassled by poverty."
4. Duncan and psychologist Jeanne Brooks-Gunn of Columbia University followed 895 babies for five years, checking family income and child development along the way. At 5, all kids took IQ tests. Findings:
   ▶ Income is nearly twice as powerful a predictor of a child's IQ as moms' education, which earlier research suggested played a major role. But "education doesn't seem to help much if you don't have money," Duncan says.
   ▶ Children raised by single moms have lower IQs than those in two-parent homes—but that gap closes when income is taken into account.
   ▶ Poor children from all racial and ethnic groups are equally impaired.
5. Census figures show that 22% of U.S. kids live below the poverty line: $13,924 a year for a family of four. That's one-third more in poverty than two decades ago, Duncan says.
6. The findings are "an ominous wake-up call," says Yale University psychologist Edward Zigler.
7. "We're scared to death on the streets of cities, but people don't see the connection between poverty and violence. These hungry, undeveloped kids become gun-toting adolescents," he says.
8. The IQ gap "is one of many compelling reasons why we need policies to end childhood poverty."

Praise from parents spurs better grades

By Marilyn Elias
USA TODAY

1. College students whose parents always assured them they were able scholars earn higher grades than classmates with the same academic ability but less supportive parents, a new study suggests.
2. "Parents' attitudes toward their children seem to affect the way students think of themselves—and self-image seems to influence performance," says psychologist Carolyn Cutrona of University of Iowa, Iowa City.
3. Cutrona's studies of 797 students, mostly freshmen and sophomores, compared their college extrance exam scores to grade point averages. Students also filled out questionnaires on their families. Among key findings:
   ▶ Students with the cheerleading parents showed less anxiety about challenges; lower anxiety was linked to more self-confidence, which predicted better grades.
   ▶ Having supportive friends or romantic partners didn't affect grade point average.
4. Few students were in daily contact with parents, says Cutrona, but findings "probably show a lifetime of being raised to have self-confidence."

Gifted kids are bored by U.S. schools

By Tamara Henry
USA TODAY

1. Talented and gifted students in the USA aren't challenged, are bored and are often ill-prepared for the workforce, says an Education Department report out today.
2. Students lag behind those in other countries while the United States is "squandering one of its most precious resources," the report says.
3. The department's Pat O'Connell Ross told the National Association for Gifted Children conference in Atlanta Thursday that educators tend to focus most of their attention on the needs of average students or slow learners.
4. Little is done to accommodate the needs of gifted children, she said.
5. Talented and gifted children typically excel in math, writing, dance, history, athletics or any other intellectual or artistic endeavors that are complex, difficult and novel.
6. In 1990, 38 states served more than 2 million gifted students at all levels.
7. The USA has an "ambivalence toward intellectual accomplishment," Ross says. "We have names for kids that we think are too smart"—nerd or dweeb.
8. Fred Brown, principal of Boyertown Elementary School in Pennsylvania, says gifted children often aren't seen as having special needs.
9. Also, Brown says "there is a problem with limited funds," with gifted programs often getting "leftovers."
10. Compared with top students in other countries, the report shows the USA's brightest students are undistinguished at best and poor at worst.
11. For example:
    ▶ U.S. seniors taking Advanced Placement courses in science were last in biology compared with top students in 13 other countries; 11th out of 13 in chemistry and ninth out of 13 in physics.
    ▶ In math, the top 1% of U.S. students ranked 13th out of 13 in algebra and 12th out of 13 in geometry and calculus.
    ▶ When comparing U.S. and Japanese high school seniors enrolled in college preparatory math classes, Japanese students at the 50th percentile scored slightly higher than the top fifth of U.S. students.

GETTING THE MESSAGE

A. After reading Article 1A, list three factors that, according to the article, do not affect IQ.

1. _____

2. _____

3. _____

B. According to Article 1B, who is likely to get better grades—the student who worries a lot about grades or the one who doesn't worry much?

C. Considering Articles 1A and 1B, what seems to have the greater impact upon a child's academic success, the home environment or school programs?

D. What evidence does Article 1C offer to show that the top American students are academically weaker than the top students from several other countries?

PLAYING WITH WORDS

A. Decide what each italicized word or phrase from Article 1A means by rereading the paragraphs indicated in parentheses. If you cannot determine the meaning from context, use a dictionary for help. Circle the best definition.

1. *gap* (1)
   a. a hole or opening
   b. a distance or difference

2. *chalked up to* (1)
   a. written on a board
   b. attributed to; caused by

3. *cognitive development* (2)
   a. mental growth
   b. emotional growth

4. *taken into account* (4)
   a. put into the bank
   b. considered

5. *impaired* (4)
   a. mentally empowered
   b. mentally weakened

6. *two decades ago* (5)
   a. twenty years ago
   b. two hundred years ago

7. *an ominous wake-up call* (6)
   a. a threatening morning phone call
   b. information that calls attention to a dangerous condition

8. *compelling reasons* (8)
   a. strong, convincing facts
   b. violent, forceful facts

B. Reread paragraph 7 in Article 1C, paying special attention to the word *ambivalence*. Then, in small groups, discuss the answers to these questions.

1. What does the word *ambivalence* mean?

2. What does the combining form *ambi-* mean?

3. What does the first sentence of paragraph 7 mean?

4. What are some experiences or ideas you feel ambivalent about?

5. What do you think the words *ambidextrous* and *ambiguous* mean? (If no one in the group knows, check a dictionary.)

DIGGING BENEATH THE SURFACE

A. Article 1A tells about a study that indicated that poverty impairs IQ. Why do you think this might be true? Write a list of five experiences that a poor child might not have that could affect his or her IQ .

1. _____

2. _____

3. _____

4. _____

5. _____

B. The researcher discussed in Article 1B compared students' college entrance exam scores with their grade point averages. Why was this step necessary before the researcher could draw the conclusion she did?

C. In Article 1C, what does the report mean when it says that the United States is "squandering one of its most precious resources"?

GOING BEYOND THE TEXT

A. *Learning Together*

1. Can you help a preschool child develop a higher IQ? Find out if you can volunteer at a day-care center to work with children that need more intellectual stimulation. (An alternative might be to work with a neighborhood child or a relative.) Read a few books about early childhood development to get some ideas for valuable activities. Share your ideas and experiences with classmates who also volunteer to work with preschoolers.

2. One recent study suggested that listening to music (particularly highly structured music such as classical and jazz) can help raise the IQs of young children. Another study revealed that there are intellectual benefits from listening to the music of Mozart. Try listening to some classical music in your classroom before or during a test. Then discuss whether or not it helped you to do better work.

3. At one time, ability grouping was very common in American schools. Today, there is a movement toward inclusion. Children with a wide range of academic abilities remain in the same classroom for most of their school day, though gifted students and those with special needs may participate in pull-out programs. In some schools, students with physical and mental disabilities are being put into the same classroom with so-called "normal" children, if the school believes that the handicapped children will benefit from inclusion. Considering the needs of all types of students, what type of

educational system do you think is best—grouping students according to their abilities and/or disabilities or keeping classrooms as inclusive as possible? In other words, just who should learn together?

B. *Responding in Writing.*   Choose one of the following writing projects.

1. Describe your relationship with the person who was most influential in encouraging you to learn (or in discouraging you from learning).

2. Poverty may tend to lower IQ, but all of us have known (or heard about) a person who became successful and well-educated despite an impoverished childhood. Write about such a person you have known or read about.

3. According to Article 1A, paragraph 7, "People don't see the connection between poverty and violence." What connections do you see? Why are poor kids more likely to become violent teenagers and violent adults?

MAKING CONNECTIONS

1.   Article 1A points out that poverty lowers IQ scores. What other factors do you think might make an IQ test inaccurate? Read "Immigrants' status: Many factors in the mix" (Article 3 in the "News" section). As our nation becomes more ethnically and linguistically diverse, do IQ test scores become less and less reliable as a method of measuring innate ability? (Clearly, it is difficult to write a test that is free of cultural bias, that does not give an advantage to the person who has always lived in the United States and who is a native speaker of English.)

2. Article 1B suggests that students with less anxiety are likely to get better grades in school. Compare this article to the information in Article 2 of the "Science" section, which deals with the effects of stress.

ARTICLE 2A
Panel: Extend school year

ARTICLE 2B
Report gives "A" to longer school year

PREVIEWING THE ARTICLES

How much time do American students spend in school? What do they study while they are there? The answers suggest to many educators that we need to improve both the quantity of time spent in the classroom and the quality of material studied during that time.

If you ask students, they will tell you they are always in school. But what is the reality? For American kids, less than half the days in a year are school days. Moreover, less than half of each school day is spent learning core academic subjects such as math, science, social studies, foreign language, and language arts.

There is widespread concern that American students are not keeping pace with European and Asian students in the most developed countries that are our closest economic competitors. This could mean, down the line, that the United States could fall behind economically. In a high-tech world where jobs that pay well require sophisticated skills, we could be educating students to stand in unemployment lines.

Many tests and surveys indicate that American students do, in fact, know less than those in several European and Asian countries. Defenders of American education say that American schools teach a lot besides facts. In good schools, creativity is fostered, problem-solving techniques are practiced, and social skills involving teamwork and leadership are an important part of the curriculum. Some educators argue that if Americans fall behind in academics in high school, they catch up in college. Nevertheless, there is a back-to-basics movement afoot to put more academic work into the elementary and high school curricula. Recently, some improvement has been noted. Students' standardized test scores are a little higher, and more high school students are taking more core academic courses (as a result of more stringent graduation requirements). Can we do even better if we keep kids in school for a longer year? The following articles take up that question.

BEFORE YOU READ

Discuss what would help you get more out of school. Is some of the time students spend in school wasted? Is a longer school day and/or year needed? Do teachers need to improve their teaching techniques? Does the school need more equipment and new books? What do you think is needed most?

AS YOU READ

Note the various ideas for changes in American education. Jot them down, and, after each one, write *yes* or *no* to indicate your approval or disapproval. After classroom discussions of these articles, look back at your notes to see if you have changed your mind.

Panel: Extend school year

By Dennis Kelly
USA TODAY

1 A federal commission today will call for nearly doubling the time students spend in "core academic courses"—and even changing the length of the school year if that's what it takes to help kids learn.

2 That likely means a school year longer than the traditional 180 days, says Milton Goldberg, executive director of the National Education Commission on Time and Learning.

3 "If reform is to take hold, the 6-hour, 180-day school year should be relegated to museums," he says.

4 Congress created the commission partly out of concern over the longer school years of economic competitors like Germany, with 200 to 225 days, and Japan, with 230 days.

5 The report found the time kids devote to core academic courses such as English, math, science and history averages three hours a day—less than half their international peers.

6 "If we want excellence for our children, we need more learning time in school, at home and in the community," says Education Secretary Richard Riley.

7 The commission recommends students spend 5½ hours a day in core subjects.

8 But how? "Reclaim the academic day," says Goldberg, noting it's filled with non-academic requirements: "personal safety, consumer affairs, AIDS, family life, driver's training."

9 Many are worthwhile topics, but communities should offer them after the "academic day," he says. The report also:

▶ Calls for more time for teacher training.

▶ Attacks the premise that all kids need the same amount of time to learn: Some need more than 180 days, some less.

10 The report concedes the recommendations will cost money, but doesn't say how much.

11 The commission has no power to change education, which is still largely under state and local control.

12 But Goldberg led research on the landmark 1983 report, *A Nation at Risk,* which helped the push for tougher academic requirements. *Risk* also called for longer school years, and little happened.

13 "It's the hardest nut to crack," says Goldberg. "It's more tied up with tradition than anything else."

Report gives "A" to longer school year

By Barbara Nachman
USA TODAY

1 Summertime and the livin' won't be so easy for some school kids in the USA.

2 New findings from California researchers show that increasing the school year from 180 to 223 days leads to significant gains in achievement for at-risk students.

3 The controversial year-round schooling plan, which has been operating in three California elementary schools since 1988, also improves parent and teacher satisfaction, says the study's author, University of California professor Patricia Gandara.

4 Gandara, who reports her finding in the current issue of *Educational Evaluation and Policy Analysis,* calls her plan a "radical restructuring of the schools. We were trying to do a number of things," she says. Gandara says her program, called the Orchard Plan, also addresses the problems of overcrowding, teacher dissatisfaction with low pay, and a statewide shortage of teachers.

5 In the Orchard program, students attend classes for 60 days, then have a 15-day vacation. Children with academic problems can attend enrichment programs during these breaks.

6 All students and teachers share a four-week summer vacation and one week off during the winter and spring.

7 Gandara says her program is not a model for all USA schools but believes aspects of the plan could be adopted by many schools.

8 "Schools shouldn't be afraid to try something new," she says. "Parents will come along if they're involved."

GETTING THE MESSAGE

A. After reading both articles, mark the following statements true or false.

_____ 1. Students in some countries spend more than six hours a day on academic subjects.

_____ 2. The federal commission is going to require a longer school year.

_____ 3. In the United States, public elementary and high school education is controlled by the individual states, not by the federal government.

_____ 4. A federal commission has suggested that subjects such as safety and driver's education be eliminated from high school programs.

_____ 5. Article 1B tells about an example of a recommendation made in Article 1A.

B. Are the ideas listed below in either, neither, or both of the articles? Put a check (✓) in the appropriate column if the article contains the idea.

	Article A	Article B
1. The article supports the idea of year-round school.	_____	_____
2. The article makes recommendations that haven't been tested.	_____	_____
3. The article says that all children need to spend more time in school.	_____	_____
4. The article recommends eliminating summer vacation.	_____	_____
5. The article suggests that parents don't like year-round schools.	_____	_____

PLAYING WITH WORDS

A. Decide what each italicized phrase from Article 2A means by rereading the paragraphs indicated in parentheses. If you cannot determine the meaning from context, use a dictionary for help. Circle the best definition.

1. *federal commission* (1)
   a. group established by the national government to study a particular matter
   b. an official action taken by a state government

2. *nearly doubling* (1)
   a. slightly less than twice as much
   b. more than twice as much

3. *that likely means* (2)
   a. probably
   b. certainly

4. *should be relegated to museums* (3)
   a. is valuable and must be carefully preserved
   b. is out-of-date, no longer works well, and should be discarded

5. *concern over the longer school year of economic competitors* (4)

   a. worry that a longer school year will harm our competitors
   b. worry that, in the future, American workers won't be able to compete with better-educated workers from other countries

6. *reclaim the academic day* (8)

   a. spend more of each school day on core academic subjects
   b. reestablish a special day for academics

7. *attacks the premise* (9)

   a. shows what is wrong with this commonly held belief
   b. spends too much time fighting ideas

8. *the report concedes* (10)

   a. disagrees with a particular premise
   b. admits the validity of one argument made against its proposal

9. *the hardest nut to crack* (13)

   a. the most difficult thing to accomplish
   b. the strongest part of the program

10. *tied up with tradition* (13)

    a. related to the way people have done it for a long time
    b. impossible to separate from tradition

B. With a partner, discuss the meanings of the following phrases from Article 2B. The paragraph number where each phrase appears is indicated in parentheses.

1. *at-risk* (2)

2. *radical restructuring* (4)

3. *addresses the problem* (4)

4. *enrichment programs* (5)

DIGGING BENEATH THE SURFACE

Discuss these questions in groups of three or four.

1. Did these articles convince you that American schools should be in session about 220 days per year instead of 180? What is good about the idea? What problems might this change create? Besides disliking a break with tradition, do you think there are other reasons parents may object to this change?

2. Do you think that a longer school day is a better idea than a longer school year?

3. Do you think that subjects such as first aid, consumer affairs, and driver's education should be taught in schools? What about cooking, sewing, and carpentry? What about music, visual arts, drama, and athletics? Would American schools be better if all these skills were taught in after-school programs instead of during the school day? Which ones would you remove from the curriculum?

4. Do you think that, for some high school students, algebra and organic chemistry may be less important and useful than subjects such as cooking, carpentry, sex education, and family life?

A. *Learning Together*

How much effort do you put into academics? To find out, form groups of four or five and complete the following list of statements by adding three more. Then use the nine statements as a test. Give yourself from one to five points for each, with five meaning your behavior is closest to the statement. Put each of your scores on the blank line after each statement. Compare your final score to the scores of the others in your group. Does there seem to be a correlation between high scores on this test and high grades in school?

1. I spend much more time per week doing homework than watching TV. _____

2. I always complete my homework on time. _____

3. If I do not understand how to do some assigned schoolwork, I always ask for help from a parent, teacher, tutor, or friend who can explain it to me. _____

4. I always listen to my teachers' explanations. _____

5. I always get enough sleep so that I don't come to school tired. _____

6. I always eat breakfast and lunch to give me energy for my school day. _____

(Add three more statements your group thinks of. Then take the test.)

B. *Responding in Writing.* Choose one of the following writing projects.

1. In June 1994, Eva Wilkinson of Huntington, West Virginia, was sentenced to one hundred days in jail because her eight-year-old missed fifty-nine days of school. In many other communities, parents are being punished if their children are truant. Sometimes the punishment is a fine or the loss of welfare payments. The ultimate punishment is losing custody of one's children. Do you think parents should be held responsible for the truancy of their children? If so, what is appropriate punishment for the parents? Give your opinion.

2. If you have ever attended school in another country, compare that system with the American system, pointing out the strengths and weaknesses of each.

3. Write a letter to your state Board of Education recommending a change in the way that schools are operated.

MAKING CONNECTIONS

Tradition causes parents to prefer the 180-day school year, according to Article 2A. In the "Lifestyles" section, the article entitled "Chapel offers simple way to say 'I do'" talks about the traditional wedding, which has a hold on couples even when they cannot afford the time and money it requires. In what other areas of American life does tradition seem to control behavior? Which traditions do you think should be "relegated to museums," to quote Milton Goldberg. The preceding articles urge Americans to reform their educational system, not to cling to tradition and fear change. In what other areas of American life do you think change is drastically needed?

ARTICLE 3
Where values are the first, most important lesson

PREVIEWING THE ARTICLE

What are high schools supposed to teach? Once the answer was simple: information and skills. Today the answer is quite complex: whatever kids need to learn in order to have a decent future. Some educators believe the high school curriculum should include instruction in ethics, self-love, love of others, and a positive philosophy of life. How can schools do all that? The following article is about some schools that have tried, using a unique program called "Character First."

Some people would say that character and ethics should be taught by parents and religious institutions, not schools, and especially not public schools. After all, in a multicultural society, ideas about what is moral and admirable behavior can vary immensely from one ethnic group to another. But the principles that "Character First" espouses may be universal.

Other critics would say that public high schools in the U.S. are having enough trouble teaching subject matter and basic skills to their diverse population. They do not need an additional educational assignment. But the proponents of "Character First" say that you cannot teach subject matter to students who have no values and no appreciation of their own value.

"Character First" involves students, teachers, administrators, and parents in a joint effort to improve schools and save troubled kids. Those who have tried it say it works. That makes it worth reading about.

BEFORE YOU READ

Before reading the article, read the basic principles of the Hyde "character curriculum" (in the box). Ask questions about any of these points that are not clear to you. Do you believe all of these traits are worth developing?

AS YOU READ

Look for activities that make the Hyde program different from the typical high school program. Jot these down for later use in your group discussions and writing.

Where values are the first, most important lesson

By Tamara Henry
USA TODAY

1 BATH, Maine—The sign hanging on the wall of the elegant Georgian brick mansion that serves as the Hyde School says simply: *The truth will set you free but first it will make you miserable.*

2 Matthew Radasch, a freshman at the private boarding school, can vouch for that. Radasch slowly rises during Friday's required weekly meeting in the Student Union, where any of the 200 students have the chance to discuss concerns, problems, achievements and other Hyde "family business." He admits cheating on a recent math test.

3 "I'm going to be here hopefully 'til I graduate. I didn't want (the guilt) weighing me down the next four years. I knew it was best for me to get it off my chest," explains Radasch, who says he had been too "achievement-oriented."

4 Radasch's discipline was a 5:30 a.m. workout for two days.

5 Truth is not the only value promoted. The 28-year-old high school operates on the premise that if you teach students values such as courage, integrity, leadership, curiosity and concern, then academic achievement naturally follows.

6 Hyde School founder Joseph Gauld claims success with the program at the $18,000-a-year prep school, known best for its work with troubled youngsters.

7 "We don't see ourselves as a school for a type of kid," says Malcolm Gauld, Joseph's son, who graduated from Hyde and is now headmaster. "We see ourselves as preparing kids for a way of life—a set of principles that can affect all kids."

8 Now, like an itinerant preacher, Joe Gauld is trying to spread his Character First doctrine to public, inner-city schools willing to use the tax dollars spent on the traditional program for the new approach. The first Hyde public school program opened in September 1992 in Gardiner, Maine, a 2,800-student school system. Within months the program was suspended. Teachers protested the program's demands and more intense work.

9 This fall, the Hyde Foundation is slated to pilot a public school program in Baltimore. Teachers will be trained to later work throughout the entire Baltimore system. Other U.S. school superintendents are eyeing the program, too.

10 Last fall, the Hyde Foundation opened a magnet program within a public high school in suburban New Haven, Conn., over parents' protests. The community feared the school would attract inner-city minority and troubled students.

11 About 100 ninth- and 10th-grade students now occupy the spacious building that once housed a Catholic middle school. As in Maine the quest for truth is also prevalent at the Hyde Leadership School in Connecticut.

12 In teacher Melissa Keating's math class, the 11 students spend the last five minutes in an energetic exchange evaluating their class performance for the day on a 1–10 scale.

13 "I get a 10."

14 "I challenge that. You didn't do your homework."

15 "OK, a seven."

16 "You should get a six."

17 "Wait, I put my best effort forth here."

18 "Yeah, but you didn't ask questions today."

19 Explaining his approach to education, Joe Gauld says the USA's traditional education system cannot be reformed. He notes "no amount of tinkering" with the horse and buggy "will produce an automobile."

20 The Hyde School assumes "every human being has a unique potential" that is based on character, not intellect or wealth. Conscience and hard work are valued. Success is gauged by growth, not academic achievement. Students are required to take responsibility for each other.

21 To circumvent the controversy of other character programs used in U.S. schools, Gauld says the concept of *doing your best* has nothing to do with indoctrination.

22 The Hyde curriculum is similar to traditional schools, complete with English, history, math (pre-algebra, algebra and calculus) and science (biology and chemistry). But all students are required to take performing arts and sports and provide a community service. For each course, students get a grade for academic achievement and for "best effort." At Bath, 97% of the graduates attend four-year colleges.

23 Parental commitment is a key ingredient in the Hyde mix. For the student to be admitted, parents also must agree to accept and demonstrate the school's philosophies and concepts. The parents agree in writing to meet monthly in one of 20 regional groups, go to a yearly three-day regional retreat, and spend at least three times a year in workshops,

By Robert Deutsch, USA TODAY

COMMUNITY SERVICE: Tommie Artis, 16, visits Bernadette Braslin, 84, through Hyde School in suburban New Haven, Conn.

encounter groups and seminars at Bath.

24 Parents of Maine students have an attendance rate of 95% in the many sessions.

25 Steve Cavalli of Danville, Calif., along with about two dozen other parents, spent the Easter weekend at Bath. Cavalli's 18-year-old daughter came to Hyde two years ago after involvement with drugs and alcohol, bouts of depression and an attempted suicide. She graduates in May.

26 "At the time I didn't really realize what I was getting myself in for, as I think most of the parents who come into this program would agree," Cavalli says. "I sent my daughter here basically to get the school to fix her because I wasn't doing a very good job at home, and found out, in the process, that I required a lot of fixing myself.

27 "My family has grown back together. My daughter is a different person. . . . Something wonderful happens here. There's a process that takes place here and I think parent involvement is important."

28 Joe and Malcolm Gauld both say children tend to seek excellence when they see their parents making similar efforts. The biggest hurdle for many parents, they say, is to realize their own weaknesses.

29 The process for public school parents is still being worked out, with a lot more difficulty because there are few ways to motivate parents to participate.

30 Of the 100 students enrolled in New Haven, about 30% of the parents attend special meetings. The low attendance is in spite of commitments they made when Hyde officials initially interviewed 300 families.

31 Eric Winchester, 16, says "my dad loves it. He's totally committed. He does everything he possibly can to help. He attends all the meetings."

32 "Mine are the complete opposite," admits Gloribelo Lopez, 15. "For my freshman year I transferred out of two schools. I was just looking for something and I think I finally found it. (My mom) says this is just another school. They are fed up with me. I tell her

The character curriculum

Hyde expects all students to develop these traits:
▶ The *courage* to accept challenges
▶ The *integrity* to be truly themselves
▶ *Concern* for others
▶ The *curiosity* to explore life and learning
▶ *Leadership* in making the school and community work

With these traits, five principles develop:
▶ Destiny. Each of us is gifted with a unique potential.
▶ Humility. We believe in a power and a purpose beyond ourselves.
▶ Conscience. We attain our best through character and conscience.
▶ Truth. Truth is our primary guide.
▶ Brother's keeper. We help others attain their best.

Expected results for students:
▶ Core knowledge and skills
▶ Capacity to use education and a reverence for learning
▶ Self-confidence, perseverance, creativity and personal vision
▶ Integrity of relationships
▶ Responsible and effective citizenship

Expected results for parents:
▶ Personal liberation from children's challenges
▶ Vision beyond parenthood
▶ Simultaneous personal growth with children

what's up and she's trying her hardest to understand it. She doesn't get the concept of any of it."

33 Once the kinks are out, Hyde should work well in public schools, says Gary Kent, a government teacher in Bath who taught 14 years in public schools. Once parents make a commitment to the program, they can daily be role models for their children, unlike parents whose children are in boarding school.

34 John Russell, a former inner-city high school teacher who now works in the New Haven program, says teachers also benefit. "Here we really begin to focus on relationships with students. Our focus is really about teacher to student and then we together deal with the . . . academics. In the traditional high school setting, it's teacher to the material and then to the student."

35 The teacher-student relationship is taken even further at Hyde. Faculty evaluations are conducted by the students.

36 Jimmy DiBattista, 19, Philadelphia, is amazed he will graduate this May from the Bath campus and plans to attend Drexel University. Years ago, he had seen his future as "jail, not college."

37 DiBattista remembers his first days at Hyde.

38 "When I came here, I had my middle finger up to everybody. Every other school was, 'Get out, we don't want to deal with you at all.' I came here and they said, 'We kind of like that spirit. We don't like it with the negative attitudes. We want to turn that spirit positive.' "

GETTING THE MESSAGE

A. After reading the article, mark the following statements true or false.

_____ 1. The Hyde Foundation is the only program for teaching character in American schools.

_____ 2. The Hyde curriculum has been used in both public and private schools.

_____ 3. If parents do not come to meetings regularly, their children cannot remain in the Hyde program.

_____ 4. The Hyde program can be used only in boarding schools.

_____ 5. The character curriculum that Joseph Gauld is promoting can be used for an entire school or as a program serving only some students attending a particular school.

_____ 6. The main goal of the Hyde Foundation is to help inner-city students improve their grades and do better on standardized tests.

B. Answer the following questions about this article.

1. Why is this program getting journalistic coverage at this particular time? Is there anything that makes this piece especially timely?

2. What evidence is presented in the article to support the claim that this program helps students?

3. Which do you think is more important as a motivating force in the Hyde program: competition or cooperation? Which paragraphs helped you reach that conclusion?

4. What are some unusual aspects of parental involvement in the program?

5. Why might teachers find working at a Hyde school more difficult and time-consuming than in a typical public school?

PLAYING WITH WORDS

A. Decide what each italicized word or phrase means in this article by rereading the paragraphs indicated in parentheses. Circle the best definition. If you cannot determine the meaning from context, use a dictionary for help. Then reread the paragraphs to look for context clues that you missed on your first rereading.

1. *vouch* (2)
   a. offer evidence that a statement is false
   b. tell you that the statement is true

2. *too "achievement-oriented"* (3)
   a. more concerned with grades than is appropriate
   b. moving toward a successful future

3. *discipline* (4)
   a. punishment
   b. self-control

4. *premise* (5)
   a. promise
   b. assumption

5. *itinerant* (8)
    a. old-fashioned
    b. traveling

6. *eying the program* (9)
    a. setting up a program with similar features
    b. looking at and considering the program

7. *prevalent* (11)
    a. widespread, generally practiced
    b. disregarded, scorned

8. *potential* (20)
    a. possible source of power
    b. ability that could be developed

9. *circumvent* (21)
    a. get around, avoid
    b. come into conflict with, fight

10. *commitment* (23)
    a. a prison term
    b. continuing involvement with

B. With a partner, discuss the meanings of the following words found in the boxed section labelled "The character curriculum." Also, say the words aloud. If you are not sure of the pronunciation, check the pronunciation symbols in a dictionary.

1. *integrity*

2. *destiny*

3. *conscience*

4. *perseverance*

5. *simultaneous*

DIGGING BENEATH THE SURFACE

A. Writers commonly develop their general ideas with reasons, results, examples, comparisons, statistics, or other details. Reread Article 3 to study the ways in which the ideas are developed. Then indicate the paragraph(s) in which you found the following types of development. After you have found at least one example of each in the article, check your answers with a partner.

1. example: _____

2. statistic: _____

3. result (cause and effect): _____

4. comparison/contrast: _____

B. Did this article convince you that the Hyde program should be tried in more communities? If so, what information was most convincing? If not, what additional evidence would make the case stronger? Jot down your ideas first. Then discuss these questions with two classmates.

A. *Learning Together*

    1. Discuss these questions in small groups:

        a. If your school had a Hyde program would you want to get in it? Why or why not?

        b. Do you think your school fosters good character and self-esteem? If you think it does, in what ways? Or does your school unwittingly encourage the development of negative traits and attitudes? If so, tell how.

        c. Do you think public boarding schools would have a better chance of helping inner-city teenagers than public day schools do? In Chicago, plans to open public boarding schools were underway in 1994. If you had the opportunity, would you choose to attend one?

    2. Divide into small groups. Then select one of the traits that the character curriculum hopes students will achieve. Brainstorm together to think of activities that would help to develop the trait you have selected. Each group should then select its best idea and explain it to the class. Choose one person to be your group spokesperson. From the ideas presented, choose one or two to put into practice in your class. After several weeks, evaluate the results.

B. *Responding in Writing*

    1. Choose one of the character traits in the Hyde curriculum, and write about why you think it is essential (or not essential) to a successful happy life.

    2. What do you expect to gain from your present school year? Are you hopeful that you will get what you want and need? Write a brief essay answering these questions.

    3. Write a letter to Joseph Gauld. (The address is Hyde Foundation, 616 High St., Bath, Maine 04530.) Tell him about your class's experiences with his "character curriculum." If you wish, ask for further information or advice.

A. Review the article "Learn to lighten up and live longer" in the "Science, Health, and Behavior" section. Do you think students in the Hyde program are likely to feel less stress or more stress than students in conventional high school programs? What facets of the program would increase or decrease stress?

B. Considering the three articles in the "Education" section, what changes are needed in American public schools in order for them to serve their diverse population more effectively? Make a list of six changes that you would recommend. They can involve students, teachers, parents, administration, organization, and/or curriculum.

EDUCATION

Why Schools Are News

Most Americans see education as the best vehicle for individual and social advancement. Parents generally give their children's education greatest priority. A great percentage of Americans are involved in education as full-time students, part-time adult learners, or teachers. Others, affected less directly, take a general interest in what is happening in one of society's major institutions. All things considered, it is not surprising that what happens in the nation's schools frequently makes news.

We look to newspapers and magazines for evaluations of our educational systems. How do today's standardized achievement scores compare to those of a decade or two ago? How do American students compare to their peers educated elsewhere? We look to the news media for insights into new methods of teaching and new programs, for the latest educational problems and challenges, and for the latest experiments to find solutions.

Exercise 1: A Week's News in Review

For a week, look through *USA TODAY.* Make a list of the stories you find on education, and read each one carefully. Then write a paragraph summarizing the news in education for that week. (In *USA TODAY,* articles on education are sometimes in the first section and sometimes in the "Life" section. Articles about schools are often published under the heading "Education Today.")

Exercise 2: Education News and a Follow-up Story

In *USA TODAY* or your local newspaper, find a major story about schools or education. During the next week, look for a follow-up story on this topic. Follow this particular story for as long as it is in the news. Check the editorial page(s) of the paper to see if there is editorial commentary and/or letters from readers about this topic. When coverage of the story is complete, write a paragraph about this piece of news and its long-term significance. Tell if you think it received more or less newspaper space than it deserved.

Exercise 3: Analyzing an Article about Education

Select an article about education from a recent newspaper, and answer the following questions about it. Hand in the article along with your answers.

1. What key words in the headline helped you predict the content?

2. What is the purpose of the article (for example, does it report on a problem, explain a new school policy, or describe a new type of school)?

3. What is the main idea of the article? (Try to state it in your own words in one sentence.)

4. What did you find interesting about the topic of this article? (Why did you select it to analyze?)

5. Did the article leave you with unanswered questions? What else would you like to know about the topic that the article did not tell you?

Advertising Education

Newspapers run many advertisements relating to education. These include private schools that offer training in particular careers and facilities that teach particular skills, such as a foreign language or study skills. Shortly before the beginning of a new school year or semester, newspapers may have an education insert with advertising and articles about career opportunities, trade schools, and regular academic programs.

Exercise 4: Responding to an Education Ad

Find an advertisement for some kind of skill, trade, career, or academic program that you might be interested in now or in the future. Respond to the ad by calling or writing to get more information. If you find more than one advertisement for competing programs that interest you, get information from both sources. Then write a paragraph telling whether your research stimulated your interest or caused you to lose interest.

SCIENCE, HEALTH, AND BEHAVIOR

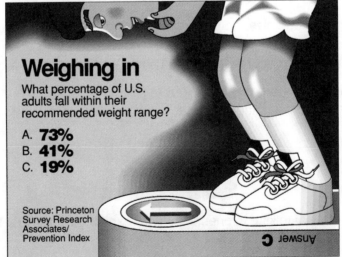

ARTICLE 1
Look who's talking to themselves: Just about everyone

So you talk to yourself. Does that make you crazy? Not at all. In fact, it may help you stay sane. Talking to oneself is such a natural human activity that almost everyone does it, according to this article.

There are many reasons why people talk to themselves: to clarify a thought, release angry feelings, rehearse future conversations, even scold themselves for past mistakes. Alone in a room, some people say a prayer. Alone in a shower, some people sing. Seated at an uncooperative computer, many have been known to swear, threaten, or otherwise psychologically abuse their disobedient machine. But even if you do all of the above, don't panic. You are not only sane; you are actually typical.

To support her claim that the average person is a "mumble mouth," the author of this article cites evidence from many sources. For members of the silent minority—those who don't talk to themselves and doubt that most other people do—the author offers testimony from psychologists (the experts) and from ordinary people (whom the skeptical reader might be more willing to believe).

BEFORE YOU READ

1. Take a survey in your class. Students should provide anonymous written answers indicating whether or not they ever talk to themselves and, if so, how often (about how many times a day, week, month, or year). Tabulate the results on a graph.

2. Discuss the kinds of situations that might make you or someone in your family talk to himself or herself. Do you think computer users do this often? Why? Do you think stress causes this behavior?

AS YOU READ

Notice the various uses of talking to oneself that are explained in the article and try to think of some others not mentioned.

Look who's talking to themselves: Just about everyone

By Karen S. Peterson
USA TODAY

1 Do you talk to yourself?

2 Never?

3 I'll bet you denied it aloud.

4 Why not just admit it? Almost everybody does it at one time or another.

5 Psychologist Thomas Brinthaupt admits he does, and is quite OK with it. That's one reason he is studying the topic. "Talking to one's self is an experience we all share," he says. "It is tied to our everyday functioning as adults."

6 All but one of the 102 college students he surveyed at Middle Tennessee State University confess to having muttered aloud to themselves under some circumstances. Frequent places cited: in a car, alone in one's room, at work, in the shower. Brinthaupt does it "in my office—with the door closed," stuck behind a slow driver or working on his computer.

7 Stress makes us babble: "I find I'm talking to myself more in the last two weeks, maybe from sleep deprivation. We have a 2-week-old baby," he says.

8 The computer age is breeding a whole new generation of mumblers, says Mike Bruckner, 37, Keene, N.H. "All of these thoughts run through my head at the computer. And when things are not going right, I'll swear at it."

9 In the car, his musings are about "things I have to remember to do. And I might pray a little bit aloud. I'm not really religious, but there is solitude, a time to talk to God a bit."

10 Psychologist Shirley Sanders talks to Aristotle instead—her computer. "Sometimes I get blocked in my writing, and I think it through aloud."

11 She even has Aristotle programmed to respond—with helpful comments and reminders to take deep breaths to alleviate frustration.

12 And she is quite sure she is not bonkers. "We all talk to ourselves. Some do it in their heads, some talk out loud. It's a matter of style and preference, and both are appropriate," says the University of North Carolina researcher.

13 Brinthaupt considers talking behavior part of a continuum, from talking internally to talking aloud. So does Richmond, Va., psychologist Alan Entin. "Talking to yourself is just thinking aloud. It's a way of problem-solving, of answering your own questions, arguing with yourself, seeing different points of view. So don't worry about being crazy."

14 We readily use "private speech" as kids, Brinthaupt says. As we mature, the habit doesn't disappear but "goes underground," and resurfaces from time to time. Among the "normals" he cites who talk easily aloud:

▶ **Thinkers.** People who like "to think about things, contemplate mysteries, solve problems and puzzles." And people who are concentrating intensely, "as a way to keep themselves on task."

▶ **Athletes.** Many athletes psych themselves up out loud before and during the fray of competition.

▶ **Perfectionists.** People who lecture themselves when they miss the mark. "I could have gotten an A if I had studied harder."

▶ **Those with low self-esteem.** They berate themselves: "You dummy! How could you have forgotten the keys!"

15 A common reason for us all to self-talk is to rehearse something, Brinthaupt says: asking a boss for a raise, for example.

16 Others review aloud something that has just happened to do better next time. "It's something like a replay," he says. " 'Why did I say that? In the future, I'll put it this way.' "

17 We also "self-regulate" by talking aloud, "give ourselves commands, directives," tell ourselves what to do next.

18 Contrary to what most think, talking aloud is "a way of preserving our mental health," Sanders says. "We burst forth spontaneously; if we didn't have that outlet, we'd be in trouble."

19 So feel free, mumble mouth.

A. After reading the article, mark these answers true or false.

_____ 1. People should try not to talk to themselves.

_____ 2. Paragraphs 1–4 suggest that many people who talk to themselves deny it to themselves and others.

_____ 3. Stress is related to talking to oneself.

_____ 4. According to paragraph 6, psychologist Thomas Brinthaupt studied people from all walks of life.

_____ 5. Psychologist Shirley Sanders equates talking to a computer with talking to oneself.

B. Write your own statement of this article's main idea. Then write two pieces of evidence that support the idea.

PLAYING WITH WORDS

A. After reading the article and looking up the meanings of words that are new to you, circle the best word to complete each of the following statements.

1. People may (*commit, contemplate, admit, deny*) that they talk to themselves because they think it is embarrassing to (*admit, deny, experience, review*) it.

2. When people talk to themselves, they often speak quietly. Therefore, the author of this article describes the habit as (*musing, mumbling, lecturing, functioning*).

3. Some people like to think about mysteries and puzzles and try to solve them. They like to (*contemplate, concentrate, cite, survey*) difficult matters.

4. People sometimes talk to themselves while driving alone in a car because (*competition, behavior, solitude, embarrassment*) encourages talking to oneself.

5. Where are people most likely to talk to themselves? Some of the common places (*psyched, sited, cited, slighted*) in this article were the privacy of a car, one's own room, or one's private office.

6. Some people self-regulate their behavior by giving themselves orders, also called (*solitude, directives, frustration, replays*).

7. People who don't have much confidence in themselves have low (*self-esteem, self-regulation, self-awareness, self-reliance*).

8. People sometimes talk to themselves to decrease or (*deprive, survey, alleviate, contemplate*) frustration.

9. Before asking the boss for a raise, some people (*replay, rehearse, admit, block*) the request they are going to make.

10. Athletes sometimes talk aloud during the (*solitude, replay, babble, fray*) of competition.

B. See how many compound words beginning with *self-* you can list in four minutes. Work with a partner and compete against other teams in your class. When the four minutes is up, each team should list its words on the board. After determining the winner of the game, discuss the meanings of the more difficult words.

C. Discuss the meanings of the following phrases with a partner. Try to get the meanings from context. If necessary, use a dictionary for help.

1. In paragraph 7, what does *sleep deprivation* mean? Do you ever suffer from this problem? When?

2. In paragraph 8, what does *run through* mean? Is it used literally or idiomatically?

3. In paragraph 14, what does *private speech* mean? Can speech ever be private?

4. In paragraph 14, what does *psych themselves up* mean? Do you ever psych yourself up? When? Why?

5. In paragraph 18, what does *burst forth spontaneously* mean? Do you ever do this when you are watching a baseball or basketball game on TV, when you stub your toe, or when you receive very good or very bad news in the mail? Give some examples of spontaneous outbursts you have uttered.

D. Discuss the meanings of the homonyms *sight, cite,* and *site.* Identify the part of speech of each word—noun, verb, or both. Then use one of these three words to complete each of the following sentences. Add third-person singular endings or plural endings where they are needed.

1. The author of this article _____ many examples of times when people mumble to themselves.

2. That man is alone in his car, and he is talking to himself. What a funny_____ !

3. Why do you think Thomas Brinthaupt chose a college campus as the_____ of his study?

4. When you did your research paper, did you _____ a lot of sources for the information?

5. Did you _____ the North Star in the sky last night?

DIGGING BENEATH THE SURFACE

A. The author begins and ends this article by talking to you, her reader. In the first four paragraphs, what is she saying to you? What is she telling you in the last line? Do you find the opening and closing of this article funny? Insulting?

B. Write an outline of the major headings of this article and a few subheadings under each. Work with a partner to find three major headings and some specifics to go under each heading. Number the major headings with Roman numerals and the subheadings with capital letters. Write a topic outline, which uses phrases and clauses, not whole sentences.

C. Pretend you were the psychologist who surveyed 102 college students and found that 101 of them talked to themselves. What conclusions would you draw from this data? Can you assume the results would be the same for all age groups and nationalities? Discuss these questions with a partner.

D. Reread the article to determine its tone. Is the author treating this subject with a great seriousness or with a light, humorous touch? Make a list of three examples of the writing style to support your answer. Then compare your list with those of two classmates.

GOING BEYOND THE TEXT

A. *Learning Together*

1. In small groups, discuss whether you think that factors such as age, ethnicity, sex, level of education, or occupation affect talking to oneself. Is a middle-aged Italian opera singer more likely to talk to herself than a young Japanese wrestler? Why do you think babies babble to themselves so much?

2. Work with a small group to plan a survey to conduct in your class. (You might ask about behavior, attitudes, values, leisure-time activities, and so on.) Prepare a form with questions for your classmates to answer. Duplicate this survey form and distribute it. What do you think the results of your survey will be? Write up your hypothesis. Then, from the information you get back, write up the results of the survey. Create a graph to present your data visually. Finally, evaluate your project, indicating its strengths and, perhaps, ways in which it could be improved. Present the results to the entire class.

B. *Responding in Writing.* Choose one of the following writing projects.

1. Write about a time when you talked to yourself. Did it help? Did anyone hear you? Did you reveal a secret?

2. Reread paragraph 18. Then write a paragraph about what you do to preserve your mental health. What do you do for an emotional outlet when you are angry or anxious?

3. Write about how you interact with a computer. Does working on a computer cause you to feel stress? How do you respond? Do you think of a computer as a person? Do you give it a name, get angry with it, scold it, consider it your best friend?

MAKING CONNECTIONS

The article that follows this one—"Learn to lighten up and live longer"—also deals with the mind-body phenomenon of stress. After you read that article, ask yourself why Dr. Eliot doesn't recommend, as one of his techniques for dealing with stress, that people talk to themselves. From "Look who's talking to themselves: Just about everyone," do you conclude that people decide to talk to themselves in order to get the psychological benefits? Or do they simply respond aloud without thinking and, as a result, derive psychological benefits?

After reading both articles, make a list of six ways to reduce stress in your life.

ARTICLE 2A
Learn to lighten up and live longer

ARTICLE 2B
Translating blushes, belches, and other body language

PREVIEWING THE ARTICLES

Who is more stressed out—the Asian teenager or the American teenager? Surprise. The American teen wins this contest, hands down. According to a recent study, almost three-quarters of American high school juniors said they felt stress at least once a week, some almost daily. Fewer than half of Japanese and Taiwanese eleventh graders reported feeling stress that often.

The phenomenon of stress is just one example of the constant interaction between mind and body. And the influence of one upon the other can be either positive or negative. What can the mind do to the body? Studies have proved that watching funny movies can reduce pain and promote healing. Conversely, worry can give a person an ulcer, high blood pressure, even a heart attack.

The mind and body work together to produce stress, which is a bodily response to a stimulus, a response that disturbs the body's normal physiological balance. Stress is not always bad. For example, a stress reaction can sometimes save a person's life by releasing hormones that enable a person to react quickly and with greater energy in a dangerous situation. In everyday situations, too, stress can provide that extra push needed to do something difficult. But too much stress often injures both the mind and the body. How can stress be kept under control? "Learn to lighten up and live longer" has several good suggestions. "Translating blushes, belches and other body language" also deals with ways to control the physical responses to stress.

BEFORE YOU READ

1. Article 2A mentions four general causes of stress. One of them is fear. Try to guess what the others might be.

2. Discuss the sources of stress in your life. What makes you feel angry, hostile, depressed, or nervous? What do you do to make yourself feel better?

AS YOU READ

1. Look for the major causes of stress mentioned in Article 2A. Did you guess some of them before you read the article?

2. In Article 2B, note the bodily responses that are related to stress.

Learn to lighten up and live longer

By Nanci Hellmich
USA TODAY

1 If you often feel angry and overwhelmed, like the stress in your life is spinning out of control, then you may be hurting your heart.

2 And if you don't want to break your own heart, you need to learn to take charge of the areas of your life you can—and recognize that there are many things beyond your control.

3 So says Dr. Robert S. Eliot, author of a new book *From Stress to Strength: How to Lighten Your Load and Save Your Life* (Bantam Books, $22.95). He's director of the Institute of Stress Medicine in Jackson Hole, Wyo., and clinical professor of medicine at the University of Nebraska.

4 Eliot says there are people in this world whom he calls "hot reactors." For these people, stress may cause dramatic and rapid increases in their blood pressure.

5 "Your brain writes prescriptions for your body," says Eliot. "There are people who write prescriptions like they are fighting saber-toothed tigers 20 to 30 times a day. They are hot reactors. Those people are walking time bombs because they can look cool as a cucumber on the surface and are as hot as chili peppers underneath."

6 Hostile people activate their fight-or-flight response more intensely and more frequently during the course of everyday life than other people do, says stress expert Dr. Redford Williams, Duke University Medical Center, Durham, N.C.

7 They respond to petty annoyances like supermarket lines, traffic jams and children who don't clean up their rooms as though it were a threat to life and limb, says Williams, co-author of *Anger Kills: 17 Strategies for Controlling the Hostility That Can Harm Your Health* (Times Books/Random House, $22).

8 Williams' studies and others show that hostility is bad for health. "In patients who have heart disease the emotion of anger can cause the heart function to deteriorate."

9 Eliot says researchers have found that stressed people have higher cholesterol levels, among other things. "We've done years of work in showing that excess alarm or stress chemicals like adrenalin can literally rupture heart muscle fibers. When that happens it happens very quickly, within five minutes. It creates many short circuits, and that causes crazy heart rhythm. It beats like a bag of worms instead of a pump. And when that happens, we can't live."

10 Eliot, 64, suffered a heart attack at age 44. He attributes some of the cause to stress. For years he was a "hot reactor." On the outside, he was cool, calm and collected but on the inside stress was killing him. He's now doing very well.

11 The main predictors of destructive levels of stress are the FUD factors—fear, uncertainty and doubt—together with perceived lack of control, he says.

12 For many people, the root of their stress is anger, and the trick is to find out where the anger is coming from. "Does the anger come from a feeling that everything must be perfect?" Eliot asks.

13 "That's very common in professional women. They feel they have to be all things to all people and do it all perfectly. They think, 'I should, I must, I have to.' Good enough is never good enough. Perfectionists cannot delegate. They get angry that they have to carry it all, and they blow their tops. Then they feel guilty and they reset the whole cycle."

14 People who are unassertive or people pleasers also often get angry. "They say yes all the time when they really want to say no. All of the sudden they get mad and they resent the system."

15 Others are angry because they have no "compass in life. And they give the same emphasis to a traffic jam that they give a family argument," he says. "If you own anger for more than five minutes—if you stew in your own juice

What's your quality of life?

Dr. Robert S. Eliot developed this quiz to help people evaluate stresses and make adjustments. For each category, choose a number that accurately reflects your feelings, from 1 (most stressful) to 9 (least stressful).

1 . . . 9

Relationship with spouse, companion or significant others:
1. Not going very well   9. Going very well

Relationships with children:
1. Unrewarding   9. Very rewarding

Social relationships with friends, neighbors and others:
1. No real friends, feel distant   9. Have friends, feel close

Reltionships at work with co-workers, boss and others:
1. Frequent discord   9. Usually harmonious

Major life crisis in past six months, such as loss of job, divorce, moving:
1. One or more   9. None

Finances:
1. Getting out of control   9. Manageable

Perfectionism:
1. Things should be done right   9. I do the best I can and that's OK

Assertiveness:
1. I have difficulty saying what I think   9. I can usually say what I think

Self-esteem:
1. I often don't feel sure about myself   9. I rarely think about myself

Personal aspirations:
1. I'm not fulfilling my potential   9. Fulfilling my potential.

Career/work:
1. Often does not meet my expectations   9. Usually meets my expectations

Time management/ circuit overload:
1. I can't get everything done   9. I can pace myself

YOUR SCORE

Evaluating your score: Review the list and figure out which areas you'd like to get better control over. Then for an overview, add up your numbers and divide by 12. **Anything below 5 indicates low energy and a heavy stress burden. Scores of 8 or 9 indicate low stress loads and high energy and optimism.**

Source: *From Stress to Strength*, Dr. Robert S. Eliot. Copyright © 1994 by Robert S. Eliot, M.D. Used by permission of Bantam Books, a division of Bantam Doubleday Dell Publishing Group, Inc.

By Elys A. McLean, USA TODAY

with no safety valve—you have to find out where it's coming from.

16 "What happens is that the hotter people get physiologically with mental stress, the more likely they are to blow apart with some cardiovascular problem."

17 One step to calming down is recognizing you have this tendency, William says. Learn to be less hostile by changing some of your attitudes and negative thinking.

18 Eliot recommends taking charge of your life. "If there is one word that should be substituted for stress, it's control. Instead of the FUD factors, what you want is the NICE factors—new, interesting, challenging experiences."

19 You have to decide what parts of your life you can control, he says. "Stop where you are on your trail and say, 'I'm going to get my compass out and find out what I need to do.'"

20 "He suggests that people write down the six things in their lives that they feel are the most important things they'd like to achieve. Ben Franklin did it at age 32. "He wrote down things like being a better father, being a better husband, being financially independent, being stimulated intellectually and remaining temperate—he wasn't good at that."

21 Eliot says you can first make a list of 12 things, then cut it down to six and

---

How to control hostility

Stress expert Dr. Redford Williams offers these suggestions for trying to control your hostility:

▶ **Damage control.** When you start to get angry, distract yourself. When you're getting irritated while you wait in line at the grocery store, read a magazine. Tell yourself to stop having negative thoughts. Meditate.

▶ **Try and change those negative attitudes.** Change your cynical thoughts into positive ones. Use humor. Go through a day pretending it's your last day on Earth. How would you spend the last 24 hours if you had to go through a normal day—you couldn't take off for the beach? "We've yet to find anyone who says they would get even with all their enemies."

▶ **Reduce the situations that will make you angry.** In general, improve your relationships with other people. If you have better relationships, you'll be less angry.

---

set your priorities. "Don't give yourself impossible things, but things that will affect your identity, control and self-esteem.

22 "Put them on a note card and take it with you and look at it when you need to. Since we can't create a 26-hour day we have to decide what things we are going to do."

23 Keep in mind that over time these priorities are going to change. "The kids grow up, the dog dies and you change your priorities.

24 "If you're having a hard time setting priorities, imagine yourself as 65 or 70 years old, and looking back and say to yourself, 'What would I really feel good about?'"

25 "Eliot says the other key to controlling stress is to "realize that there are other parts of your life over which you can have little or no control—like the economy and politicians."

26 You have to realize that sometimes with things like traffic jams, deadlines and unpleasant bosses, "you can't fight. You can't flee. You have to learn how to flow."

Translating blushes, belches and other body language

By Karen S. Peterson
USA TODAY

1 How does your body do that? And for heavens sake—why?

2 Take blushes, for example. They're genetic, a legacy from mom or dad.

3 During stress, the mouth gets warm and dry, triggering a "blush" message to the brain. To prevent an embarrassing glow—when you're about to tell a whopper, for example—suck an ice cube. The drop in temperature stops the action.

4 Blushes are just one of 400 "feelings" or quirky ways your body uses to talk to you, says Dr. Alan P. Xenakis. He reviews about 60 in his new *Why Doesn't My Funny Bone Make Me Laugh?* (Villard, $18).

5 Most of the quirks—from "butterflies" in the stomach to yawns—are normal. Xenakis explores some scary, serious ones but dwells on the funny. His goal: to get people relaxed about their bodies and "receptive to health care information." From his panoply of peculiarities:

▶ **Goose bumps.** They're a legacy from a Neanderthal ancestor whose body hair rose to trap heat and to look like the toughest kid on the prehistoric block.

▶ **Yawns.** They fill the body's need for fresh oxygen and can often seem contagious. Our evolutionary ancestors used them to warn each other of danger.

▶ **Burping.** The biggest cause is swallowing air. An hour of stress will cause the swallowing of five balloons' worth of air; 10 minutes of chewing gum brings in enough air for one glorious belch.

6 Additional facts, tidbits, anecdotes, cures and trivia about the body:

▶ **Cravings.** When a pregnant woman craves pickles, it's probably because she needs salt to retain water—and she needs that increased water when she is carrying a child.

▶ **Heartburn.** When you next have heartburn—a backing up of fatty acids from the stomach—flap your arms like a bird. "When it comes to putting out pyrosis (heartburn), the flying exercise often takes off when most antacids leave

us grounded."

▶ **Hiccups.** Nobody really knows why they happen. They usually stop in a few minutes, whether you try a cure or not. However, the *Guinness Book of World Records* records one case that lasted 60 years.

▶ **Tickles.** Tickling is caused by stimulating fine nerve endings beneath the surface of the skin. Psychology is a big part of the tickle game. If you like and trust the tickler, you open yourself up to enjoying the tickles. But if you try too hard to overcome the urge to laugh, you can actually make the experience unpleasant. You block the tickling sensation and confuse the same nerve fibers that respond to pain.

▶ **Thirst.** One of the greatest examples of the body regulating itself. The body is 70% water. When it feels deprived, the brain sends a message to your salivary glands to stop doing their thing. The resulting thirst sends you to the designer water bottle.

7 Did you also know that laughter releases natural chemical painkillers; chicken soup can cure a hangover?

A. After reading Article 2A, mark these answers true or false.

_____ 1. Destructive stress is a problem for everyone.

_____ 2. "Hot reactors" can change.

_____ 3. A person can and should control every aspect of his or her life.

_____ 4. Ben Franklin's list of priorities probably helped him to live a long life.

_____ 5. There is an alternative to the fight-or-flight response.

B. After reading Article 2A, decide which of the following activities would be likely to increase stress and which would not, in Dr. Eliot's opinion. Put a check in the correct column.

Would these activities increase stress?	Yes	No
1. Trying to please everyone.	____	____
2. Allowing others to make important decisions for you.	____	____
3. Putting annoying experiences out of your mind.	____	____
4. Delegating responsibility.	____	____
5. Yelling at others when you are angry at them.	____	____
6. Pretending it is your last day on Earth.	____	____
7. Always behaving in a calm, controlled manner.	____	____
8. Deciding what is most important to you.	____	____
9. Striving to be perfect.	____	____
10. Accepting what you cannot change.	____	____

PLAYING WITH WORDS

A. Use context clues and a dictionary if necessary to determine the meaning of each italicized word as it is used in the articles. Circle the best definition. The paragraph in which the word is used is indicated in parentheses.

Article 2A:

1. *deteriorate* (8)
   a. get better
   b. get worse

2. *perceived* (11)
   a. the way a person views something
   b. complete

3. *physiologically* (16)
   a. related to the body
   b. related to the mind

4. *temperate* (20)
   a. moderate
   b. extreme

5. *priorities* (23, 24)
   a. an ordering of things in terms of importance
   b. an ordering of things in terms of what happened first

Article 2B:

1. *genetic* (2)
   a. inherited
   b. embarrassing

2. *legacy* (2, 5)
   a. inherited money or possessions
   b. traits a person has received genetically

3. *whopper* (3)
   a. a huge sandwich
   b. a big lie

4. *quirks* (5)
   a. common occurrences
   b. peculiar habits

5. *receptive* (5)
   a. related to TV reception
   b. willing to accept

6. *panoply* (5)
   a. a complete array
   b. a few examples

B. When writers compare two things that are not really in the same category, they are using figures of speech. When *as* or *like* is used in a figurative comparison, it is a *simile*. A comparison without *as* or *like* is called a *metaphor*.

Literal comparisons:

Joe is as hostile as his father. Joe has a bad temper, just like his father.

Figurative comparisons:

Joe is a walking time bomb. (metaphor)

Joe is as gentle as a saber-toothed tiger. (simile)

Scan Article 2A, looking for three similes and three metaphors. Write them down. Then evaluate them. Which are trite (common, not original)? Which ones are fresh? Which ones create a picture in your mind? Which ones are funny?

DIGGING BENEATH THE SURFACE

A. In Article 2A, what do the following phrases mean? Discuss them with a partner. The paragraph in which each phrase is used is indicated in parentheses.

1. *break your own heart* (2)
2. *"hot reactors"* (4)
3. *Your brain writes prescriptions for your body.* (5)
4. *fight-or-flight response* (6)
5. *Perfectionists cannot delegate.* (13)
6. *no compass in life* (15)
7. *a 26-hour day* (22)
8. *setting priorities* (24)
9. *learn how to flow* (26)

B. Compare and contrast the words *anger* and *hostility*. Is anger always hostile? Does hostility always involve anger? Consult a dictionary. Then discuss the words with a partner. Share some examples of each emotion.

C. Put a check in the appropriate column to show which of the following statements applies to Article 2A, Article 2B, or both.

Statements	2A	2B
1. The information in the article comes from a recently published book.	___	___
2. The book's goal is to help people understand their bodies better.	___	___
3. Another major goal is to amuse the reader.	___	___
4. The article gives advice.	___	___
5. The article is mostly about how to handle stress.	___	___
6. The article is trying to help people live longer.	___	___

GOING BEYOND THE TEXT

A. *Learning Together*

1. In small groups, tell about a time when you got very angry. Tell what you did about your anger. Discuss your behavior in light of the advice in Article 2A. Group members should comment and make suggestions about each situation.

2. Would Dr. Eliot (the author of the book discussed in Article 2A) agree with the following quotations? Discuss your answers with a partner.

   a. "The only thing we have to fear is fear itself," from President Franklin Delano Roosevelt's First Inaugural Address, 1933.

   b. "If you would be well served, you must serve yourself," from "The Courtship of Miles Standish" by Henry Wadsworth Longfellow.

B. *Responding in Writing.* Choose one of the following writing projects.

1. Keep a record of your emotions for one week—especially of the negative feelings discussed in Article 2A. At the end of the week, read over your notes and decide if you are a "hot reactor." Decide if you need to do something to reduce your stress responses and indicate what you might do to accomplish this.

2. Write about someone you know who is a "hot reactor."

3. Write a short composition about various cures for hiccups. You can research the topic in the library, ask a doctor or nurse, or interview some people who have found remedies that work for them. Look in books about folk remedies for interesting ideas from other cultures in past centuries. You can also incorporate your own experiences.

MAKING CONNECTIONS

The preceding article, "Look who's talking to themselves: Just about everyone," also touches upon the topic of stress. What are some situations in which you might talk to yourself to reduce stress?

ARTICLE 3
Children committed to cleanup

April—springtime—is when the cycle of life begins anew. Appropriately, Earth Day is celebrated on April 22 to remind people the world over that, by working together, we can assure ourselves a future rich with colorful, song-filled springs. Earth Day began in 1970, the brainchild of Gaylord Nelson, a former Wisconsin governor and U.S. senator. On the twenty-first anniversary of Earth Day, this slogan was introduced: "Make every day Earth Day." Today, the day is an international event.

Yet, according to this article, many adults are losing interest in environmental protection. Fortunately, throughout the country, children and teenagers are setting an example for their elders by remaining dedicated to the cause. This article offers ample evidence of that.

Not all adults have been forgetful and negligent. In 1994, Congress worked on new protection standards to include in the Clean Water Act and the Safe Drinking Water Act. The Clean Air Act, amended by Congress in 1990, gave many cities a deadline for decreasing smog. Cities are keeping these deadlines in mind and making progress in reducing air pollution from auto emissions. Still, young people are leading the way, as they continue their individual and group efforts to create a safer, cleaner world.

BEFORE YOU READ

1. Have you ever been involved in a group effort to improve the environment? Have you heard of any that you would like to participate in? If so, tell about it.

2. Discuss the meaning of the word part *eco-*. Scan the article for words beginning with this word part and discuss their meanings. Think of other words you know that contain *eco-*.

AS YOU READ

The author of this article says that young people are more committed to saving the environment than adults are. As you read, look for the evidence she gives to support this statement.

Children committed to cleanup

By Anita Manning
USA TODAY

1 Another Earth Day. More green hoopla. More hype about pollution and recycling.

2 Big deal.

3 Even amid today's tree-plantings, concerts and neighborhood cleanups, there are signs that for some adults at least, the message is growing monotonous. Once-active supporters of eco-causes are suffering energy depletion.

4 Memberships in the largest environmental groups, which doubled and tripled in the 1980s, are falling off.

5 Eco-magazines founded in the green glow of Earth Day 1990 are gasping for air.

6 An annual poll by National Opinion Research Center shows the number of adults who think more should be spent on environmental protection peaked at 75% in 1990. By 1993, only 56% thought so.

7 But there's one group of Americans for whom environmental activism is no fad: kids.

8 "This is their mission," says Annie Brody, who, as director of The Children's Earth Fund and vice president of Earth Force, has spent three years working with young people.

By Michael Wyke

NOT KIDDING AROUND: Ashley Hightower at a pond cleanup at Holland High School in Tulsa, Okla. A recent Louis Harris Poll found nearly 60% of kids try to get their parents to recycle.

"They know the Earth's in trouble. They feel it's their generation's pivotal chance to change things."

9 "We're not passing through a stage," says Catherine Markham, 17, a senior at National Cathedral School in Washington, D.C. "This is something I feel is part of me."

10 In a recent Louis Harris survey of 10,375 students in grades 4–12, only crime topped the environment in a list of topics children think about "a lot."

11 The poll found kids are activists—they want to help fix problems such as polluted beaches and oceans (74%); polluted air (72%); chemicals in the ground that hurt people or animals (62%); and garbage (58%).

12 Teachers have seized on the environment as a way to teach science and math as well as social studies, government and citizenship skills.

13 They're celebrating Earth Day 1994 in a big way—from a parade in Birmingham, where 3,000 schoolkids will march in costume, to hundreds of school, youth group and community events today, this month and all year round:

14 ►Girls United to Save the Environment, a project of the National Coalition of Girls' Schools, involves 25,000 students, grades K-12, in projects that range from building birdhouses for the National Zoo to cleaning rivers in Tennessee, Massachusetts and Colorado.

15 "We feel we can change our environment, and that we can change the country and the world," says Sarah Cobey, 13, an eighth grader at Castilleja School in Palo Alto, Calif., where students today are stenciling Palo Alto storm drains with the words "No Dumping: Flows to Bay."

16 ►In north St. Louis, the Dolphin Defenders, a group of 55 pre-teens who live in a world of guns, drugs and turmoil, will spend Saturday creating a wildlife habitat in a vacant lot, complete with evergreen trees, flowering trees, berry bushes, brush to provide shelter for raccoons and possums, and an in-ground water dish to be refilled regularly. It's their fifth such habitat, one of several projects they've done since being founded seven years ago by neighborhood worker Neil S. Andre.

17 The Defenders meet weekly and have made it their business to clean up their corner of the world. Says Icarius Johnson, 9: "I like helping save the world. God made the earth and we should care for it."

18 Under Andre's direction, they've cleared more than 12,000 pounds of glass from streets, returned more than 100 abandoned shopping carts to local grocery stores and recycled more than 1,000 tires (at a cost to them of $1 or more per tire). And that's just since last September, Andre says.

19 ►Roots and Shoots, a project launched in the U.S. this month by primatologist Jane Goodall, has chapters in 40 countries. Its goal, says Goodall, is "to generate concern (among children) for the environment, for animals and for each other." The project, she hopes, will "bring back meaning and values into the world" by teaching children concepts like responsibility, compassion and a connection with different cultures. "We have kids in Tanzania writing to kids in Munich and America," she says.

20 "Kids are now beginning to realize there are kids their age all over the world just as concerned with doing something for the environment," says teacher Tim O'Halloran, leader of a Roots and Shoots club at Holland Hall School in Tulsa, where kids who "look like swamp things" are cleaning algae out of a pond on the school grounds today.

21 ►Tree Musketeers in El Segundo, Calif., plants trees in the city in memory of a loved one or celebration of a birth. The group began seven years ago, when 13 Brownie scouts had "a vision of how the earth could be more beautiful," says founding member Sabrina Alimahomed, 15.

22 "When I was a kid," Alimahomed says, stories about environmental destruction frightened her. "I thought the world would be in flames, people would be getting skin cancer. I got this horrid idea in my head about having to live underground. I couldn't even imagine it—I couldn't play soccer underground!

23 "Then I realized I could do something about it. . . . We just went with our vision."

A. After reading "Children committed to cleanup," mark each of the following statements true or false.

_____ 1. According to this article, kids are more concerned about pollution than adults are.

_____ 2. The main idea of this article is that the Earth is in terrible condition.

_____ 3. The student activists quoted in this article are optimistic about the future of the environment on Earth.

_____ 4. The current interest of young people in ecology is just a fad, according to the author of this article.

_____ 5. This article tells about the cleanup efforts of a few small youth groups.

B. The author of this article says that adults seem to be losing interest in the message of Earth Day. Find three pieces of evidence that she gives to support this claim.

C. The author also says that children are very concerned about saving the Earth. What evidence does she give to support this claim?

A. Study the meanings of these combining forms. Then use these word parts to complete the words in the sentences that follow. To find the word (or a variation of it) in the article, refer to the paragraph number in parentheses.

com-, con- = together, with

de- = removal, separation, away from, out of, down, decrease

eco- = environment, natural habitat, ecology

en- = to cause to be in a place or condition

gen- = to be born, to become, to produce

mono- = one, alone, single

re- = again, back, backward

1. Jane Goodall wants to_____ erate concern for the _____ vironment. (9)

2. When the supply of water is _____ pleted, animals and plants may suffer. (3)

3. It is possible to _____cycle glass, rubber, paper, and many other products. (18)

4. When one person feels concern for another and shares the person's feelings, that ability is called _____ passion. (19)

5. _____ tonous (3) music has little variety. It all sounds the same.

B. Use an unabridged dictionary to help you answer these questions.

1. What is the difference in meaning between the words *earth* and *Earth*?

2. In paragraph 1, are *hoopla* and *hype* synonyms or antonyms? What is the original French meaning of *hoopla?*

3. What does *peaked* mean in paragraph 6?

4. What is a *pivot*? What does *pivotal* mean in paragraph 8?

5. In paragraph 12, does the word *seized* suggest that the teachers acted reluctantly or eagerly?

6. What was the old meaning of the word *habit*? What is a *habitat*? Do you see any connection between the old meaning of *habit* and its modern meaning?

7. What does *launched* mean in paragraph 19?

8. What does *vision* mean in paragraphs 21 and 23?

DIGGING BENEATH THE SURFACE

Discuss the answers to these questions with a partner.

1. Does the headline on this article, "Children committed to cleanup," seem funny to you? If so, tell why.

2. Paragraphs 1 and 3 suggest two reasons why adults might have lost interest in environmental protection. What are they?

3. In paragraphs 3 and 5, the author uses two phrases in an unusual way. Phrases generally used about a person or animal are used instead to describe an organization (paragraph 3) and a group of magazines (paragraph 5). What are these two phrases? Why is this usage so appropriate?

4. What are some differences between a fad and a mission? Do you know anyone who has a mission? What is it?

5. Paragraphs 22 and 23 quote a girl who was frightened. How did she deal with her fears? Have you ever dealt with your fears in a similar way? Share some examples.

GOING BEYOND THE TEXT

A. *Learning Together*

1. Brainstorm with the entire class and make a list of ten to fifteen major national or world problems (crime, pollution, high cost of college education, overpopulation of the earth, and so on). Make your list into a survey form and conduct a classroom survey to find out which ones students rate as most serious. Compare your group's responses to those discussed in paragraph 11. Which problems do the students in your class think about most?

2. Brainstorm in groups of six and select a good project your class can do to improve the environment. Choose a group spokesperson to tell your group's best ideas to the class. Then vote to select one or two projects for the whole class to work on. Set up committees to handle various types of tasks related to the project. Set a deadline for completion.

3. Study endangered species in groups of six. Each group member should choose an endangered animal to tell the rest of the group about. (Be sure there are no duplicate selections.) Bring a picture of your animal when you talk about it.

B. *Responding in Writing.* Choose one of the following writing projects.

1. Think up some good slogans for next year's Earth Day. Enter your slogans in a class contest. After some of the group's best slogans are selected, use them on posters and banners to post around your classroom and school now or shortly before Earth Day.

2. Write to one of the organizations mentioned in the article or to one listed below for more information about how to help clean up the environment:

The Children's Rainforest
P.O. Box 936
Lewiston, ME 04240

Kids Against Pollution
c/o Tenakill School
275 High Street
Closter, NJ 07624

Green Seal, Inc.
P.O. Box 1694
Palo Alto, CA 94302

When you get a response, write a summary of the information to post in class.

3. Call a local recycling center. Find out what can be recycled in your community and where people can take materials for recycling. Must materials be prepared for recycling in any special way? Is there any payment? Get the whole story and then write up step-by-step instructions for people who want to recycle.

4. Write about the various ways that people deal with fears about the future or about how you deal with your fears about the future.

MAKING CONNECTIONS

Compare the depiction of teenagers in this article with the portrayal of teenagers in Article 2A of the "News" section ("Cities deciding that its time for teen curfews"). Which view of teens do you think is more accurate?

ARTICLE 4
Attempts at liquid breathing

PREVIEWING THE ARTICLE

Breathe under water? It was no problem for the mermaids and mermen of European folklore, but they had the distinct advantage of being imaginary. Could real human beings ever really breathe oxygen from a liquid? Fluid respiration, now in experimental stages, is a promising medical therapy for patients with various kinds of lung disorders. The following article explains how and why it works.

This article reminds readers that scientific progress does not always travel the expected path. Sometimes scientists first decide what society needs, and then they try to develop it. This is what happened with the polio vaccine. But sometimes additional uses for various discoveries and inventions are not made until much later. For example, many technologies created for the U.S. space program have proved extremely beneficial right here on Earth.

This kind of scientific serendipity is what happened with a group of synthetic chemicals called *perfluorocarbons.* They were developed during the Manhattan Project (the code name for the American effort to build an atomic bomb during World War II), designed to carry heat away from electronic components in bombs. Today, these chemicals are being used in experiments involving liquid breathing. Someday they may save lives and assist in interplanetary exploration.

BEFORE YOU READ

Compare and contrast the meanings of these pairs of words commonly used in health-care professions: *chronic/acute; syndrome/symptom; intensive/extensive; trauma/disease; respiration/ventilation.*

AS YOU READ

Note that the information presented in this article covers three time periods: past research and discoveries, current experiments and treatments, and future possibilities for the uses of this technology. Be sure that you distinguish between what has already been done with perfluorocarbons and what may be possible in the future.

Attempts at liquid breathing

By Tim Friend
USA TODAY

1 The intensive care nursery of the future may hold rows of dark, bubbling aquariums.

2 Inside, babies born too soon will breathe special fluids that allow their premature lungs to develop without harm, just as if they were still in the womb.

3 While that's definitely a science fiction scenario, scientists are in fact well on their way toward developing liquid breathing technologies.

4 "We breathe liquids in the womb for the first nine months of our lives," says Leland Clark Jr., a pioneer of liquid breathing research. "As our knowledge of lung function increases and as the fluid compounds get better every year, we get closer to a really simple method of breathing liquid out of the womb."

5 Clark is credited with first recognizing that a class of chemicals called perfluorocarbons, developed in the Manhattan Project, make a perfect medium for liquid breathing. Perfluorocarbons are like liquid Teflon and are excellent carriers and dissolvers of oxygen and carbon dioxide. They also seem harmless.

6 Breathing fluids that can deliver controlled levels of oxygen to the lungs and carry away carbon dioxide could mean the difference between life and death for premature infants with underdeveloped lungs. Liquid breathing also may rescue adults who fall victim to acute respiratory distress syndrome, experts say.

7 Approximately 80,000 infants are born prematurely each year. The main cause of their deaths is premature lung development. Also, approximately 600,000 people in the USA must be put on mechanical ventilators each year because of trauma or disease that causes their lungs to fail. Of these, about 150,000 to 200,000 develop acute respiratory distress. Liquid breathing in these cases could give doctors time to treat whatever condition is causing the lung failure.

8 Liquid breathing may benefit premature babies because their lungs don't yet make surfactant, a substance which keeps the air sacs in their lungs from collapsing and causing respiratory distress.

9 Today, a surfactant drug can be given to reduce the chances of dying, but doctors still must use mechanical ventilators to help the infants breathe. These ventilators must be turned to high, and ultimately damaging, pressures to get air into the underdeveloped alveoli even after surfactant is given.

10 A small group of scientists reason that since the lungs at this early stage in development are better suited to breathing liquid, then perhaps a premature baby could do much better if not forced to breathe air.

11 Researchers are already showing "very promising" results in a five-center clinical trial of premature babies treated with an experimental perfluorocarbon called LiquiVent, says Thomas Shaffer, Temple University School of Medicine and St. Christopher's Hospital for Children, Philadelphia.

12 Shaffer conducted the first studies of premature babies in 1989 after giving up on the development of a liquid breathing device for deep sea divers. He created a full liquid breathing method and used a different perfluorocarbon than in the current human studies. And though his severely premature infants eventually died, Shaffer demonstrated that humans can indeed breathe a liquid; the babies survived longer than anyone expected.

13 "In 1968, I first became interested in liquid ventilation for diving applications. I tried to develop a demand-regulated

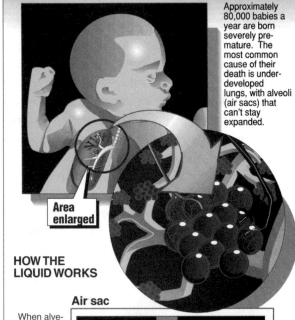

Fluid respiration

The lungs are one of the last organs to mature in a fetus. When babies are born severely premature, their lungs are often incapable of breathing air. New research with synthetic fluids called perfluoro–carbons suggest liquid breathing techniques could dramatically improve the chances of survival in infants with underdeveloped lungs.

Approximately 80,000 babies a year are born severely premature. The most common cause of their death is underdeveloped lungs, with alveoli (air sacs) that can't stay expanded.

Area enlarged

HOW THE LIQUID WORKS

Air sac

When alveoli collapse in the immature lung, blood circulating in surrounding capillaries cannot release carbon dioxide or pick up oxygen.

Collapsed   Normal

Air sac after treatment

LiquiVent expands alveoli at very low pressures allowing doctors to fill the lung with air. The fluid also exchanges oxygen for carbon dioxide.

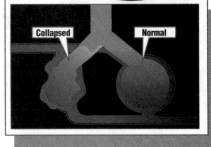

Source: American Chemical Society   By Suzy Parker, USA TODAY

device and that's what the movie and book *The Abyss* picked up on," Shaffer says. "Then I became interested in looking at applications for abnormal lungs and I started studies in the 1970s with premature lambs. We had remarkable findings. Not only did they breathe the fluid, they did better."

14 Shaffer's animal research and subsequent human study in

1989 sparked interest at Alliance Pharmaceutical Corp., which one year ago began the current five-center study.

15 The latest research employs LiquiVent and a partial ventilation technique developed by Bradley Fuhrman, Buffalo Children's Hospital, Buffalo, N.Y. In this technique, LiquiVent, which is considered more bio-compatible than most perfluorocarbons, fills the lungs and expands collapsed air sacs.

16 With each breath, LiquiVent travels in and out of the airways and eventually evaporates from the lungs. This allows air to be ventilated into the lungs at much lower pressures than would be possible with conventional ventilation, says Marla Wolfson, who works with Shaffer at St. Christopher's.

17 Scientists in the study believe the partial ventilation method will make Food and Drug Administration approval faster since it involves approval only of the perfluorocarbon drug. Shaffer's full ventilation technique would require approval of both the liquid and specialized equipment to circulate it in and out of the lungs and remove carbon dioxide and add oxygen.

18 Results of the five-center trial will be submitted this fall to a medical journal, says Hal DeLong, executive vice president, Alliance Pharmaceutical Corp., San Diego, which developed LiquiVent and sponsored the study. Further studies of LiquiVent on adults and less premature infants may begin this summer.

19 Liquid breathing technology also has implications for lung-related diseases, including lung cancer and cystic fibrosis, Wolfson says.

20 "We're moving toward being able to suspend various drugs in the fluid," says Wolfson. And it may be possible to add chemotherapy agents to deliver anti-cancer treatment directly to the lungs, or perhaps to add genes to deliver gene therapy directly to the air sacs or lung's lining.

21 Agents that break up mucus in the lungs also may be added. People theoretically could undergo partial liquid breathing for short periods to deliver any drug to the lungs.

22 And perhaps one day liquid breathing will aid deep-sea divers as originally envisioned by Shaffer. It may even help humans adapt for long interplanetary space flights or prevent the lungs of pilots of future high-speed aircraft from compressing during rapid acceleration.

23 And maybe there will be the aquariums, bubbling in the dark, temporary havens at last for those who come into the world too soon.

A. Complete the sentences below by adding a clause that completes the sentence. You can find the information you need in the paragraph numbers indicated in parentheses.

1. It is logical to assume that premature babies could get oxygen from a fluid because (2, 4, 10) _____ .

2. A perfluorocarbon is an ideal medium for fluid respiration because (5)

   a. _____ ,

   b. _____ , and

   c. _____ .

3. Mechanical ventilation only (without perfluorocarbons) is not very successful in saving premies with immature lungs because (9) _____ _____ .

4. We know that some animals can breathe liquids because (13) _____ _____ .

5. The technique developed by Bradley Fuhrman is called *partial ventilation* because (15, 16) _____ _____ .

6. The words *perhaps, maybe,* and *may* are used in paragraphs 22 and 23 because _____ .

B. In this article, two kinds of breathing treatments are discussed: (1) full liquid breathing and (2) partial ventilation. Read paragraphs 12 and 15 through 17 carefully. Then discuss the differences between these two techniques with a partner.

C. Besides helping premature infants to breathe, several other possible uses of liquid respiration are mentioned in this article. List as many as you can find. Then check your list with two classmates to see if you missed any.

A. Match each word listed with its synonym or definition by writing the letters from the second column on the appropriate lines in the first column. The paragraph in which each word is used is indicated in parentheses.

____ 1.	*alveoli* (9)	a.	increase in size
____ 2.	*breathing* (3)	b.	way of working
____ 3.	*expand* (15)	c.	liquid
____ 4.	*findings* (13)	d.	information learned from research
____ 5.	*fluid* (2)	e.	respiration
____ 6.	*function* (4)	f.	method
____ 7.	*intensive* (1)	g.	increasing in amount

_____ 8. *technique* (15)   h.   immature

_____ 9. *trauma* (7)   i.   air sacs in the lungs

_____ 10. *underdeveloped* (6)   j.   a condition caused by sudden physical injury

B. Find each italicized phrase in the paragraph indicated. Try to determine its meaning from context clues in the paragraph(s) surrounding the phrase. If you are unsure, use a dictionary for help. Then circle the correct meaning for each phrase.

1. *intensive care* (1)

a. an increased amount of medical and nursing care for seriously ill patients
b. any medical care given to hospitalized infants

2. *acute respiratory distress* (6, 7)

a. sudden, severe difficulty breathing
b. a chronic lung disease

3. *mechanical ventilators* (9)

a. machines that use pressure to force air into the lungs
b. an experimental form of fluid respiration

4. *"very promising" results* (11)

a. results that have been proved successful
b. evidence from research that strongly suggests a particular method will work

5. *clinical trial* (11)

a. an experiment on human patients
b. a conclusion based upon logical analysis

6. *liquid ventilation* (13)

a. getting oxygen from a fluid
b. pumping air into a liquid

7. *more bio-compatible* (15)

a. less likely to kill the patient
b. better able to create life

8. *chemotherapy agents* (20)

a. people who sell drugs
b. drugs that fight cancer

DIGGING BENEATH THE SURFACE

A. Are the following statements facts or opinions? (Remember, a fact is information that can be proved.) Discuss the statements with a partner. Then label each either "F" for fact or "O" for opinion.

_____ 1. Liquid breathing for deep-sea divers is a technology that is not worth developing.

_____ 2. Premature babies can breathe liquids.

_____ 3. Someday lung cancer will be cured by breathing in fluids containing anticancer drugs.

_____ 4. High-pressure ventilation can damage immature lungs.

_____ 5. The survival rate for premature infants will increase greatly once the partial ventilation system is widely used in the United States.

_____ 6. Surfactant drugs make it easier to breathe.

_____ 7. The lungs become fully developed late in the nine-month lifecycle of a human fetus.

_____ 8. Adult human beings will eventually learn to breathe liquids.

B. From reading this article, what did you learn about how scientific research on new medications is conducted? Discuss this with two classmates.

GOING BEYOND THE TEXT

A. _Learning Together_

You are going to nominate someone for the Nobel Prize in science for research in the area of liquid breathing. Which of these people mentioned in this article do you consider most deserving: Leland Clark Jr., Thomas Shaffer, Bradley Fuhrman, or Marla Wolfson? Discuss the matter with a partner until you agree on your candidate. Then have the class vote to select the winner.

B. _Responding in Writing._ Choose one of the following topics to write about.

1. Read about the human respiratory system in an encyclopedia or biology text. Then do one of the following: (a) write a summary of how the respiratory system works, or (b) make a list of ten interesting facts about human respiration.

2. Write a narrative essay about a scary situation when breathing was a problem for you or someone you knew.

3. Interview a nurse or doctor who has taken care of premature infants recently. Then write about the latest techniques in intensive care for premies.

4. Watch a videotape of the 1989 movie _The Abyss._ Describe the two scenes that deal with liquid breathing. One scene closely parallels real scientific research. The other is science fiction, at least so far. Tell which is which.

MAKING CONNECTIONS

All the articles in the "Science, Health, and Behavior" section of this book show how the research of scientists and social scientists can help people live longer, happier, healthier lives. How much do you remember of what you have read? Review the titles of the articles you read, but do not reread the articles. With the book closed, list as many ideas as you can that were discussed in the articles.

SCIENCE, HEALTH, AND BEHAVIOR

When happenings in the sciences and social sciences are important, when new discoveries, inventions, or occurrences will have a significant effect upon the lives of many people, the information will appear in the daily paper. In fact, even discoveries that are not important may be the subject of journalistic investigation if they are interesting factual tidbits. Some scientific discoveries or research lead to such practical suggestions that people change their behavior (exercise more, quit smoking, check their homes for radon gas, and so on). When scientific news has something of interest or importance to tell the general public, it warrants space in the daily paper.

Where will you find articles about the sciences and social sciences in the daily paper? Sometimes the news is important enough to get front-page space. Sometimes a news story—for example, about surgery on a famous person—will result in a related medical article about that condition in general. Some newspapers have a special section or a special page for articles on the sciences and social sciences. Many papers have columnists who write regularly on these subjects, and some of these columnists answer questions from readers seeking advice on health care, parenting, or social relationships. In addition to being the subjects of news stories, important scientific discoveries and inventions can also inspire editorials and letters to the editor.

Exercise 1: Scanning the Newspaper for Scientific Information

Scan today's *USA TODAY* (or your local daily newspaper) for scientific information. Then write down the following information about each article or column that you find: the title of the article, the reason why this scientific matter was news today, the section and page of the paper you found it on, the type of article it is (news article, feature article, interview, book review, advice column, editorial, and so on). Then, from articles you read, choose the topic that interests you most and do further research and reading about it in the library. Ask the librarian what indexes will lead you to more articles or books about your topic. Then write a summary of your research. Include a bibliography of your sources.

Science for the Nonscientist

When journalists write about the sciences or social sciences for the general public, they often have to translate complicated technical information into words and ideas that the nonscientist can understand. This can be quite a challenge. Some journalists have advanced college degrees in scientific or technical writing.

Exercise 2: Science Made Simple

Find a scientific article in a daily newspaper. Write an evaluation of it in terms of its success in getting its message across to nonscientists. Were there definitions, comparisons, examples, or illustrations that helped you understand? What was missing that would have clarified the findings for you?

Exercise 3: Analyzing a Scientific Article

Find a newspaper article about research or a discovery in a field of science or social science. (Choose an article at least ten paragraphs long.) Then complete the following chart about the information it contains. Hand in the article you analyzed along with your completed chart.

Did the article include	Yes	What did it tell you?	No
1. a definition?	____	_____	____
2. a comparison?	____	_____	____
3. a reason?	____	_____	____
4. a result?	____	_____	____
5. a statistic (a numerical fact)?	____	_____	____
6. a problem?	____	_____	____
7. a solution?	____	_____	____
8. a discovery?	____	_____	____
9. a recommendation?	____	_____	____
10. opposing points of view?	____	_____	____